Enlightened Life

Contents

Part 4: The Dzogchen Teachings

Part 5: Greater Commitment and Assurance

Part 6: The Flourishing of Recognition

Editor's Introduction to *Enlightened Life*

It is with great joy that we present to you the latest book in the Dzogchen Series from Ziji Rinpoche, *Enlightened Life*, which follows the previous book in the series, *When Surfing a Tsunami*.

This new Dzogchen text comes from talks that Ziji Rinpoche has given in recent years on a weekly basis and live streamed to a worldwide audience. A team of volunteers, including Rinpoche herself, is responsible for what you have before you, beginning with the group that recorded the audio and video and made the talks available for viewing and listening, followed by a team that transcribed each of the talks into text form. Once enough texts had been collected, a critical mass of material was available, and these brilliant texts were then shaped into the book you are reading now.

This enthusiastic and passionate group of people has seen the great benefits and the immense changes in their own lives, and they are entirely dedicated to bringing these wisdom Teachings to a broader audience. It is important for them to acknowledge the abiding presence of Rinpoche all the way through. It is her complete devotion to the enlightenment of all that forms the basis for this book and for any other book that will be created through the Short Moments Teaching and organization.

The process of formulating any of the books begins with the heartfelt wish from Rinpoche herself to benefit all. She has wholeheartedly dedicated her life to bringing this incredible message to the world, and we would like to take this occasion to offer our immense gratitude to Rinpoche for all that she has contributed till now and for all the extraordinary innovations she will surely bring about in the coming years.

The book is divided into six parts with generally four or five chapters in each section. The chapters in the beginning section of the book present the core elements of the Teaching: open intelligence, data, the short moments practice, complete perceptual openness, leaving data *as it is*, and the practices that best support the flourishing in this Teaching. After the introductory chapters, the book continues to lay out the fundamentals of an enlightened life and how this enlightenment is already an accomplished fact. In Part Four, the Dzogchen Teachings are more specifically presented and elucidated. The later chapters further clarify the Teachings in ways that go more fully into important aspects of the practice and with a more depthful nuancing.

As was stated earlier, this book is the second in the series of Dzogchen books that the Short Moments organization will be bringing out in the coming years; however, the word "Dzogchen" rarely appears in many of the chapters of this book. How could that be? It is evidence of the fact that the very ancient Dzogchen Teaching, which had its basis in Tibetan culture and was often intertwined with Tibetan Buddhism, is here being presented in a new way—for a modern audience, using language suitable for participants worldwide who would likely have very little previous contact with Dzogchen. It is free of references that might cause confusion for a person unfamiliar with Tibetan symbology and terminology.

The content of the book is filled to the brim with Dzogchen, but possibly not always identified as such. So, for instance, the first twelve chapters lay out the core of the Dzogchen Teaching in language that imparts the wisdom Teachings, but without distinctive cultural markers referring back to traditional Dzogchen and even without using that specific name.

As Ziji Rinpoche has said, "Dzogchen hasn't always been called 'Dzogchen.' It has also been called by other names." Depending on the era, depending on the culture, the Teachings of Dzogchen are given in a way that is suited to those who are hearing it in their particular circumstance. This modern expression is, one could say, a *furtherance* of Dzogchen, such that new skillful means and communication methods are being used to impart the ancient wisdom of Dzogchen in a way that will be most effective in the specific time and place.

One key teaching component which should be acknowledged at the outset is the skilled use of repetition. The message is one of utmost simplicity, and the same basic instructions are true and valid all the way along. The Dzogchen Teaching is approached from many different angles, but the core message never wavers. It is extraordinary that a tool like this—repetition of the primary key points again and again—does not grow old or blunted. Exalted instructions such as these are ever fresh and new, and hearing them repeated over and over again brings more opportunity for insight and clarity.

Key terms such as "open intelligence," "short moments," "data," "resting," "reification of data" and others will be clarified in the introductory chapters. One additional aspect of the Teaching which needs to be introduced here at the outset is the Four Mainstays. The Four Mainstays are the core support structure for anyone interested in gaining assurance in open intelligence. They are 1) short moments of open intelligence, 2) the trainer, 3) the training and the training media, and 4) the worldwide community. When in the earlier chapters in the book the Four Mainstays are referred to or a "Four Mainstays lifestyle" is described, in brief, these are the essentials that are being referenced. A more complete presentation of the Four Mainstays comes in the chapter "The Preciousness of the Four Mainstays."

As you begin the reading of this book, the most important reading tool is simply to be open. Openness, interest and easeful relaxation are the best possible stance. We hope that you, dear reader, enjoy your journey through this wonderful book. Thank you once again, brilliant Rinpoche, for devoting yourself to the benefit of all, and for the gift of this book in deepening and furthering that benefit.

Foreword

THE FURTHERANCE OF DZOGCHEN

The enlightenment Teachings have been present for thousands of years. They aren't anything new, but they have looked different in the cultures where there was a teaching. In each of these practices, there is a mystical teaching of enlightenment, if someone can find it. No matter what it is—Hinduism, Judaism, Christianity, Buddhism, Islam—they all have mystical teachings that state this Dzogchen truth.

However, they are not usually given openly in this clear and straightforward way, so I feel greatly fortunate to have been introduced to the Dzogchen Teaching. We in this Teaching have a very simplified approach to Dzogchen, and this simplified approach is something that was encouraged by my guru, Wangdor Rimpoche. Thank you, Wangdor Rimpoche!

We don't even really need to call it Dzogchen, but we are Dzogchen practitioners, so we use that name. Wangdor Rimpoche has emphasized for us what is called "furtherance of Dzogchen." Furtherance of Dzogchen means betterment of Dzogchen, and "betterment of Dzogchen" isn't entirely focused on only one culture. The Teaching needs to be made accessible to people all around the world.

With any new language or culture that is dissimilar to the culture we grew up in, at first it takes a while to become acquainted with that new culture and to grasp its logic. And so it is with these Teachings, which were being sustained and cherished in a culture very different from our own. These are very old Teachings, and Dzogchen practitioners have practiced Dzogchen for many thousands of years. It is truly a very long lineage.

The word "Dzogchen" means "great perfection." That's how it is usually translated, but its actual meaning is "utter completion of one's own intelligence." The profound meaning of this sentence is that for human beings there is nothing else to be. Dzogchen tells us that we are perfect as we are—open intelligence pervaded by love.

There may be a creating and advancing of Dzogchen knowledge today, but Dzogchen itself is never advanced. Dzogchen is *as it is*. Dzogchen understanding is advanced, but Dzogchen is not advanced. Dzogchen, great perfection, is always present, declaring everything as perfect.

Although Dzogchen is still being taught by some within the framework of Tibetan Buddhism, now it is also being taught independently and separately from Tibetan Buddhism. In order to give everyone a sense of context and community, we in our Teaching talk about Dzogchen because we are part of the Dzogchen community, but we're a unique expression, one could say, and one that is very important to the future of the practice. It's a time of new systems, including this new system for Dzogchen.

Wangdor Rimpoche and others have stated that Tibetan Buddhism may possibly disappear, and that Dzogchen, as termed "Dzogchen," may also disappear. But let's keep in mind the subtle meaning of this statement. Dzogchen has only been called by that name for 1200 years. Before that it was called something else, and before even that time, it was called yet again something else. This is an era of great change in which there is now a global audience, and the great Rinpoches feel that Dzogchen needs to bring its message to a wider community using terms and language that are understandable for a worldwide audience.

As Wangdor Rimpoche's specific concern was for the furtherance of Dzogchen, he asked me to write a Dzogchen Teaching for a global audience, and to write it in English. To this end, I have written thousands of pages of Dzogchen Teachings for a new era. I have been given the opportunity and permission to reformulate the Teachings so that they are more accessible in this modern age.

I personally have great respect for the tradition of Dzogchen in its many, many forms and technologies over the years; however, for a global audience, many of these words and Teachings of traditional Dzogchen are no longer easily understandable. Instead of applying all kinds of reified explanations to the Teaching, we have taken Dzogchen and rendered it into a language that is understandable to as many people as possible. They can then be introduced to the practice and take it up, and thereby amplify and elevate their own mind as a mind of open intelligence and love.

Dzogchen practitioners throughout the ages have seen the importance of passing the Teachings on to the next generation. Due to that, new technologies were developed so that they could serve a new generation and meet the needs of people of that time, as well as those to come. For example, when Padmasambhava came to Tibet with the Dzogchen Teachings, he looked at everything that was present in Tibet at that time, and he adapted to what was wanted and needed by the people there. They had been practicing a shamanistic form of religion, and Padmasambhava had to look at the entire situation and see what was most suited in that context. He could see that it wouldn't work to just take people away from what they already knew; instead, it would be more skillful to include the things with which the people were already involved. As a result, he put together a form of Buddhism with the shamanistic elements, and that's how Tibetan Buddhism and Dzogchen were formed in the way that they were and how they became so colorful and unique.

Before there was writing and only an oral tradition in Dzogchen, the early masters would carry small paintings with them so they could illustrate the metaphors, similes and analogies that were used in the Teaching. When they would refer to metaphors like "a rainbow in the sky" or "the sky and the color blue," they would hold up the painting to clearly illustrate what the metaphors were pointing to. It was the technology specifically suited to its time.

Throughout the history of Dzogchen, many of the great innovations have occurred from sources that were peripheral to the tradition itself. In order for something new to occur, what is required is the capacity to see that the current ideas in a particular culture are not necessarily the apex of all ideas. Just as there were big changes in Tibet with the Dzogchen Teachings over the centuries, so too now there are very great changes occurring. New and even revolutionary ideas about furthering Dzogchen have emerged, and through these revolutionary innovations we now have many ways of presenting the symbology of Dzogchen that were previously unavailable. Dzogchen has always adapted to where it is, but it always stayed totally pure.

I've approached this furtherance of Dzogchen not knowing for sure what the consequence would be, but "taking action without knowing the consequences" is another Dzogchen practice! Everything occurs spontaneously in Dzogchen without any kind of attachment to a consequence. In that context, everything is considered and nothing is left out. I have tried to make this Teaching as simple and as pragmatic as I can. I really completely believe in pragmatic philosophy, and as a philosopher, it's very important to me that philosophy be pragmatic, applicable and beneficial.

I am not interested in perpetuating common misperceptions. I'm engaging in a revolution that leads to the benefit of all; I want everyone to know that they are competent and that their mind is a space of ultimate wish-fulfillment. This is what the Dzogchen Teaching states, and I am a Dzogchen practitioner as well as a lineage holder. I know that the practice achieves results.

We can think of all of the Dzogchen creators of knowledge— Rinpoches, thangka-makers, artists and creators of all of the cultural symbols of Dzogchen, all of the practitioners—and our gratitude is extended to everyone who has carried forth this knowledge. The authentic Dzogchen teachers who are direct lineage successors of the Dzogchen Teachings and who are authorized by their guru to teach Dzogchen are rare and precious, and their teachings are rare and precious, and the community of practitioners is rare and precious! Heart gratitude to the profound Dzogchen masters who have served to carry to us the message of Dzogchen!

Part One

THE INTRODUCTION TO
OPEN INTELLIGENCE

LIVING AS OPEN INTELLIGENCE
CHAPTER ONE

Always-on open intelligence is the birthright and natural state of every human being, and relying on open intelligence is made easy in the following way: in short moments, repeated many times, open intelligence becomes increasingly obvious. As a human being we have a most important choice to make, and every single person can elect to make this most important choice with every thought or experience they may have.

Open intelligence has always been our only reality, and it always will be our only reality, whether recognized as such or not. Wherever we are, open intelligence is; wherever open intelligence is, we are. We are unborn open intelligence; we always have been, we are now and we always will be only that. There is no destination anywhere in sight.

Open intelligence is the power to know, and the power to know is the exact nature of intelligence. Open intelligence never comes together nor separates from anything; it does not come together with us nor does it separate itself from us. There is not a single thing anywhere that can be found to be apart from open intelligence. This brilliant intelligence is open and unlimited, hence an "*open* intelligence." It is completely permeated with love, hence the term "open intelligence and love."

To introduce open intelligence very directly, stop thinking just for a moment. What remains? A sense of alert knowing—powerful open intelligence—that is open like a clear sky. This is the pervasive, inexhaustible and undistracted singular intelligence that knows, sees and does. Our own knowing is that of open intelligence itself, so how could we possibly be apart from that?

Open intelligence already is. It does not require being or doing in any certain way. Even when we are sleeping, dreaming, unconscious or dying, the reality is that we are never apart from open intelligence. Open intelligence is in all things, without there being separate "things" in which it could exist! By living as open intelligence, we live in basic harmony with all, and this harmony is not something that is contrived. It comes from the realization of equalness and evenness. What could be more harmonious than equalness and evenness, the reality of everything?

No matter what our feelings or our thoughts or any other kinds of experience might be, our refuge and natural resource is in open intelligence. Whether we are happy and carefree, or writhing in pain and misery, this is the resource we need to call upon. Our natural state of unborn open intelligence is our go-to in life. Instead of trying to construct a life, we live as the seamless benefit and empowerment of open intelligence.

Once we are introduced to open intelligence, we realize it as our primary identity, and by gaining confidence in it, a vast power of pure benefit and love is illuminated within us. Open intelligence and love is the core competence for living a beneficial life, and yet, we do not need to "know" anything about open intelligence, for it cannot be known in that way. Recognition of its obvious nature through short moments many times is the key point. There is no need to figure anything out.

If we have never been told about our true nature, how could we know what it is? How would we know anything other than what conventional society has taught us to be true? But yet now, here, in these few words, we *are* being introduced to our real nature— loving open intelligence. What good fortune that we should be introduced to the great beauty of everything *as it is*! Open intelligence is already present, so "being introduced to it" is just an expression.

Open intelligence is the singular reality of everyone and everything; it is just that we have not noticed it. Why? Because no one ever told us about it. Why? Because the people who were educating us didn't know about it themselves.

MOST IMPORTANT CHOICE

Always-on open intelligence is the birthright and natural state of every human being, and this is made evident in the following way: in relying on open intelligence for short moments, repeated many times, open intelligence becomes increasingly obvious. As a human being we have an important choice to make, and every single person can elect to make this most important choice with each thought or experience they have. One choice is to see data *(all thoughts, emotions, sensations and experiences)* as something that has an independent nature and which is real and has meaning, and the other choice is to rely on open intelligence, no matter what appears. We can choose for open intelligence to be obvious for us or not.

No matter what happens, there are these two choices: to rely on open intelligence or to perpetuate the story of appearances. That's it. Whether the appearances are conceived to be mundane or special, in either situation there is an equal opportunity to realize the nature of one's own being.

We don't need all kinds of ways to find open intelligence. Actually, nothing is needed. We keep it simple: short moments, many times. If we have positive data, that's fine. If we have negative data, that's fine. There is no need to control the natural flow of data. Place the emphasis on short moments of open intelligence; that's all. The data just flow along doing whatever they do. Open intelligence is naturally at rest. Leave everything *as it is*.

A short moment of open intelligence eventually grows longer and longer, until open intelligence is obvious in our everyday experience. The first time the choice is made to rely on open intelligence, rather than emphasizing data, there is a sense of the great power of complete relief that is to be found. By persisting in this one simple choice, benefits are seen from the outset, and by the power of resting as open intelligence its recognition becomes increasingly obvious.

REST AND RELAX!

There is only one message here, and that is to stop seeking. Stop seeking! There is no search to be undertaken. Everything to be known or realized is already known and realized. There is no destination and there is no one going there. All there is, is stainless, flawless ever-present open intelligence. If you choose to relax body and mind completely and rest naturally as open intelligence for short moments repeated many times until it becomes obvious, open intelligence will become more and more evident.

When the terms "rest" or "resting" are used, they mean to allow short moments of open intelligence, many times, leaving everything just *as it is*. Short moments increasingly open up the balanced view, clarity and insight of open intelligence. Short moments repeated again and again become spontaneous, and clarity becomes increasingly obvious until it is evident at all times. We gain deep confidence in the power of short moments to bring benefit to our lives. We keep it simple: resting, or we could also say relaxing, for short moments, many times.

All of our life we may have been completely lost in this dizzying maelstrom of data—thoughts, emotions, sensations and all phenomena of experience—but suddenly through relying on open intelligence, we begin to enjoy ease of being. Even if in the beginning this ease isn't experienced all the time, it will at least be there some of the time. With each short moment of ease, we begin to see that we have power over all these thoughts, emotions, belief systems and ideas that we thought we were at the whim of.

We start out with the desire to benefit ourselves through resting as open intelligence, and through that practice of self-benefit we open up to the benefit of others, without having to try to do anything. When we have complete ease and complete perceptual openness in all our experiences, especially the negative ones, we throw open the floodgates of compassion for ourselves and for others.

Enjoying short moments of open intelligence is like finishing a hard day's work or relaxing in a warm and soothing bath. We are completely relaxed with nothing more to do. Relaxed open intelligence can be recognized in any circumstance—walking, running, working, thinking, parenting, studying, eating, making love and all daily activities. By the power of short moments, we are no longer derailed by disturbing emotions. Instead, we remain as we are, stable, clear and at ease. Unchanging open intelligence becomes our vantage. It is the easy way to live.

We need to simply allow the moment of the uncontrived naturalness of open intelligence. Instead of focusing upon it, it is simply allowed to naturally be *as it is*. The more we have confidence in the natural presence of open intelligence, the less we need to deliberately rely on short moments, and the easier it becomes to recognize that open intelligence is self-sustained.

Simply stated, short moments of open intelligence are soothing, while constantly having to micromanage data is uncomfortable. By the power of a short moment of open intelligence, we directly experience freedom from ups and downs and we begin to have a balanced outlook. We are better able to be of benefit to ourselves, our family, community and world. When we rely on open intelligence, we tap into our innate strengths, gifts and talents and contribute them for the benefit of all.

No matter how frenetic or calm the mind is, and no matter how crazy or calm the emotions are, and whatever the circumstances may be, they are the perfect circumstances for relying on open intelligence. The more we rely on open intelligence, the more there is the naturally occurring appearance of a warm sense of ease and well-being that pervades everything. More and more there is the ability to be in all situations without impediment. So, why would we want to go back to what didn't work: the constant micromanaging of endless thoughts and emotions? Why would we want to go back to being disturbed by disturbing states? There is no reason whatsoever to do so.

When we completely relax our body and mind in a natural way, we taste definitively and decisively the nature of everything. That's all that is needed; there is not a single other thing that is needed. Even though this may perhaps sound too easy compared with some of the other approaches to life you may have been using, just know that throughout history many, many people have come to realize the fundamental nature of their mind through this practice, because it is so simple and direct.

This essential practice of resting imperturbably as open intelligence stretches like a chain of golden mountains from one generation to another. This is the epitome of all practices of understanding our true nature. It is the practice that is accompanied by unerring instruction so that we always have the practical know-how of how to rest. Short moments is a practice that anyone can do. Never underestimate the power of this simple practice.

Open intelligence is not dependent on whether someone is Jewish, Buddhist, Christian, atheist or agnostic. We could be the most virtuous person on earth or we could have just murdered twenty people, but in the next moment we still have the opportunity to gain assurance in open intelligence. Whether we're a saint or a sinner, totally immoral and unethical or the opposite of that, people of every kind have flourished in this

23

practice. We all live in, of, as and through open intelligence. That is just the way it is.

IN THE BEGINNING

To rest the mind completely means to rest without description. When a description comes up, continue to rest without elaborating on the description. Rest as that which has no descriptions. Rather than trying to contrive a separate period of rest, like for instance only when one is sitting in meditation, rest repeatedly with all the many situations in everyday life until open intelligence becomes obvious.

At first, taking short moments may be only intermittent. Very rarely does total confidence in short moments come about immediately. For most, in the beginning it is intermittent, and then with repeated return to the practice it becomes spontaneous and obvious. So, one could choose this approach of taking short moments, or it could be a choice of continuing just to hear the message of the way things really are until conviction dawns, or a combination of the two. Whatever it is for you, it is absolutely fine. The short moments of open intelligence gradually grow longer. Initially there may be just a few seconds of open intelligence, but in a simple way, increasingly there will be more and more recognition.

Even though in the beginning it may seem like not much progress is being made, most assuredly progress *is* being made. It's very easy to eventually develop confidence in the practice, because it doesn't take a long time to see the benefits. You come to the point of wanting to rely on open intelligence more and more because of the benefits you have derived. It isn't like having to force yourself into a discipline; it is instead a very natural flow.

The best approach comes not through lots of thinking about it or through philosophizing about it. We can understand a little bit through words, but when it comes right down to it, what we truly are is completely beyond words and concepts. There is no mental achievement or avenue of doing that will lead to it. The only avenue of swift accomplishment is to rest imperturbably for short moments many times until the resting becomes spontaneous.

When we rely on open intelligence, less and less do we feel ourselves to be so defined by all the stirrings within us that say, "I am me; I am somebody; I need certain thoughts to make me feel good." This identification with being somebody who always needs more and more to make her or himself feel good is like an addiction. This self-centered identification doesn't tell us the truth of who we are, and it gives us an extremely limited way of seeing ourselves.

Please don't worry if you don't understand what is being described here. You don't need to do anything. Just show up and continue to rely on short moments, and conviction will dawn. Just with a little openness, these instructions will come fully alive for you.

NOTHING NEEDS TO CHANGE

Nothing needs to change. No matter how we are living now, we begin by relying on open intelligence. We don't have to live in any special setting—like being remote from other people or renouncing the world—to enjoy our true nature. We can do that if we want to, but it doesn't produce any cause for realizing our true nature. All lifestyles are primordially pure. We can be a great saint, a computer programmer, a ditch digger, a cake baker or whatever it is, and it's the perfect circumstance for the realization of our true nature. Indeed, there is no practice or lifestyle that is necessary, and at the same time, no practice or lifestyle is to be excluded.

As we recognize our natural state just *as it is*, all effort to "find open intelligence" or "become aware" gradually ceases, and open intelligence is seen to be permanent and obvious at all times. Open intelligence becomes predominant in the natural flow of all data that appear.

Many of us have been living in such a way that our life has been a constant self-improvement project, and so when we want to find out about the nature of our being, we may assume that it is also another self-improvement project. In that case, we will naturally go somewhere where we will be told that we have to be improved. However, it is a great relief to know that no improvement is necessary. Nothing need be done. The greatest saint and the greatest sinner are equal in open intelligence. Open intelligence is the true equal opportunity for everyone!

When we recognize open intelligence, we go right to the basis of everything we need to know and be. If we try to force open intelligence by contriving it in a certain way through changing our behavior or lifestyle, we are just creating more conditions. We are saying that open intelligence can only be in certain conditions; however, open intelligence is not dependent on anything and is not based on conditions.

This is absolutely accessible to everyone. It doesn't depend on anything else. It doesn't depend on being learned enough to understand philosophical concepts. It doesn't depend on being intellectually bright. All we have to do is to rest. We don't need to make our thoughts, emotions and experiences be like someone else's, like those of an exalted historical figure. Nothing needs to change.

QUESTION AND ANSWER

Q. I am a bit unfamiliar with you and this teaching. Could you tell me a bit more about how all of what you are doing got started?

Ziji Rinpoche: Yes, and I could begin just by speaking about the unfoldment in my own life. Even as a child I had a great passion for the benefit of all, and I could never forget that passion. No matter what anyone did, I couldn't see anything but their innate brilliance and power.

Later on in life when I was a young woman, I experienced an enormous leap into a completely new space of open intelligence that had previously been unfamiliar to me. I was sitting in a Denny's restaurant in Eureka, California, and in a moment my entire life flashed before me—every single incident, every single person, every single thing I had ever done, and it all made perfect sense to me. I could see that every single thing in my life, no matter what it was, had brought me to that point of sitting in the Denny's restaurant and having this incredible experience. Suddenly I didn't know what anything was, and that was just fine with me! Yet, in not knowing what anything was or is, what came about was a rain of self-benefit. It occurred in a peculiar, personal way that was completely beyond either the personal or the impersonal.

I saw that whether I had taken a right turn or wrong turn in my life, or whether I had liked people I met or didn't like people, or whether my thinking and my emotional life had been good or bad, none of it mattered. No matter what description I could apply, it all described the same thing. And really all I could say was "Wow!" That's how profound it was. That's all I said for about an hour: "Wow! Wow!"

There arose the power of complete willingness, I would say, to be of profound benefit. With that power also shone forth incredible lucidity; they co-emerged inseparably. I could see that all negative thoughts and afflictions had open intelligence and love as their core. At some point I said to myself, "I am going to make sure that everyone in the world knows this, too."

I walked along the docks by the oceanside until about four in the morning. I looked up at the sky and I instinctively understood what "eternal" means—that we always are and always have been and always will be. This was very real and very true for me.

I wanted to make sense of this experience, and over the next years I went through all the great texts from the major religions. I wrote the texts out beginning to end by hand, even though they might be hundreds of pages long. I also wrote these texts out in the first person, rather than in third person, and that was a powerful means of integration.

The relationships that I began to have with others were fulfilling and satisfying and filled with love, wisdom and energy beyond anything I could have cooked up or contrived. Without hesitation I committed my entire life to what will be of greatest benefit to all. That's what I see as the touchstone for all my actions: what will be of greatest benefit to all. Many people have a dream and want to make that dream a reality, and so it was for me too.

I am married and have children and grandchildren; yet, that is not where I chose to put all of my attention. I have a much broader concept of family, and that is due to the development of beneficial potency and comprehensive intelligence within me.

I knew for sure that the message I am committed to would have to come from the grassroots of humanity and could never come from an institution, a corporation or a large organization. It would have to come from you and me and from all those who resonated with such a message. Then it became a matter of going out and finding what people really wanted for themselves and how they wanted to live their lives. Very often the response from people was, "I want to be of benefit in some way." This is conclusive;

people want to be of benefit, and we want to be of benefit because we are beneficial by nature. So, here we are now, a worldwide community of people committed to benefit.

Many people told me that it would be impossible to do what I wanted to do and that it would never happen. Yet, I knew it would happen. I didn't care what anybody said, because I could see the great exaltation in everyone, and now this message has spread throughout the world. Through everyone gathering together from the grassroots, coming in contact with one another, listening, reading, hearing and adopting this lifestyle, this training is spreading around the world. Through the reach of the internet and telecommunications, now anyone can participate. The seeds are planted, the roots are very, very strong and the plants are flowering. There was a special way for each of us who are now in the Teaching to be reached, and just as there was a special way to reach us, there are other ways to reach many more people.

Some people may want to just be soothed and temporarily relieved of their pain, but I know for sure, because I am one of them, that there are people who have incredible passions in life. They have passions that burn within them, and they long to find what they are capable of. However, that capacity isn't going to come about by merely thinking about our passion or talking to our friends about it or writing essays or books about it. It is going to come about by allowing everything to be *as it is* in complete reliance on open intelligence.

To deeply rest in the realization of the reality of who we are is absolutely essential. The ideas presented to us about who we are often are very off-base. Very often we have a jumble of all kinds of things that we have heard about ourselves—ideas that have been presented to us about who we are, things that we think about ourselves, and data streams that are running here, there and everywhere.

29

We have to acknowledge that in fact *we* are the ones who have allowed ourselves to be trained up in these data streams; no one else made us do it. Many people balk at giving up their right to be a victim, but when it comes down to it, we all have a choice. If we keep it very simple, we can say that at any moment in our lives we're either choosing to be ruled by our data or we are choosing to rest as open intelligence. Rather than getting into all these trips about blaming other people, parents, spouses or negative events, if we just say, "My data are my data," then there's no one to blame. It's up to us as to how we respond to the contents of our minds.

We give up our right to be a victim of anything that has occurred in the past, which in fact goes against the way we have been trained as human beings, which is to think about our identity as being the sum of everything that has occurred in the past. It is of course true that many people, including myself, have had very violent and traumatic events occur in their lives. Terrible and inexcusable things may have happened, but what is our vantage in relationship to that event *right now*? To say to oneself, "I give up my right to be a victim," is a very powerful stand to take, because first of all we are no longer allowing the data about a person or an event to rule us. We are taking responsibility, and there is no instinctive realization that will ever occur unless this responsibility is taken. To give up the right to be a victim is very, very powerful.

We may have been taught not to talk openly about some of our deeply personal thoughts, emotions, sensations or other experiences, including the one just mentioned of feeling oneself to be a victim. We may feel shame or embarrassment when we look deeply at these things. People have been taught to keep these personal data streams to themselves, and they so often don't want to talk about these things openly. When facing reality straight on, it doesn't always feel good, because it's so much different from what we've been taught, but the great beneficial power of open intelligence lies in facing everything and avoiding nothing.

Support in all its forms is so crucial. That same support has been crucial for me personally. It took many decades before I felt I had someone in my life who would really stand behind me, but then that person came—my revered guru Wangdor Rimpoche. He said to me, "I will make sure that you can do anything you want to do." When he said that to me, I was so profoundly touched by the statement and the openness and love in it, but I was also very inspired, because I wanted to make it possible for every single person to hear those words from someone at some point in their life. Now we have people all over the world who are those someones.

COMPLETE PERCEPTUAL OPENNESS IN ALL EXPERIENCE

CHAPTER TWO

Whatever appears within the all-encompassing pure view of open intelligence is pure in and of itself. Even if we have learned that data are positive, negative or neutral, this idea is all made up. All labels, all words and all descriptions exist as a single expanse of evenness in which there has never been anything that is uneven or not equal. This expanse of evenness and equalness is pure love and the natural state of every human being.

No datum has an origin independent of open intelligence. It makes no difference what data arise; in open intelligence data vanish naturally, leaving no trace, like a line drawn in water.

In realizing the inseparability of open intelligence and data, confidence is gained. This confidence leads to a deep caring about life and about our effect on the world. Open intelligence, relaxed and enormously potent, is the source of mental and emotional stability, insight and skillful qualities and activities, and by the power of the instinctive recognition of open intelligence, these become increasingly evident.

The super-completeness of open intelligence in and of itself and the data that appear within it are like the air and a breeze which blows through it: there has never been any separation or division. It is impossible to say where the breeze began, where its middle is and where its end is. Just so, no matter what data appear within open intelligence, they have never been anything other than the basic space of open intelligence.

"Data" is the term we can use for all thoughts, emotions, sensations, experiences, people, places and things. "Data" are anything that occurs within the all-encompassing view of open intelligence. The thoughts, emotions, sensations or other experiences can be related to inner or outer events, but they are never anything other than the dynamic energy of open intelligence. To rely on thoughts, emotions and sensations—data—is the learned activity of the mind that drives us into a life of reification and suffering. We learn to reify thoughts, we learn to reify emotions and we learn to reify sensations and experiences. "To reify" means that we give people, places, things, thoughts, emotions and experiences an independent nature.

Prior to knowing any other way to be, the reification of thoughts, emotions, sensations and experiences has informed everything we do. We use data to define who we are and how we will identify ourselves. Most often we don't realize that we have even done this or that we could be something other than how we have always described ourselves to be.

All data appear and vanish naturally, like the flight path of a bird in the sky. Thoughts, emotions, sensations or other experiences can be simply recognized as data—the illumination of open intelligence. So, rest the mind and body naturally without pushing away thoughts and without seeking anything. This is all that is required, whether activity is strenuous, relaxed or in-between. What remains is clarity and alertness that is open like a clear sky. *This is what open intelligence is!* When the next thought comes, it appears due to the clarity and alertness of open intelligence.

This is similar to the vast sky being present regardless of what appears within it. Whether aware of having thoughts or not having thoughts, both modes require open intelligence.

When we stop thinking for a moment, the clarity and presence of open intelligence is obvious. This clarity that is present when we are *not* thinking is also present when we *are* thinking. All thoughts appear and vanish naturally. At the very moment data form, recognize spacious open intelligence shining from within each datum.

DATA ARE THE DYNAMIC ENERGY OF OPEN INTELLIGENCE

Data are the dynamic energy of open intelligence and nothing else. They are inseparable from open intelligence like the color blue is inseparable from the sky. There is no need to try to separate out the color blue from the sky, and there is no need to try to separate out data from open intelligence.

Whatever appears within the all-encompassing pure view of open intelligence is pure in and of itself. Even if we have learned that data are positive, negative or neutral, this idea is all made up. All labels, all words and all descriptions exist as a single expanse of evenness in which there has never been anything that is uneven or not equal. This expanse of evenness and equalness is pure love and the natural state of every human being.

All emotional states completely resolve in open intelligence, and in that resolution there is a knowledge about what to do and how to act in each time, place and circumstance. We have built up our defenses to try to protect ourselves and stay safe; however, it isn't like there is something wrong with us or that we are bad or flawed. This is just an assumption about data that has come about over time. It's important for us to be gentle with ourselves. We allow the natural ease of our being to become more and more obvious.

Open intelligence is comfort and ease, no matter what the display may be. As the ease of our own being becomes more and more obvious to us, we come to know what pure love is. Pure love and ease are equal; they are synonymous. We were meant to love others and ourselves in this way without exclusion—without excluding anything about ourselves, whether it be our thoughts, our emotions or our experiences, and whether they are past, present or future. Nothing needs to be manipulated or coaxed to another level or changed. As long as we are living within a need to change everything, we can never know the ease of our own being.

Each moment undoes everything that has gone before. If you have done all sorts of horrible things in your life or you are a great saintly being, the next moment is equal for everyone. To live a life permeated with self-criticism can't help but also lead to criticism of others. That's just the way it is. To gain familiarity with the open intelligence that is at the basis of everything gently relieves us of that self-criticism. We come into the wholly positive goodness of our own being, and as we do so we feel that same gentleness and kindness for other people as well, because we see that other people are just like us.

INDULGING, AVOIDING AND REPLACING DATA

We have four choices in how we respond to the data that appear for us. One choice is to indulge the data, a second is to avoid the data, a third is to replace the data with something else, and a fourth is to rely on flawless open intelligence until all is seen as flawless open intelligence.

Let's give two examples of indulging, avoiding and replacing: one with anger and another with fear. So, say that anger is a strong appearance that comes up frequently, and it has possibly been coming up for us all our lives. One response is that we can indulge the anger, and maybe we've had a habit of doing that. This is what we have learned to do, and so when we get angry we indulge the anger by blowing up at someone and letting them have it.

The second way is to renounce the anger, to shut it out, to avoid it. When the anger comes up, we don't want anything to do with it; we are just not going to go there, and we are going to steel ourselves and make ourselves not get angry. Maybe we also internalize the anger and hold it within.

The third approach is to replace the negative state of anger with a positive state. We get angry, but while engaging in the anger, we try to cultivate positive data, like happiness or compassion or whatever it might be. We might say, "I am going to think happy thoughts and replace the angry thoughts with these happy thoughts."

Now let's also take it from another angle, that of fear. The indulgence of fear would be that, when fear comes up, we start thinking about why we are afraid. "Oh, I'm afraid because there are these nuclear missiles and the world might come to an end. All these countries are at war, and people just can't get along, and it is a terrible world where pandemic and harm are around every corner." The fear is indulged and it's described, and then we really get afraid. We start out just with the thought of fear, and then it can be spun out into a freefall of terror.

The second thing to do with fear is to avoid it. So, fear comes up and we say, "Okay, now I am going to stay in solitude or avoid all potentially risky situations, and that way I won't have to deal with all this fear I am experiencing." That might temporarily neutralize the fear, but it does not resolve it.

The third approach would be to replace the fear with a positive state—an antidote. The fear comes up, and we say, "Okay, I am going to cultivate courageous thoughts now and in that way I will get rid of the fear," or, "Maybe if I go on to the internet for five or six hours, I can numb the fear by becoming knowledgeable about all the causes of fear."

So, whether it is anger or fear or whatever else it might be, these are three ways of dealing with a data stream. All three of these approaches require that there be a doer, someone who is doing something to try to manage, manipulate, analyze or transform whatever data are appearing. But this is a lot of work! When we approach life in this way, we are always sorting out the data, and we're trying to get more positive data and less negative data so that eventually we will only have positive data. But that can never be done. It is absolutely fruitless and it leads to exhaustion.

These three approaches—indulging, avoiding, replacing—are only half measures. In fact, they are not even half measures; they are completely fruitless in the end. They are measures that go nowhere; they just lead to more of the same. Even if the thoughts and emotions around fear and anger are neutralized and they seem a little bit better, "a little bit better" is still a matter of bouncing back and forth within a world of opposites. Whenever we are thinking that something needs to be replaced, that we need to do better, that we are not the right kind of person, that we need to improve, that we need to change, each of these is a detour away from the only real solution, which is to rely on open intelligence.

Only the fourth approach conclusively situates us in the unimpeded essence of our own being, and the fourth approach is: from flawless open intelligence, we see all as flawless open intelligence, until everything is flawless open intelligence. Said another way, as we rely on open intelligence for short moments many times, we come to see all things as being open intelligence, until all is spontaneously recognized as open intelligence. In this way, we are easily and effortlessly able to realize that everything truly is a single expanse of open intelligence, including all of the afflictive states that we have previously wanted to indulge, avoid or replace.

We rest as the ultimate basis of the fear and the anger—open intelligence—and in doing so, more and more the fear and anger are seen as the dynamic energy of open intelligence and as inseparable from it, just as the color blue is inseparable from the sky. The basic space of the fear is primordially pure open intelligence, but that can only be recognized and decisively experienced through complete assurance in open intelligence. It can't be experienced through indulging, avoiding or replacing it with any other state.

If there is anything that we are identifying as impure within the pure expanse, then we're taking a wrong turn. As everything is already pure, there has never been anything that is impure. There has never been anything that is needed to be done in order to make what is already pure become pure.

Rather than focusing on the things that were so troublesome in the past that we felt we needed to avoid or replace, now there is just resting as the open intelligence of those data streams, with no need to change them. When we rely on open intelligence, a whole new world opens up; it is a secret world that has always been present! It has only been a secret because we haven't known it is there.

FREEDOM IN IMMEDIATE PERCEPTION

The great fulfillment of human life is the total openness to reality *as it is*. There is only the primordial unborn source, and "unborn" means always *as it is*, never entering into any kind of process, such as being born, living and dying. No matter what our feelings or our thoughts or any other kinds of experience might be, and no matter whether we are happy and carefree or writhing in pain and misery, our refuge is in open intelligence.

We allow everything to be *as it is*, and here we find freedom in immediate perception and complete perceptual openness in all experience. We are not running around trying to find release from negative data through replacing them with other kinds of data. Instead, we are allowing everything to be *as it is*. In freedom in immediate perception we abide as open intelligence as the datum arises, and the ground of its being—open intelligence—is allowed to shine forth. We see the datum come, then it stays for a while, then another datum comes, it stays, and then it too goes away. This direct encounter with all data streams while resting as open intelligence is complete freedom in immediate perception. There is nothing to work with or work on, because it is seen that the coming and the going are all data streams as well. In resting naturally without seeking anything, there is nothing to do; there is complete effortlessness and complete perceptual openness in all experience.

We start to notice from there that the data are self-releasing and that we really never had to do anything at all to the data. We could not hold on to anything even if we wanted to. The self-releasing of data allows one to enter into the realm of spontaneous existence with everything being exactly *as it is*. This does not mean all the data streams turn into ones with nice names; it is just that we have realized that all we are is beneficial potency, and there isn't anything else going on.

The here-and-now is spontaneously self-releasing, and it cannot be captured in any way; there is no way to measure it or take hold of it and keep it. Only open intelligence is certain, and by letting everything be *as it is* and seeing that everything does self-release, open intelligence's beneficial potencies become more evident. That is when we really start to have the ability to respond spontaneously and directly and to have the immediate solution in each situation. That allows for spontaneous existence; that allows for open-ended knowledge and benefit creation; that allows for the benefit of all to be our only priority.

We can realize the profundity in allowing all data to be *as it is* in the shining forth of all of its dynamic energy. In this recognition is the power of great benefit. It is not a benefit put together in a contrived way; it is the ultimate benefit of open intelligence. We rely on open intelligence, and we come to see that everything is the great shining forth of open intelligence itself. All the ideas about who we are and what we are doing now, what we are going to do and what we did last time, all this is equal and even. Data simply flow on by.

In open intelligence, data streams are already naturally pure, perfect, empowered, harmonious, indivisible and beneficial. Countermeasures to our data streams are completely unnecessary, unless of course it is the ultimate countermeasure that reveals that all data are in fact open intelligence! We no longer go into the deep cave of ignorance because of a lack of education in the nature of mind; we give ourselves permission to be as we truly are. There isn't any longer the belief in the independent power of data.

It is a very simple way of life. Instead of going around trying to find the right data to relieve our anguish, we see that by allowing data to be as they are, our anxiety is naturally relieved. Real freedom has its root and source in open intelligence and nowhere else. Freedom does not need to be sought, and no kind of freedom can be constructed. The only freedom there is is unborn great freedom and great fulfillment.

LIFE SATISFACTION AND FLOURISHING

Simple, straightforward open intelligence is clarifying and empowering. When we look at the results of the short moments practice, we find that they are very powerful indeed. Through short moments, we as a global human culture are tapping into a form of knowledge that can give us complete mental and emotional stability, insight, compassion, natural ethics and beneficial skillfulness in all situations and the consistent ability to fulfill beneficial intent.

Human life is a precious opportunity, and the two things that make it so are the opportunity to benefit oneself and to benefit others. Now, that's very simple, isn't it? When we look at the fact that we have this precious human opportunity, we need to know how to go about benefitting ourselves and benefitting others. This self-benefit and benefit of others is already present within us, and it isn't something we get from somewhere else. Getting in touch with that benefit and tapping into it is very straightforward and simple. What is already present isn't something that we need to strive to achieve.

When we rely on open intelligence for short moments repeated many times in a totally uncontrived way, we have more and more love in our life. We have more and more energy, wisdom and ability to be of benefit to ourselves and to others. A shift occurs from the thinking, speaking, qualities and activities of a life focused on the individual self to the wisdom mind—open intelligence—which has as its naturally occurring focus the benefit of all. From the practice of short moments comes genuine life-satisfaction and flourishing.

Open intelligence burns like a wildfire through all conventional designations. There isn't a conventional designation that can stand in its fire. All the dreamed-up things about how powerful our emotions and thoughts are are just burnt to nothing. Why should we depend on emotional states to inform who we are? Why not depend on wisdom? For anyone who wants to feel better, why not seek to feel better on a *permanent*, rather than temporary, basis?

It is like a scientist who has a hypothesis and tests it to see the result. In the same way, here is a hypothesis for you to test, and you can see for yourself what the results are.

WHAT'S LOOKING

Our true being is directly accessible and is not something that is out of reach. If we think that it is out of reach and we are looking somewhere for it, then we have to just relax as *what's looking*. If what's looking is looking at a cat or a dog—or at an ego or a self-identity or at a goal of enlightenment—it is all rooted in open intelligence. What's looking is the complete free form perceptual openness in each moment that is pure, simple, complete and identical just *as it is*.

If you get in touch with what's looking, you will see that what's looking is what is seeing you! It is not only seeing all this that seems to be around you, what's looking is what's seeing you as well. If you rest as what's looking, you come to see that what's looking is not limited to you and is not trapped within the skin line of your body. It has seemed as though it was trapped there because you have trained yourself to believe that it is and because you have been exposed to a lot of other people who have trained themselves to believe the same thing.

Over the course of our lives we have looked in a mirror again and again, and even as our physical appearance has changed, what's looking has never changed. The reflection in the mirror may have become old, wrinkled and gray, but what's looking is completely unaffected. When we rest as what's looking, the all-pervasiveness of the seeing starts to penetrate everything, without our needing to be thinking about how all of this is coming about.

No matter what appears, it already is timelessly free, so why be troubled by the appearances? The only troublesome aspect of what appears is the description of it, which is just another data stream. In the restful enjoyment of super-complete open intelligence, whatever appears is A-Okay! When we look at what appears and we say, "This is a bad appearance, this is an acceptable appearance, this is an unacceptable appearance," we obscure the naturalness of our own being, which is beyond all these descriptions.

In a very simple way, this is complete perceptional openness in all experience. It is complete ease with no need to cling to anything or push it away—the relaxed openness of all experience.

What's looking is a natural resource of indestructible wisdom. If we are looking for natural resources, it is important to look for the ultimate natural resource first and rely on that. When we rely on wisdom, we are of benefit to ourselves. The things that once bothered us and really got us revved up, like spinning stories to do with fear, anger, jealousy, pride, desire and so on, we see that we are not affected by these things to the same degree anymore.

Where we used to have a story, there isn't a story running any longer. When feeling distracted by thoughts or emotions, we rest as what's looking without continuing to build a story or a description about what is appearing.

If we rest as the equilibrium of what's looking, it's much easier to allow all of these unpredictable thoughts and emotions to be whatever they are without getting overwhelmed by their apparent importance. Whether we label an impression of the mind as "sadness" or whether we label it as "joy," it is the same basic space. It's only when we start to think that some things are good and other things are bad that we seem to have fallen out of the total simplicity of the great equalness. We drain ourselves of our vitality when we persist in holding to the significance and importance of things. The only timeless freedom there is is the natural rest of complete and utter availability that is right here.

The looking and seeing of everything *as it is* occurs whether the eyes are open or shut. It has nothing to do with the eyeballs. If it were only a matter of the eyeballs, then what would be seeing in dreams? When we dream there's all kinds of seeing, smelling, tasting and touching, and yet we are sound asleep. So, what is seeing, hearing, tasting, touching and smelling then? It is ever-present open intelligence. We are completely timelessly free already in the immediacy of what's right here. There is complete freedom in immediate perception, and that freedom in the immediacy of perception is not tied anywhere or to anything. It can't be affected by anything or diverted by anything or conditioned into anything else. It can never be fixated or identified or destroyed in any way.

AN ISLAND OF GOLD

In relying on open intelligence, what is taking place is a process of enrichment, in which our fundamental nature is gradually becoming more and more manifest. Through this enrichment, the island of gold—the great intrinsic radiance, insight and discernment—is seen. On an island of gold, nothing but gold can be found; there isn't a single thing that is not gold, including us! Here we have a very powerful metaphor that has the capacity to disintegrate all of the erroneous ideas we have had about ourselves.

If someone were to take you to live on an island of gold, would you decide instead to live on an island of garbage? We each have to decide where we want to live. Living on the island of gold we recognize that all data are gold, no matter how they are described. Wherever we go on an island of gold, everything is golden, and we're not going to find anything other than gold.

QUESTION AND ANSWER

Q. The fact that people have trouble realizing their original purity leads me to believe that something happened in time to hinder this realization. To what do you attribute this loss of purity?

Ziji Rinpoche: Now, let me please tell you a few things that I learned when I was a girl. One thing I learned is that everyone wants to love and be loved. The second thing I learned is that everyone wants to belong, in other words, to not be ostracized or set aside in any way. Then the third thing that I learned was that everyone had tremendous gifts to give, and it was through love that these gifts would be recognized. I knew these things, but I didn't really know anything much about practically applying them until I was much older. But wherever I went, I looked at what I saw in these terms.

I thought, "Well, this is interesting, because everywhere I look— school, church, family, institutions, government, companies— they are not organized this way. In fact, they are organized as structures of fear, saying, 'If you don't toe the line and behave like everybody else, you won't be able to belong here and we will send you away.'" How could we possibly learn about our strengths, gifts and talents in an atmosphere like that?

I felt that, because there is something about each of us that is only love, if we just get familiar with that love, then all of these other things would become possible. If we know ourselves as love, then our families, our communities, our institutions, our countries and our world would become love-filled. We realize that love in ourselves, and then we realize that it is possible for everyone else, and then everything, no matter what it is, can become love-filled.

I stayed with this belief until it became an actuality. I know that today I am one of many participants in a worldwide movement that is filled with love and caring, where everyone is mutually supported to succeed. The simple suggestion of this Teaching for all of humankind is to become acquainted with the wisdom at the basis, and from that wisdom to live together.

So, more directly to your question, all of our ideas about everything have led us as a human culture to where we are today. Why not get to know that about ourselves that is completely beyond all concepts, but yet is the root of all concepts? *That* is what we need to know. What needs to be actualized today is the wisdom power that is at the basis, the wisdom power that is completely beyond all ideas about everything and which is completely beyond all the systems that have been put together that have led us to where we are today.

All of my own study from a very early age of philosophy, religion, spirituality and psychology led absolutely nowhere ultimately. When I ended up in a critical moment of the absolute failure of everything, what I found to my great joy was that the underlying basis of it all is complete relief and complete purity. Rather than being stained, marked, tainted and incomplete, at the basis of everything is super-completeness in and of itself. In that super-completeness, all belief systems are completely set aside.

When I had a very traumatic and unexpected event occur in my life, all my thoughts, emotions, and experiences were just completely running wild. None of the very accomplished strategies that I had developed for dealing with life worked at that point at all. In the hopelessness and powerlessness of that, I suddenly realized that these thoughts and emotions that were so troublesome to me all had the same underlying basis and the same basic space. I saw that if I just rested as that, there was complete relief.

I didn't even know about nondual philosophy or Dzogchen or that it was possible to be completely free from assessing and judging everything that happens, but resting as this relief I found complete freedom as everything. It was just so amazing that everything is *as it is*, and I could see that this is the way it is *for everyone*, whether they are aware of it or not. It is so natural, and for me it occurred in my own mind stream in a time of great upset. I became very interested in that, because I knew that there must be many other people who had also realized the inseparability of all things. Indeed, there are, and there is a tradition and practice having to do with inseparability that has been handed down for thousands of years.

So, again, in terms of your question about purity, I found that in every single moment of all of my seeking there had been an urge to freedom, and I saw that that urge was completely pure in and of itself. All ideas about purity and what it means are completely subsumed in primordially pure open intelligence.

As It Is

CHAPTER THREE

Data are allowed to be as they are in equalness and evenness, and in this way data are left unrejected. Through allowing a data stream to be as it is, however it is, while simultaneously and instinctively recognizing open intelligence as its only nature, the certainty of inexhaustible open intelligence and its benefits will bloom.

Data are the dynamic creative energy of open intelligence and are inseparable from open intelligence, and everything is *as it is*—a fabulous all-in-one combination. Every data stream is the creative energy of open intelligence and is spontaneously free in its own place, like a line drawn in water or like the flight path of a bird in the sky. A data stream could not be held in place even if we tried to do so.

When we allow the mirage-like existence of data to be *as it is,* we realize the vast expanse of mind. Everything, no matter what it is, is primordially pure from the beginning. "Primordially pure from the beginning" is what *"as it is"* means. When we hear the term *"as it is"* repeated again and again, that doesn't mean the definition of something as it is in a reified sense. It means as it *actually* is, which is primordially pure. To repeat, "leaving a data stream *as it is"* doesn't mean leaving the *definition* of the data stream *as it is.* It means the data stream *as it is* is like inexhaustible space. This is the true import of leaving data streams as they are: to see them as nothing other than open intelligence.

If you let everything be *as it is,* you will see that there is nothing wrong with you at all! Those things that you thought were contaminated and that you should not indulge or you must avoid or replace with something else, when allowed to be as they are, those very things are seen to be the magnificence of your own beneficial potency. By allowing everything to be *as it is*, you are able to see that everything blossoms into the incredible power of benefit and exaltation.

The result of a one hundred percent commitment to open intelligence is the assurance that open intelligence actually does exist, and *you are it*. Then there are also the incredible skillful capacities that come into play, as well as your capacity to notice these very things. You are able to handle situations as they arise, and you have things that come into your mind to do or to say that you know could not have come out of reified intelligence. They could only have come out of an intelligence that is always expanding inexhaustibly. Thus, through your commitment to open intelligence you become aware of a world that you may have never known was available. In your reified existence you had been facing in one direction, but now you are facing in a completely different direction.

If we do not let data be as they are, we will be stuck in whatever definition we have given the data. We do not see that letting things be as they are can carry us to great exaltation and to an inexhaustible, comprehensive and beneficial intelligence that enables us to thrive. To not let everything be *as it is* and to not accept this simple instruction leads us down the wrong road. Even though there have been positive changes in society through reified thinking, there will be bigger changes through open intelligence. We have gone as far as we can go with reified intelligence, and now it is time to carry on with something different.

The more we engage in a fix-it project of trying to alter our data into some kind of perfect data set, the more we will feel confused and unhappy, so that would not be the best plan! However, relying on open intelligence always works. It is the sure bet and the guarantee for everyone, because open intelligence is who we have always been, who we are now and who we will always be.

Essentially, what we have to do is to re-train ourselves. We say, "No, I'm not going the way of reification. Instead, I am going the way of open intelligence, and I am one hundred percent committed to that." Due to the skillful means of the trainer and training, this intelligence opens up until it is obviously one's primary identity.

DATA-DEFINITIONS SUBSUMED IN OPEN INTELLIGENCE

It is so important to understand that leaving everything *as it is* does not mean "acceptance," "surrender" or "letting go." These three reified concepts of popular culture are aspects of replacement and avoidance in which something needs to be done by a doer. Letting everything be *as it is* means simply that: letting it be *as it is*. We have to see what that means for us in our own direct experience.

To allow all the descriptions to be as they are also does not mean that we are trying to suppress them or repress them or anything else. The willingness to leave everything *as it is*—that is, to let everything be definition-free and to allow all definitions to roam wherever they may—is really important. When all of the definitions are subsumed in comprehensive intelligence, we open up into discernment, clarity, insight and skillful means that are of great benefit to ourselves and to all. There could be ten million definitions for a particular thing or circumstance, but through our skillful means we hone in on what is exactly appropriate to every time, place and circumstance.

Because everything is already *as it is,* we do not need to make it be so; it really is just a simple acknowledgment. We acknowledge and instinctively recognize clarity and the true power of our beneficial potencies. If we think that we have "gotten somewhere" when we are in some sort of elevated state and then we try to hold on to that state, we really have not fully allowed everything to be *as it is*.

Data disappear without a trace, like a flight path of a bird in the sky. Through allowing a data stream to be *as it is* however it is, while simultaneously and instinctively recognizing open intelligence as its only nature, the certainty of inexhaustible open intelligence and its benefits will bloom. Similarly, a flawless lotus blossom arises from the mud.

In everything *as it is*, no longer is there hope and fear related to any data, in other words, hope that data will change to better data or fear that specific kinds of data might occur. All data of hope and fear are allowed to be as they are in equalness and evenness, and in this way data are left unrejected.

"GOOD" AND "BAD" AS TOTALLY INSEPARABLE

We have been taught that we are supposed to become a good person through not having bad thoughts, but this clever plan is actually quite painful. Trying to have a life filled only with good thoughts does not work, because it is contrived. We are trained to believe that one thing is good and the other thing is not; yet, when we can see the good and the bad as totally inseparable, that changes things completely! We thought that we were going to get to be a good person through turning the bad thoughts off and the good thoughts on. However, there is a big difference between that way of living and letting everything be *as it is*.

Through resting, dictionary definitions are no longer seen to be our best friend and all the rules we have learned about socially appropriate behavior are now viewed more skeptically. Instead of relying on conventional reified concepts, we operate from the most comprehensive intelligence that is available—inexhaustible open intelligence. A great space opens up, and here one can freely move through life with intelligence and skillfully be in any situation.

We would be well served by seeing clearly that we allowed ourselves to be trained up in reified knowledge. But, even if we were trained up this way, it is just another experience that has occurred. Now there is a whole community of people in which the authority of reified knowledge and institutions is being questioned. We are being shown clearly that we no longer need to be a victim of our previous experience. The descriptions about things that we may have had become less and less important.

Focusing on the thinking that is troubling us or pleasing us is a very small place to live from. When we are doing this, usually we are indulging, avoiding or replacing whatever data is appearing. However, when we let everything simply be *as it is,* we are able to open up into a comprehensive order of being. "Opening up" means that instead of seeing all of our thoughts, emotions, sensations and other experiences as something particular to us, we see ourselves and our experiences as relating to everyone. We begin to realize that others are having the same sorts of experiences that we are having.

Both disturbing states and the countermeasures to them are data streams inseparable from open intelligence, and a key point is that negative data streams provide an opportunity for the recognition of open intelligence. Negative data streams indicate the *presence* of open intelligence, not its absence. This is very, very important and should be repeated: negative data streams indicate open intelligence's *presence*, not its absence. When something unwanted falls into our lap, we may have a negative datum such as hope, fear, anger, hatred, desire, pride, arrogance, envy, jealousy, upset, irritation, anxiety, depression, anguish or fear of death. Again, by just allowing everything to be *as it is*, we find that we do not have to do anything about those data, other than to rely on open intelligence.

The Innate Desire to Be of Benefit to All

We are an inexhaustible space of beneficial energy without any boundaries, without any limits, without any beginning, middle or end, without any birth, life and death. This is what we can count on—this which subsumes birth, life and death and subsumes waking, dreaming and sleeping. At some point we come to realize, "Oh, right, it is that way. I really see what that means in my own direct experience."

Each one of us is born with the innate desire to be of benefit to all, and we can know this without any thought or reasoning. When it is said that, "The desire to benefit all is innate," that means that it isn't something we need to accomplish, because it is always already accomplished. If we are going for some kind of desired state and headed for a destination of being of benefit, then it is good to know that we are already at the destination. We just naturally are of benefit because we *are born that way*! Truly, our greatest fundamental desire is to benefit all, and life can be lived purposefully, intentionally and spontaneously for the benefit of all.

It is also very important not to think of open intelligence as a destination. What is inexhaustible cannot be a destination, and the fact that there is no destination to get to is a great relief. We do not have to seek for open intelligence, because once we have found that we *are* that, this recognition ends all seeking. Open intelligence is just continuously pouring out more and more benefit, more and more complete enjoyment of life, more and more connection and familiarity with everyone and everything, more and more willingness and heartfelt desire to be of service.

In our all-encompassing, all-inclusive nature, we are able to let everything be *as it is* without any need to get wrapped up in things. It is the same with anything that occurs in life; whatever it is that is going on in our circumstances, we let all of it be as it will. No matter what the descriptions are running around in our mind or someone else's mind, they are not the reality of who we are.

If we merely contrive a way of being beneficial, we can certainly be of help to the world, but we are not realizing the great potency of supreme spontaneous benefit that exists in every human being. A contrived life may also involve striving to attain money, power and prestige, but to spontaneously leave everything *as it is* brings a treasure trove of everything that lies beyond the world of want. Letting things be as they are provides the great spontaneity and exaltation of always-on discernment, clarity, insight and all skillful means that ensure the benefit of all in this particular time, place, and circumstance without anything needing to be acquired.

Once we have left everything *as it is,* what do we do then? Are we going to become a couch potato? No; what comes next is the adventure of exploring our inexhaustible beneficial intelligence. In leaving everything *as it is,* a potent space for each and every experience is created, and we become increasingly comfortable with that space. At one point we were not comfortable with it, but now we are. This enormous space is noticed, a space that is an endless treasury of discernment, insight, clarity, potency and skillful means. If we stay in reification and don't let everything be *as it is,* all along trying to fix, define and analyze things, there is no way for that space to open up or for us to even realize that it is there.

A SKILLED RESPONSE

A very welcome consequence of letting everything be *as it is* is that everything is free from obstruction, because no storyline is created and sustained that could create obstruction. When a thought arises, in leaving it *as it is* the thought is allowed to run its course. In doing so, clarity, discernment and insight become more evident, and skillful means are freed up, because reification has been left to the side.

We now have knowledge available to us that we had not known before. That is what open-ended knowledge creation is: knowing that the knowledge that is already present *is* already present! There is no knowledge that is going to come about sometime in the future; all knowledge is present and available right now, and by allowing everything to be *as it is,* that intelligence becomes very, very obvious. There might be all kinds of data running, but when a true insight comes—one that is of beautiful discernment, clarity and benefit to all and one that leads to a solution that will greatly enhance and expand all current activities occurring—that is the welcome consequence of not trying to gather data together and make it into a story.

We strengthen ourselves considerably in complete relaxation, and we release all need to buy into the power and influence of a reified lifestyle. We just relax, and when we relax, automatically we subsume everything within ourselves and we live as this greater comprehensive order of intelligence.

The more we rely on this simple lifestyle, the easier it is for us to live with everyone, not just those who live the Four Mainstays lifestyle, but with everyone. No one is completely new or unknown to us, because we know where they are coming from. We know that if we had the same data streams that they have, we would be behaving in exactly the same way, and this recognition is the root of spontaneous compassion. Only through the inexhaustible view of open intelligence can we greet this very crucial realization: whether their conduct is wonderful, really negative or indifferent, we would be doing exactly the same thing they are doing if we had the same data streams.

QUESTION AND ANSWER

Q. I often have such intense feelings of inadequacy, and I find it very difficult to outshine this feeling and the other strong afflictions I have in the way that you are describing.

Ziji Rinpoche: In completely outshining afflictive emotions, through the empowerment of strengths, gifts and talents, we have the ability to do things that we have never done before. It could be that we didn't even know what our strengths, gifts and talents are, and then suddenly they pop out and are in full bloom! It could be compared to a beautiful white lotus flower suddenly emerging from the mud with not a speck of mud on it.

There is an example from my own life of this, and I like to tell these anecdotes because people feel supported by these real-life examples. So, at one time I did not like to speak in front of people, and I would go to any lengths to not be in that position. For example, when I was in primary school and we would have to give a speech in front of a class about something that we had written, I would do anything to avoid it. When it was my turn, I would run out to the bathroom!

Later in life my sons were born, and I was working at a university and we needed to start a daycare center. It was decided by the group who had started the daycare center that I was going to be the president of the board, and so as a result I had to give a talk in a church in front of a large group of people. I was sitting in the back of the church and my knees were shaking, and I really felt like I was going to the guillotine. I thought that this was it. My head would be lopped off and that would be the last of it! I finally made my way up front, and I had to speak into a microphone. That was terrifying, but I did it and I lived through it.

A little bit later, but not that much later, I was blessed with the recognition of all-accomplishing activity, and my entire life changed. Suddenly I was able to do things I had never done before, and I knew things that I had never known before. I don't really even know how I knew them. As you can see, now I speak in front of lots of people. I never even think about it when I come out to speak; I don't think anything really other than, "Oh wow! I get to see all these shining faces. So exciting!" Nothing else is going on.

So here we are, and we're able to have discernment and insight and all of the other very amazing gifts that accompany the outshining of afflictive data. We have to recognize that a new education in the nature of mind is possible, and a time will come when it's more than a glimmer of hope inside us, and we come to recognize that it *is* possible.

Many of us might have tried many different approaches before we find one that really works, and what we are looking for is something with *results*! The results have to be evident in the community of people that are practicing the Teaching. We want to see people who are recognizing their strengths, gifts and talents and who are able to actually demonstrate those gifts. This is key, because when we see people who are demonstrating talents in that way, then we know that it's possible for us too. This is very important. In fact, it is a profound basis for the introduction to the nature of mind to take place.

In training up in open intelligence and outshining data, the overall result is the exaltation of all data. Whereas before we may have gotten all tangled up with our thoughts, emotions and sensations, now we're just relaxed, powerful and potent, and we carry on powerfully and potently. We're able to engage life from an entirely new vantage; in fact, our whole definition of ourselves and our life changes. This is what I wish for you as well.

NEVER A VICTIM OF DATA-DEFINITIONS
CHAPTER FOUR

We begin to see things that we were never able to see before because our minds had not been clear. We learn from directly encountering all the afflictions, both the overt and the subtle ones, that in affliction there is no affliction. That is a very, very powerful insight. With that knowledge, we can never again be ruled by what we have thought to be affliction.

We have until now tricked ourselves into believing that affliction and afflictive states are real, but the more we allow everything to be *as it is*, the less we feel that afflictive states are actually afflictive. We find that these data streams that had been named "afflictions" were not really afflictive at all; it is just that we had labeled them that way. In the past we may have seen affliction as such a major part of our life, but now we can find a new relationship with this long-held belief.

We have victimized ourselves by giving these afflictive states a power they actually did not have. When we give up our right to be a victim, it is such a big step, because we are no longer blindly accepting everything we have heard about who we are. We come to recognize that we have never been a victim of the definitions of "good, bad and indifferent" that we have used to describe our data. No one is a victim of data-definitions, no one.

It is such a pivotal moment when we first leave this mirage-like existence *as it is* while realizing the vast expanse of mind. Here we realize that what we are now seeing defies everything we have learned in the past. It also puts to rest all of what we have believed about affliction, suffering and victimization. We come to instinctively comprehend that in reality we are the vast mind of open intelligence. Our confusion about this came about because there has been a little bit of a mix–up along the way!

So often when we feel afflicted, we feel we are all alone and isolated and that we are the only one who has ever felt this way. We might not want to tell anyone how we feel because we are afraid they will think we are crazy! Let's say that a particularly strong afflictive state comes up for us. In the past it has likely been a personal matter for us as we tried to figure it out in the context of being "the only person with this very big problem."

But what an insight it is to realize that there are probably thousands, maybe millions, of other people experiencing exactly the same data stream at exactly the same moment. That recognition completely changes the perspective. It is then no longer just "little me with my enormous afflictive state." There are many others who have that afflictive state, or something much worse, at exactly the same time. The realization that we are all in the same boat together is really the beginning of spontaneous altruism. Opening the affliction beyond self-concern will grant access to the great benefit of open intelligence, and to consider all the other people who might be suffering brings a real softness and kindness to the heart. This is the basis of truly real compassion.

Unless we have enough compassion for ourselves to be able to lay everything bare and to be open to everything about who and what we are, we will not discover the very profound wisdom available to us. Our capacity for complete indivisibility and intimate relating with all beings is rooted in this very profound self-disclosure of everything about ourselves that we had thought of as opposed to wisdom. That is when real humility steps in, and this is where we get to love ourselves deeply. By letting ourselves be exactly as we are, we are able to love ourselves deeply, and only through understanding and loving ourselves can we enter into true relationship with someone else.

In our natural desire to belong and to feel connected, we find that through relying on open intelligence we feel a sense of truly heartfelt belonging with everyone. We do not need to contrive that, like for example through having affirmations or positive psychology: "I am strong and loving, and I can love myself and everyone else, and I feel connected with everyone," or whatever the affirmation may be. Rather, the natural connection radiates out into the world as a wave of true empathy which includes everyone—and especially those who was feeling that same affliction at that same moment—connecting us all together in indivisible intelligence.

LEAVING AFFLICTIVE STATES UN-REJECTED

Some people come to this training with a naturally restful mind, and so the instinctive recognition is easy and increasingly obvious from then on. There are people at the other extreme who have very afflictive minds; however, people with afflictive minds are highly motivated to be free of affliction! The motivation to be able to be at ease with affliction is huge. Some people proceed in quantum leaps, while for others it is more gradual, but we do not need to try to replicate anyone else's qualities, and we do not need to compare ourselves to them. We do not need to be like anybody else; we just need to be ourselves, exalted and flawless as we are. We come to see that we no longer need to live within the context of what we "ought to do" and how we "ought to be."

Regardless of what comes up, we maintain open intelligence, because in fact, open intelligence is all that is present anyway! Everything that appears is the shining forth of open intelligence. Open intelligence accomplishes all activity, no matter what that activity is called, even if it is called "afflictive states." There isn't anything else going on, and there isn't any special separate state called "open intelligence." Open intelligence is completely inseparable from whatever is shining forth. Everything shines forth in, of, as and through open intelligence.

"To leave afflictive states un-rejected" means to leave them as they are without the need to do anything about them, without the need to explore them any further or stop them or do anything at all. When the afflictive states are left un-rejected, they become bliss, compassion, loving-kindness, lucidity and luminosity—a balanced view.

To allow all affliction to be *as it is* does not mean that we always feel "good," according to how that word is conventionally defined. We have devised all sorts of reified definitions of what "feeling good" means, but as a result we may not actually know what true well-being is. When we allow ourselves to leave the definitions as they are and we expand beyond the definitions into the vastness of the open intelligent mind, then we see what true well-being actually is.

NO AFFLICTION IN AFFLICTION

"Affliction" is a reified label, and after realizing the self-releasing nature of affliction and of all data, it is very easy to realize that, no matter what we have called it before, it is in fact beneficial potency, so we can stand tall in that. By trusting in the power of short moments and through gaining confidence in open intelligence, we realize that we do not have to do anything with affliction, because affliction is nothing other than self-releasing beneficial potency. Everything is seen as pure benefit. When we actually do realize this, it is a revelation, to say the least!

Instinctive realization of open intelligence must be simultaneous with the afflictive state, showing the afflictive state to be nothing but open intelligence. Through this vantage we can directly encounter affliction as it self-releases in open intelligence. When we have been trained to see afflictions as something really negative and horrible, it may be difficult at first to adjust to the reality that they really are nothing but open intelligence.

Sometimes, after the overt afflictions have had their day, the subtle ones may start to come up. We begin to see things that we were never able to see before because our minds were not as clear. We learn from directly encountering all the afflictions, both the overt and the subtle ones, that *in affliction there is no affliction.* That is a very, very powerful insight. With that knowledge, we will no longer be ruled by what we have thought to be affliction. "Affliction" becomes definition-free data and is seen for what it truly is, the dynamic energy of open intelligence. That recognition empowers us in seeing everything exactly *as it is* and also in being able to support someone else going through the same affliction that we had gone through. It is an opportunity to share our own experience with someone else: "Well, this is how it unfolded for me."

If we examine a data stream thoroughly, we cannot really say that there is a beginning, a middle and an end to it. In the direct encounter with our own perceptions, we can see that "beginning," "middle" and "end" are just words we apply to equalness and evenness. The benefit of evenness and equalness is always evenly pure and free of anything of a different kind. That means that open intelligence does not have anything different mixed into it, such as affliction. It is all benefit. Discerning wisdom understands all data to be free of an independent nature and that their only nature is open intelligence.

Life is filled with all kinds of things, and again, not just with things that are conventionally called "good." Because we have learned to interpret things as good, bad and indifferent, for a while we continue to do that, but then when that is outshone, we no longer interpret things as good, bad or indifferent. They are simply the beneficial energy of open intelligence.

AN ENORMOUS BREAKTHROUGH

It is an enormous breakthrough to realize in our own direct experience that afflictive states indeed do not have a power or influence of their own. By letting afflictive states be as they are, their innate beneficial potency is revealed. They have always been beneficial potency in the entirety of their appearance. We begin to see that, no matter what the afflictive state might be, it is bursting forth with beneficial potency and shining like brilliant sunshine. This is the simple, moment-to-moment enactment of empowerment in our own life. We are left exactly as we are—beneficial and filled with potency.

The saying goes, "The greater the affliction, the greater the wisdom," and this is absolutely true. The more severe the afflictive state, the more incredible the wisdom potential therein, so there is no need to hide out from anything.

Through letting everything be *as it is*, reified ideas get burnt off, and the burning off and outshining of all these old ideas is really a key. To be able to burn off data in this way brings great relief, and the greater our relief, the greater our trust. As we trust more and more in this particular capacity of open intelligence, we will not even have to think about burning off the old ideas. We find that data are automatically self-releasing and that they burn off naturally. The data streams that were so powerful when we were entertaining them so diligently eventually become preposterous, and we cannot even entertain them any longer.

Rather than continuing to wade through data streams, we rely on open intelligence and its beneficial potency, and in doing so, we are using our intelligence in a different way. Whatever the afflictive data stream is, we learn a lot more about it from relying on open intelligence than we would from going from "a bad data stream" to "a good data stream" trying to seek relief.

As an antidote to afflictive states, a person might seek out positive states, such as a non-conceptual state, bliss or clarity or some other comfortable way to be. However, all of these positive states are also nothing other than the dynamic energy of open intelligence, just as the afflictive states are nothing other than the dynamic energy of open intelligence. Even if we tried to hold onto a non-conceptual data stream of bliss and clarity, it would be impossible. Due to the law of impermanence, nothing can be held onto forever. Everything changes in each split second, so what would be the purpose of trying to hold onto something that will inevitably pass away?

To indulge, avoid or replace data is what most of us have learned, but now we see very clearly that all data can be allowed to be as they are, because all data operate equally and evenly as open intelligence. When negative states appear, we allow them to be as they are, and they instantaneously open up into the reality of pure wisdom energy. Nothing need be done for this to be the case. It is only in clamping down on a negative state and calling it something that it seems to be something. Clamping down on it only furthers reification and hence also the accompanying distress.

Simply by the power of relying on open intelligence, we see that the data are ceaseless, countless and unpredictable for ourselves and others. The data streams have seemed habitual simply because that is how we have been experiencing them for so long, but by the power of open intelligence these apparently habitual data streams are outshone. Realizations like this are countless. Just as open intelligence is inexhaustible, realizations are inexhaustible.

Positive data streams have pleasant descriptions; however, they are equal and even to the negative data streams that we have so long feared. All of these positive things may have brought a smile to our face; however, the negative data streams are just as friendly in their shining forth! All data streams are naturally beneficial, and like ripples in water, data streams leave no trace.

THE END OF INTERNALIZED OPPRESSION

When the oppression brought about by afflictive states is so internalized that we actually believe that our natural tendency is *not* to be of benefit to ourselves and each other, this is a very severe form of oppression. We could call it "internalized oppression," which means that we have taken on very strong belief systems and believed them to be true. Internalized oppression is so subtle and covert that people do not even know they have it. This is the condition for most people in the world: internalized oppression, where people have inherited and adopted the belief from the prevailing culture that they are flawed creatures, when in fact they are beautiful and exalted beings with incredible potential.

After countless years of viewing ourselves as flawed and in need of constant repair, it may come as a surprise to discover that we are flawless, exalted creatures who hold the intelligence of the universe in a usable way. The first time it enters our mind that we are exalted and flawless, it may seem like this could not possibly be the case. A period of adjustment is required as the realization of our real nature opens its vast doors. This period is called education in the nature of mind.

There may be murderers, rapists and all other kinds of others who are judged to be wrong in a conventional sense, and while it is important that the persons doing these things take full responsibility for their harmful behavior, there is not a single person who is in their essence not an exalted being. Each of us is exalted. Maybe we did not grow up with someone telling us that we are exalted, and when we think of ourselves in that way for the first time, it may seem a little unusual or strange, as in, "Well, I do not think this applies to me. It might apply to someone else, but not to me." However, through relying on and resting as open intelligence, we come to see that we are exalted, and we come to see that we do have beneficial potencies beyond anything we could have dreamt or imagined.

The normalization of the human condition, wherein all data are seen to be nothing other than open intelligence, is the end of internalized and externalized oppression. "Normalization" means to bring all data streams—positive, negative and neutral—to a field of permission wherein all things are allowed to be as they are. One of the most important aspects of normalizing data streams is that it opens for us the possibility to see our own strengths, gifts and talents and how those specifically might apply to what we want to do with our life. That is really important, because each of us is a truly great creator; we are naturally talented and gifted in our own way, and through open intelligence we get to see that. Things that seemed impossible, things that seemed like they could never happen, do come about.

NOTHING NEED BE DONE

We have heard throughout our lives that something is wrong and that we have afflictive states, an ego, samsara, sin, karma, bad parents or whatever it is that we have been told. However, there is nothing to make wrong. That is the basis of wise discernment: making nothing wrong.

This does not mean that we do not respond to all the grave problems the world is facing. We can act decisively and with beneficial intent when we have found a basis for discernment. The comprehensive intelligence that is the ability to take care of the world's problems comes from this basis of "nothing is wrong." Nothing is wrong with data, not a single thing, whether the data are described as positive, negative or neutral. It is this clarity that empowers the skillful means that are required to face all the challenges that are before us.

We do not need to be fixed or corrected. Our beneficial potency is present right here, right now, and in being aware of its presence, we experience ourselves as we actually are without constantly doubting or admonishing ourselves. We let ourselves be as we are, and for each of us that will happen in a unique way. Just as each of us is unique individually, our beneficial potencies and our strengths, gifts and talents are similarly unique. It isn't a matter of trying to get everyone rowing with the same oar and acting in the same way. By each of us letting everything be *as it is* in our own distinctive way, an infinitely varied display of beneficial potencies opens up.

By profoundly seeing that all data just simply are as they are, we do not have to take any countermeasures to anything, because the countermeasure too is just another data stream! As we rest naturally and profoundly, the vast expanse of open intelligence is what we see. In that, we have the ultimate view of open intelligence.

QUESTION AND ANSWER

Q. I suffered a lot of emotional abuse when I was younger, and I would so love to be free of that burden, especially when I consider that the stance I have taken for much of my life has been one of feeling totally victimized by my circumstance.

Ziji Rinpoche: A really great way to get started with this is for you to begin to gain some familiarity with open intelligence and then to see if that familiarity is making a difference in your life. First the introduction to open intelligence takes place, and as we get more familiar with it, we notice that more benefit is available to us.

So, for instance, when we get into a problematic situation and we rely on open intelligence and we just rest body and mind completely, rather than going into all the stories, we sense a very real benefit therein. This benefit is self-kept; we do not have to get a bunch of it together and hold on to it forever. We are simply acknowledging reality *as it is*. Open intelligence already is and does not need to be created. It is always present; it's just a matter of acknowledging it. It's very simple: we just want to see the benefits and changes in our own lives, and then eventually in the lives of others as well.

We as individuals have had all kinds of experiences in our lives. So, say you grew up in a home where there was a lot of emotional or physical abuse going on. With all of your memories of that, in the context of relying on the Four Mainstays, and most specifically the short moments practice, you let these thoughts and memories go wherever they go and you let them be as they are. You will then see that as the thoughts and memories proliferate and elaborate, they will spontaneously and naturally free themselves.

Letting everything be *as it is*, no matter what might come up or what you might feel, is an empowering step for you or for anyone. The intensity of your empowerment and freedom is in letting that data stream be *as it is*. Through that, all data and all past memories are subsumed in all-subsuming intelligence. Now all the thoughts, emotions, sensations and other experiences can be seen as open intelligence and nothing else.

Giving up one's right to be a victim is a very, very powerful action. We become able to say with conviction, "No one ever made me choose to be a victim; I chose it myself." That's a big step. It might sound scary at first, but it is the truth. We give up our right to be a victim of everything that has been laid out to us as true, and we look to see what is actually true. Through a comprehensive education in the nature of mind, we come to see ourselves as we really are, rather than as we were told we are. It does not have to look any particular way, and there is no rulebook that applies to everybody. Your way of letting things be as they are is related to your own experience and not to somebody else's experience. It's your own walk, your own responsibility, your own sovereignty, your own way of taking over the helm.

It took us a long time to memorize all this stuff about our identity as a victim, and maybe for years and years we have held it in place. However, it takes a much shorter time to let it all be *as it is*. Why? Because one way of seeing things is aligned with reality and the other isn't. One is aligned with a complete fallacy, in other words, the idea that we are a victim and thereby damaged goods, and the other is aligned with reality as it actually is.

Once again, just to make it perfectly clear, we are not a victim of our beliefs. We have chosen these beliefs, and this is a very important point for each of us to accept. The acknowledgment that we had chosen these beliefs is the key to our freedom. To be able to say, "I am not a victim," is the starting point. We are not victims of anyone or anything, and we are never too old or too young to get started living this new way.

Even if we have undergone something totally harsh, abusive and awful which never should have happened, we know that we have a choice in this present moment as to how we will respond. We know that we can take responsibility for the way we are living *now* in relation to those circumstances. No matter how horrific the circumstance, we can re-envision that circumstance as open intelligence. To open its definition as open intelligence through relying on the Four Mainstays brings so much healing power and relief.

We choose the lifestyle we want to live, and we decide for ourselves who we are. Rather than relying on lots of inherited ideas, we rely on our own direct experience of open intelligence. This provides us what we need.

Part Two

PRIORITIZING OPEN INTELLIGENCE

THE PRECIOUSNESS OF THE FOUR MAINSTAYS

CHAPTER FIVE

Through the power of the Mainstays we find a generosity that is absolutely native to us, and we know about its richness, its rareness and its precious power through our own direct experience of its immediate benefit. To be educated in the nature of mind is real riches, and through the Mainstays a vehicle has been created through which these riches can be passed along to future generations.

Special, rare and precious are the Four Mainstays because they are ultimately reliable and are there for us as a source of complete joy and comfort. And yet, if we have no familiarity with them or confidence in them, we cannot possibly understand their benefit. It is supportive to reflect on the potency, exquisiteness and rarity of the Four Mainstays—the gift of *practice, trainer, training* and *community*—and to be aware of their power and what they bring to the human community across the globe.

The Four Mainstays are a combinatory pattern that gives us a way to live everyday life in a skillful and beneficial way. All Four Mainstays are required; the reliance on each of the Mainstays, and not just one or two, is the best context for the inexhaustible display of open intelligence's beneficial potencies. The Mainstays are essential, because there are pitfalls and obstacles that are difficult to see without a system of mentorship and support. This support is something that has been lacking for many people, so the fact that there is ongoing, unending support available through the Mainstays is greatly assuring.

There is also the complete joy of having a worldwide community of people who share the same vision. We can appreciate the fact that there are trainings and media that are always available in multitudinous forms and which can be drawn on at any time to be of support with whatever is coming up in life. Then there is our own trainer who supports us in stability, reliability and spontaneous benefit. If we use the Four Mainstays as suggested by the training and trainer, we will have the full result, just as we have previously had in our lives the full result from participating in the beliefs and values provided by reified intelligence.

There is no greater splendor in life than the instinctive realization of open intelligence, and a great support for this realization comes through active participation in the Four Mainstays. One could say that the Four Mainstays are a time-tested measure, not only time-tested within this present era, but time-tested over many thousands of years. The Four Mainstays are the reliable method to bring about a full realization of fundamental reality. Down through the ages, whenever there have been great realizations in many people, these are the skillful means they have relied upon. People become involved with the Mainstays in different ways, sometimes wanting just a little, other times wanting a lot, and sometimes in–between, but however it is, it is fine.

First Mainstay: The Practice of Short Moments

The first of the Four Mainstays is a simple practice that requires no effort: short moments of resting as open intelligence many times until open intelligence is spontaneously obvious at all times. Short moments does not take a single standard form, and there is no special way of taking short moments. For some people the way short moments manifests is through listening to lots of talks. For others it might be actively practicing short moments as the moments grow longer. For others it can be getting very involved in service, or it could be a combination of all of these, and many other things as well. But however it may be, shorter moments naturally extend into longer moments, and we know the practice is working if we have increasing assurance in open intelligence.

The skilled instruction for recognizing open intelligence is "short moments repeated many times becomes obvious"; that is to say, open intelligence becomes clear and evident at all times in short moments, many times. Just to rest naturally for short moments is most important of all. There isn't anything that needs to be done, just the sparkle of who we are right here and now. That's it!

We rest naturally and completely as spontaneous wisdom benefit, without any effort and without anything needing to be done. It isn't that we have to work for years to reach open intelligence. No, it is simply a matter of taking short moments over and over again until open intelligence becomes completely, naturally and spontaneously present. At first the practice of short moments may be necessary, but eventually it won't be, because there will be the increasing realization that open intelligence is naturally present as our only identity. The wisdom reality of who we are is not something that needs to be brought about; it is the reality of who we already are. The great reality is the inseparable reality of what we are; it isn't "you" or "me" as a separate entity.

Because of what we have been taught over the course of our lives, we may have had all sorts of reified ideas, but now we need never veer from the great reality to which we have been introduced. In looking directly at the great reality, we see clearly. Very often we think "Oh gee, I'm just right here within my skin line, and that's who I am." But if we rest naturally for short moments many times, we come to see that our existence is vast and that it is beyond our skin line. One cannot really identify a point at which open intelligence begins or ends, because there isn't any such beginning or end to open intelligence.

Short moments secures us in open intelligence so that we can then see for ourselves the nature of data shining forth directly in open intelligence. In short moments we come to see that the intelligence that fuels us is vast. It occupies not only our own body, but everything else as well. That is what we really are, comprehensive intelligence, and we find immediate benefit in this comprehensive intelligence.

Short moments is a treasure, a true treasure, and with the short moments practice there is such an immense reward. The short moments that are practiced in the beginning will grow into longer moments, no matter how short they seem to be now! Many, many people have had short moments grow into longer moments and then into total spontaneity, so it is clear that the practice does work. This life as open intelligence is what one wants to be involved in. It really is, because if we never have this recognition of open intelligence, we die with empty pockets, even though we have been living all of our lives on an island of gold. We come to recognize that we are living on an island of gold through the gift of the short moments practice and the Mainstays altogether.

SECOND MAINSTAY: THE TRAINER

The second of the Mainstays is the relationship with the trainer. A trainer is a person who has actualized a complete commitment to the Four Mainstays. The trainer is someone who really cares about other human beings; they care so much that they have given their life to sharing this training of open intelligence all over the world. That is a person of totally complete character, the ultimate friend who introduces us to the realm of treasure that is available to all beings.

The preciousness and rarity of the Four Mainstays is shown very clearly in the trainer. When new participants are first introduced to the Four Mainstays lifestyle, they may not know exactly what it is that they are getting into. But if they have any questions about what it actually is, the answer is found in complete openness and commitment, and the trainer provides a living example of that. In our trainer we have someone we can intimately share with who has gone through the same process we are going through.

There needs to be a genuine sense of reliable openness at all times, or the trainer will be of no use to us. Maybe at first a relationship like this does not feel entirely comfortable, but it will. The trainer is there to assist us in every way possible, and as our confidence in open intelligence grows, with their help we become stable, reliable and potently beneficial. The trainer always supports us in being everything that we are meant to be, and they are devoted to providing us life satisfaction and flourishing. They genuinely want us to flourish in all ways.

If we want to learn something new—plumbing, cooking, playing tennis or whatever it is—it is always wise to seek the advice of someone who has more experience in that area than we have. If, for instance, we want to climb Mount Everest, we wouldn't try to do so without a guide. We would want to learn from someone who is experientially familiar with Everest and who knows exactly how to reach the summit and what the conditions are going to be along the way. The unerring and clear approach of a skilled guide can take us to the summit. In the same way, we can have confidence in the accomplishment of someone who has realized the fundamental condition and who has supported many others in doing the same.

Everyone has the same potential for open intelligence, but not everyone has the same openness to it. With a little encouragement, that openness can be fostered in just about anyone. What is required is for the trainer to first create a communication bridge with the people who are open, which requires knowing what they are interested in and where they are coming from. Then from the very place where the participants are, a trainer can walk forward with them into complete openness with no preconceived notions. It isn't a matter of having to be evangelistic or trying to get people to believe anything. It is merely a matter of pointing out the reality of what we are. When we ourselves rest deeply in the reality of what we are, we don't necessarily have to say anything to share that with anyone else.

THIRD MAINSTAY: THE TRAINING

The third Mainstay is the training itself: the media-rich offering available online and in person. There are audios, videos, face-to-face trainings, clarity calls, apps, books and texts and so many other skillful means to render support in every way conceivable, and inconceivable! The training is created and written from the basis of complete exaltation of mind, speech, body, qualities and activities, so that even a single word can evoke inexhaustible understanding and realization. When the profound meaning is understood, the words in the texts and trainings come alive, because they are the shining forth of reality itself.

One may notice that the literature in the trainings does not read like other writing, and reading it isn't like reading anything ever read before. When we finish reading a text, we may find it confusing or afterwards we do not remember a single thing; however, without ever having thought about it, we can read the text once again and it is completely clear. "Wow! This makes perfect sense to me now!"

The same topics are repeated over and over again in the texts— and then over and over and over again—but the repetition is a key aspect of the training. Somehow the repetition never becomes boring or burdensome.

The training will never mislead. No matter which text or which talk of the training we see or read, we will not be misled. Always more and more inexhaustible potent benefit will be provided, never less. Our power and energy are coming from a training source which is unlike any other thing that we have ever accepted into our lives, and suddenly we are released from having to be anyone at all. All we need to do is to be as open and available as we can possibly be.

FOURTH MAINSTAY: THE COMMUNITY

The fourth Mainstay is the community, present all over the world. "Community" is no longer limited to a place located near one's home, family and friendship circle and is not bounded by country, race, ethnicity or religion. Wherever there are people gaining confidence in open intelligence, on whatever continent they may be, there is community. This is a worldwide community of people living as open intelligence's beneficial potencies, and the community is evidence of the peace brought about by short moments of open intelligence. If we have been thinking about world peace and working for world peace, in this community of open intelligence we see world peace alive and well.

This is a worldwide community of people who can understand us completely, because they are living life in the same way that we are. Each person knows that the other person is responsible for their own data. Each person knows that it is up to them to live in accord and harmony with one other. The whole community is here to give support in being everything we want to be, and that is really quite something! When people like this come into a room together, they feel an immediate bond that is not based on the conventional notions of familiarity. More and more all of us will be able to truly see ourselves as one global community, and more and more we will see ourselves as open intelligence.

The simple practice of being with community ingrains open intelligence, rather than data, as our primary orientation. The best way to support the short moments practice is to do so while actively involved with other community members in ongoing commitment to open intelligence. This community is our home base in life. No matter what else we do or where we might go, it is home and we can count on it. The trainer, the simple practice of short moments and the profound words of the training are ways for people to join together in a great seamless community of beneficial potency. In such a community, benefit is the go-to for everyone, and everyone operates harmoniously in devotion to that.

In a Four Mainstays community one does not need to know the other person's politics or background or ethnicity or where they work or how much money they make; each person is united together through the commitment to the education in the nature of mind. No one is a stranger; there is a natural closeness that cannot be infringed upon by anything. That is the basis of empowered relationship right here. This is the priority that never fails. No matter what happens, no matter how old we get, how sick we get or what happens in life otherwise, open intelligence will never fail us. We have a life of good cheer, and there is always a solution coming clear. To have a life where we are surrounded by the Four Mainstays and to always be within the Mainstays knowing that this *is* our reality is totally amazing.

TRAINING UP IN REALITY

As we train up in the Four Mainstays, we begin to live from reality. There are not many different realities; there is just one indivisible reality: open intelligence unendingly present. The Mainstays connect us to a reality of such exquisiteness that it cannot be put into words. We have heard this word "reality" tossed around here and there, but as we gain assurance and confidence in open intelligence, we find that we have found a reality that is beautiful beyond expression. Every attempt to describe it falls short.

It is so important that we all deeply realize who we truly are, and it is so essential to be resting in the total wisdom-reality of who we are. It is important to never, ever, veer from that and to never be separate from it, and to never think that there is a reality other than the great reality of who we are. The reality that the Four Mainstays represent is inexhaustibly beneficial, and because we *are* that reality, its benefit and potency are available to us in our direct experience.

As we gain more assurance in the Mainstays, we can feel that reality in our own direct experience. The power of recognition in our own experience is very profound. The inspiration to fully take on the Four Mainstays lifestyle comes through seeing the actual result in our own life and in the lives of others. We think, "Wow, this is really so incredible! Everyone should know that this is available."

Making a one hundred percent commitment to the Four Mainstays is the doorway to actually entering that reality fully and completely. Making that commitment to the Mainstays has an immense level of power associated with it, because the commitment springs from spontaneous connection to fundamental reality. Spontaneous connection brought about through authentic introduction to open intelligence is fundamental reality. We rest therein and let data vanish on their own, like a line drawn in water.

Many people, and especially people who have children, ponder the question, "What kind of legacy will we leave for future generations?" The Four Mainstays way of being is the greatest treasure we in this present generation have to give to the next generation. Through the power of the Mainstays we find a generosity that is absolutely native to us, and we know about its richness, its rareness and its precious power through our own direct experience of its immediate benefit. To be educated in the nature of mind is real riches, and through the Mainstays a vehicle has been created through which these riches can be passed along to future generations.

QUESTION AND ANSWER

Q. I really don't understand your extreme emphasis on using the Four Mainstays. Somehow this sort of practice doesn't sound like anything that would be really helpful for me in my life.

Ziji Rinpoche: I would say first of all that by participating fully in the Mainstays, we take hold of the opportunity that they provide. This commitment guarantees that we will always have the best resources available to us for strengthening our realization of open intelligence in all its profundity. However, by isolating from them it becomes more difficult to know how to proceed, and it is more likely that one can begin to devolve into old data streams.

As I have said many times in the past, the Four Mainstays are a lifestyle choice among many other possible lifestyle choices in life. That's it, plain and simple: they are a lifestyle choice, an all-encompassing, warmhearted, lucid lifestyle choice, a place where you can finally get down to being real. It's very, very difficult to be real when everyone around you is telling you to indulge, avoid or replace data. To have the embrace of everyone being on the same page in a totally simple and clear way is a wonderful support.

The Four Mainstays are very comfortable. They're very, very, comfortable, but if we don't grow familiar with the Mainstays, we can't possibly understand their benefit. Open intelligence and the Mainstays work in mysterious ways. We don't have to figure it out, as "figuring it out" is not a tool in this training! Things simply are as they are, and we leave everything *as it is*. As we do so, an incomprehensible open intelligence—the most comprehensive intelligence of all intelligences—opens up within our own mind, speech, body, qualities and activities, vast and expansive as the sky, without any effort at all. This is because open intelligence is what is true about us. This is reality itself.

The more we allow ourselves to be open to open intelligence through the Four Mainstays, the more everything about us manifests open intelligence: the way we think, the way we speak, the way we act and our qualities and activities. They all conform naturally, without any effort, to the beneficial potency that they naturally are.

When I think about my life, there are things that have happened that I could potentially wallow in. Some years ago I had an episode of extreme violence towards my body, and so there is an example: I could have lived in that incident for the rest of my life. "Oh, wow, this thing happened to me. It was so scary and I'm afraid it's going happen again. I'm terrified."

I could have just fallen apart from what had happened. However, up until that point in my life I had lived for the benefit of all, and I knew that this was more important to me than anything else. When this unexpected violence occurred, I didn't need to just engage in extreme self-focus; I could see it in terms of the benefit of all. If I lived harboring the terror and horror of what had happened, I would just live in this self-consuming misery of being affected by this event.

Within twenty-four hours of being out of that situation, I felt nothing but complete love and—I would say "forgiveness" for lack of better word—for that other being. The only way that I could endure the entire experience was through resting and relying on open intelligence in the way that I am asking you to do.

It didn't take a long time. It wasn't like years of healing or anything like that; it was very spontaneous in me. Although there was some strong resistance in me initially to what was happening, I realized that to resist was to be harmed even more. The only thing to do was let go absolutely and have it take its natural course and then end. If I had been caught up in myself, I could have ended up dead. But I didn't. Why? The support of the Mainstays, and my recognition of raw empty seeing and raw empty knowing of the power to benefit all, with no distinction between the predator and the prey. The equalness and evenness of all. So, you can see that the Four Mainstays lifestyle can look a lot of different ways.

If I didn't rely on resting and open intelligence, I would have had to create a lifestyle based on that violent episode. I had worked in the domestic violence movement earlier in my life, and I know that it is an extraordinarily important and sometimes tragic issue in many lives. Even if the incident I am referring to in my own life was not a domestic violence issue, what I am pointing to here is the fact that, along with the healing that needs to take place after a violent episode, we need to see that our victimization is not a place to live from forever.

Get accustomed to your real identity, the identity you were actually born with, one which is not limited by all the reified notions you've learned about yourself. Stay with yourself as you are. Just rest; rest in the pure potency, the sheer benefit of what you are. Rest in the benefit of yourself as a great knowledge and benefit creator. Rest in your own empowerment.

THE LIFESTYLE WE CHOOSE

CHAPTER SIX

There has been a choice to live in a certain way based on reification, and now there is another choice being made to live an open-intelligence Four Mainstays lifestyle. We are actually making a conscious decision about how we are going to live our life; we are selecting and electing a lifestyle instead of just having a lifestyle imposed upon us.

One could say that there are always four mainstays present in whichever lifestyle we choose. If we choose a certain group of people with specific data streams, then there will be the mainstays that come from that data. There will be a pervasive data stream that binds everyone together, and there will be teachers and proponents of that data stream within the group. There will be the teaching material, whatever it is, and then there will be some kind of community collected around that pervasive data. Throughout life those mainstays will be practiced, for the most part without realizing that one is doing so.

Generally, in most people's lives, this has been a matter of being focused on reification, with teachers and teachings in reification and a community immersed in reification. Once again, "reification" means attributing a nature to data as being something that is independent of open intelligence. When we believe that data are somehow separate from open intelligence, we give them power to influence us, and in doing so we have "reified" the data, that is, given them an independent nature. So, we have been training up in reification with people we allow to train us, we have been reading or watching the many training materials based on reification and we have a community in common with other people based on reification.

We adopt the lifestyle of those around us who are practicing these mainstays because we so want to belong and be loved, and once we have a feeling of belonging and of being loved, we are afraid of losing that. Always hope and fear are present: hoping to get the love we want but then fearing that we won't. There might be the semblance of life satisfaction and flourishing in that lifestyle, but in the next moment there could be fear of its loss. True love and belonging are only completely satisfied in open intelligence, which is not bounded by the limitations of hope and fear.

Living a life based on reified mainstays is how we have been living anyway; however, now a significant number of people are no longer willing to live a reification-based life supported by reification-based mainstays. Now with the Four Mainstays of open intelligence, we are willingly and consciously choosing a specific lifestyle. We are taking a step out of the vagueness of the lifestyle based on data streams into the lifestyle of open intelligence. The Four Mainstays are an all-encompassing, warmhearted, lucid lifestyle *choice*, a place where we can finally get down to being real.

A SIMPLE BUT IMMENSE CHOICE

There are all kinds of lifestyles and all kinds of teachings about how to live based on indulgence, avoidance and replacement of data streams. There will be all sorts of abstract ideas about how we should live, for instance, "You should do this and you shouldn't do that, and you can think this but not that." To live a life of indulgence, avoidance and replacement is like having infinite passports for infinite countries, but it never leads anywhere. In a life of indulgence, avoidance and replacement we will not be able to recognize the power of the Four Mainstays lifestyle of spontaneous benefit to all.

When we recognize that the lifestyles we have had throughout our lives have been ones that we have chosen, we give up our right to be a victim of those choices. No matter what we have learned, we had to choose to learn it, and just as we chose to learn it, we can choose to be open to learning something else. We need not consider ourselves to be a victim of anything.

Most all of us were probably unaware that all along we really did have a choice about our lifestyle, but now we actually see that we *do* have a choice. It is a matter of saying, "This is the way that my life is going to be lived. It is going to be a life of short moments of open intelligence with support from a trainer, training and community. It is no longer going to be a life of adhering to false ideas of reification." This choice is so simple, but at the same time so immense. So simple, but so immense.

A Four Mainstays lifestyle brings greatly beneficial power to human society. A great turnaround has happened because people worldwide have stood up at the grassroots and said "no" to a reified life. People are actually making a conscious decision about how they are going to live their life; they are selecting and electing a lifestyle, instead of just having a lifestyle imposed upon them.

A Hundred Percent Commitment to the Mainstays

It may take some time to be able to fully commit to the Four Mainstays lifestyle, because for most people there has been a lifetime of living as reified intelligence. At first, one may be a bit hesitant, and gaining confidence in the Four Mainstays may take a while. Then for others it is more like, "Of course! This is what I've always been looking for. I want a trainer and trainings on this topic, and I want a community to share this with for the rest of my life, and I don't want anything else."

Those who live the Four Mainstays lifestyle maintain their commitment to open intelligence and develop and deepen it as well. It isn't like putting one toe in the water and continuing to stand there with only one toe immersed. No; we jump in completely! When we choose this one hundred percent commitment to open intelligence and to the Mainstays, we find that we have a capacity that we never knew we had before. We are able to take on challenges that never would have even come to mind prior to taking on a Four Mainstays lifestyle, and we are able to identify strengths, gifts and talents in ourselves that we had no idea existed. Then we are able to bring them forth in an incredible way for the benefit of all. That is just really beautiful and astounding.

We know when open intelligence becomes obvious at all times in our life; there isn't any question about it, because it is like slicing off a finger. If you slice off a finger, that is a direct cut and the finger is completely gone, and you definitely know it! This example of a direct slice—in terms of open intelligence becoming immediately and completely obvious—points to a whole world of assurance and confidence that opens up in a new way.

In the Dzogchen Teaching, for example, this is called "the thorough cut," which means a thorough cut through all conceptual boundaries and all reification. "Cutting through" means cutting through our reified understanding about our own mind and building philosophical understanding and confidence in open intelligence to the point where we can leave everything *as it is*. This takes us to the mind of great bliss seeing emptiness. When that thorough cut is complete, next comes the teaching that is called "direct crossing," which means to leap over reification. Through the direct slice and direct crossing instructions, we're able to see the spontaneous presence of everything *as it is,* the dynamic energy of the diamond mind. In cutting through we instinctively *recognize* open intelligence; in direct crossing we instinctively *realize* open intelligence.

Another excellent metaphor is one of a bird learning to fly. A bird has wings and it sees lots of other birds flying around and so believes that it can also fly; however, until it actually flies it may not have confidence that it can. But once it has flown, it has full assurance of its ability.

With a one hundred percent commitment, we have committed ourselves to a kind of lifestyle that brings out our best innate abilities and which fosters our naturally exalted nature. We find ourselves gaining more and more assurance in the power of the Four Mainstays to let data streams be as they are, which is the shining forth of open intelligence. We get to the point where we are just gliding along with great ease, and we know that no matter what each moment brings, a profound equalness and evenness beyond all description is available to us. To live together like this is our birthright, our most basic human right.

Supreme commitment is always already-on, always already accomplished, always already present and always already evident. It can be called "commitment outshining preservation," as it does not require anything to keep it in place. Open intelligence's beneficial potency exists as the reality of supreme commitment. In the beneficial potency of open intelligence, we live as the natural commitment inherent in the great reality, the commitment that is always already made. When we make a one hundred percent commitment to the Four Mainstays lifestyle, it is not a contrived commitment. It is the full-on acceptance of the commitment of open intelligence's beneficial potency *as it is*.

A UNIFIED LIFESTYLE

Through a commitment to the Mainstays, we come to have a lifestyle of sanity. "Sanity" actually means "health and soundness of mind," and then to that we could add soundness of speech, soundness of the body and soundness of qualities and activities. A sane mind gives forth sane speech and sane qualities and activities. Sanity itself is the soundness of mind brought about by open intelligence's beneficial potency.

The Four Mainstays lifestyle offers the possibility of potent answers to the fundamental questions: Who are we? What is our actual fundamental basis? What are we capable of really and truly? What is our most optimal conduct? What can each of us individually bring to the world? This inquiry does not have to do with intellectual constructs, philosophies or political ideologies, but with the reality of what it means to be human in each and every moment.

When we elect to live the Four Mainstays lifestyle, we do not try to live one Mainstay, then another Mainstay, then the third and the fourth. It isn't that way at all. The Mainstays are an indivisible algorithm in which all the component parts are included. We elect a unified lifestyle that will clarify for us with increasing profundity that open intelligence and beneficial potency are alive and real. This is the reality of everyone and everything—the reality of every thought, every emotion, every sensation, every action and every quality.

No matter what we are doing, no matter what we are involved in, if we are committed to a life lived as open intelligence, it is essential to have the basis of the Four Mainstays lifestyle, because it is this lifestyle that will reinforce and affirm for us what our commitment is every step of the way. It could be that every day we are dealing with people who live lifestyles that are based on ordinary kinds of commitments which involve limitations, partialities, efforts and struggles. However, when we have our basis in the Four Mainstays lifestyle, we are able to know what to do and how to act with all people and in all circumstances.

It is through open intelligence that we find complete dignity as a human being. So, here we stand: we know who we are and we know what our identity is, and within the context of this newly discovered lifestyle we find dignity and integrity. Love, wisdom and energy are real and alive, and the more we rely on open intelligence, the more we find the love, wisdom and energy that allow for open-ended knowledge and benefit creation.

A LIFESTYLE HOME BASE

The Four Mainstays serve as a lifestyle home base with no entry requirements! There is lifelong access; in other words, people are assured of a sense of belonging along with the always-on, always available Four Mainstays lifestyle support system. This provides an incredible amount of freedom, which is really fantastic when one considers that many of us have had a lifetime of feeling uncomfortable within the systems and structures of organizations.

The Four Mainstays lifestyle is rooted in the introduction to and the instinctive recognition of the power to benefit all. It is not rooted in the body or the mind and is not rooted in all other data and information associated with the body and mind. There is total release into spontaneous natural perfection that nourishes and refreshes us in every single moment without any effort at all— without asking, without praying, without beseeching. It is an always-on gift.

Within a Four Mainstays lifestyle a setting has been created where everything is normalized. All the things that have been unspoken and taboo are now spoken to directly. Whatever it is that could not be talked about with others is now talked about, and that is so vitally important, because this capacity activates truly beneficial speech—the speech that cannot be forgotten.

In relying on open intelligence, we can see more and more how we flow from goodness to goodness in a way that is inexhaustible. When the goodness is first recognized, it really strikes the heart. Then over the long term it is recognized even more deeply; it is recognized all the time, day and night, waking, dreaming and sleeping. When we just relax and take it easy, everything is seen to be a part of the vitalizing energy of beneficial potency. We do not struggle; we rely on open intelligence in the face of whatever is appearing. Beneficial energy isn't in some cutoff state that we have called "open intelligence"; it is in whatever is happening right now. We can simply show up for who we really are, whatever the circumstances may be.

Acknowledgement of our always-present real identity guarantees that we are of revolutionary benefit in every instant. Therein is a life-altering disposition that is recognizable to ourselves and to others in terms of our action in the world. Our way of being is uniquely available for relationship, because we are transmuting our reified identity into our authentic, genuine identity. This is a life that is a *love-style,* a love-style where anything is possible.

We become accustomed to exaltation; we are able to walk down the street feeling completely connected and always in full relationship with ourselves and with everyone else. We can share the delight that is reality. We live our lives and do whatever we do, and within that is greater and greater delight. There is no push or drive to try to get somewhere or to get away from something.

We choose to be happy rather than being right. That sounds very simple—being happy instead of being right—but it is very profound. How often have we stood our ground and said, "I am right and you are wrong!" No matter how provocative the data streams might be, open intelligence in its obviousness at all times is always content, always relaxed and always able to be fiercely or peacefully responsive in the way that is required by that time, place and circumstance.

Instead of trying to abide by constructs that have never led any of us to complete and permanent happiness and the ability to be of benefit to all, we rely on what we can find to be absolutely true about ourselves. We find what is always established, never changing, absolutely real and always available to provide immediate benefit that is beyond all kinds of ideas of good or bad, right or wrong. In this we find the ultimate rightness and goodness, and it is completely uncontrived. Uncontrived; we are not trying to contrive being good or being right.

AN AUTHENTIC WAY OF BEING

Realization of open intelligence is the authentic lifestyle of benefit to all. Completely letting go of the need to be somebody, completely relaxing, opening to the reality of who we really are, this is what it means to be genuine and authentic and to not have a contrived identity. A contrived identity is, "Oh, they expect me to do this, so I better do it." An uncontrived identity is, "Well, here we go!" There is no need to write a script and then fulfill it; instead, we let it all be *as it is* and respond from complete spontaneity.

There may have been worries that were nagging us at every turn; even if they were not conscious, they may have been churning underneath and ready to cause us anguish at any moment. They are what could be called an under-mutter. Living confidently as that to which we have been introduced, worries begin to dissipate and to no longer disturb us, and the incessant under-mutter quietens.

We see others who live without worry who can be role models for us. We are a human being just like they are, so when we see that they can live without worry, we know it is possible for us. Worrying can be exhausting, but without worry we are sprightly and energetic. When we do begin to live without worry, it is helpful for us to ponder this enormous change in ourselves and to see how very far we have come.

We might occasionally return to old ideas of reification, but only because this has been a long-held habit for us. Through the power of open intelligence, over time the habits of reification are erased.

There may have been one particular habit that we had struggled with, maybe for years, yet through reliance on open intelligence, not only does it disappear, but many other long-held habits disappear along with it.

When someone introduces us to open intelligence, in that introduction the person is merely confirming what we already know. At last we have actually found someone who can confirm what we already know! Fortunately, through the Four Mainstays we can have confirmation of open intelligence throughout our entire life. All aspects of our life whatsoever are the presence of open intelligence, and we have every single tool for mastery of all of these aspects.

This supreme path of the complete confirmation of open intelligence is the journey of all conquerors past, present and future. When we speak of "conquerors" we are not talking about military conquerors. We are talking about the all-victorious ones who through the instinctive realization of open intelligence's supreme benefit conquer the notion that everything has an independent nature. Once we gain assurance of open intelligence's beneficial potency, we become the fortunate ones certain of empowerment.

QUESTION AND ANSWER

Q. I have a deep love for my family, but at the same time also a strong resentment towards them, well, actually especially towards my mother. I find that these strong feelings that have been with me for so long keep me from experiencing the sort of easefulness and openness that you are describing. Is there any way that you can help me with this?

Ziji Rinpoche: For each of us it is the same: we have lived life the way that we have only because we had trained ourselves to do that, and we didn't know anything else to do. The same has been true for all of us; it has been true for me, true for you and true for your mother. We lacked education in the nature of mind, and that's the only reason we have lived life as we did.

It is so very, very empowering to see that if we had the same data streams another person has, we would be doing exactly the same things they are doing. In that way we can put ourselves in another person's shoes; we can see that if we were pressed by the reification of data as they are, we would be doing exactly the same thing they're doing.

Certain discomforted relationships may be present in our lives, and in some of them we know we've done something that we feel badly about or something has been done to us, while in other relationships it is not clear to us why we feel discomfort. Some relationships are ones in which we have been harmed, although we have not harmed anyone ourselves.

If we still resent the situation, we rely on open intelligence and the Four Mainstays lifestyle to harmonize and bring powerful benefit to that relationship. Becoming willing and committed to harmonize avoided relationships with people, places and things is really freeing, because usually we have had things that greatly irritate us in these areas, and to be free of that burden is such a joy.

The Four Mainstays lifestyle is all about creating a new way of life for people to choose, so now here you are involved in that lifestyle. You have recognized the immense empowerment that comes from a growing confidence in open intelligence, and you can see the value in harmonizing all your relationships, including this broken relationship with your mother.

It is important for us to stop avoiding relationship as a means of dealing with afflictive emotions, and our commitment to this must be unflinching. We face everything and avoid nothing, and we empower our lifestyle through the Four Mainstays. We let data flow on by and we allow beneficial open intelligence to bring skillful means and insight to all situations. By the power of open intelligence we empower our relationships and focus on the potential harmony in all of them, rather than avoiding relationships through emphasizing data streams.

Instead of a vague sense of other people, we have a very clear and openhearted sense of each and every person and a feeling of connection to an indivisible family of all beings. This is so touching, so powerful and so revolutionary, and it is great fun, too!

There are valuable tools that can be used to harmonize any relationship at all. For instance, we are able to identify clearly the relationship that we want to be empowered and harmonized. Through relying on open intelligence, we stop blaming others and ourselves for the challenges in the relationship. In this way we release the compulsion to think or speak about past data associated with the person, place or thing. Instead of carrying around our big bag of resentments, we just let it fall to the ground and we open up to our direct connection with individuals, places and things.

By first taking on the harmonization of an avoided relationships, the previous avoidance in the relationship may be noticed for the first time. Rather than continuing to avoid, we are able to stand firmly in our commitment to harmonize the relationship. We see that any person, place or thing that we have avoided is naturally indivisible open intelligence, and that's it. Whatever else we think they are, they are shining forth as open intelligence.

In regard to being together with one's family, the key really is in building a bridge of communication through listening. The more open intelligence grows in us, the more we are able to listen. Open intelligence doesn't have an agenda; hence, there doesn't have to be any agenda to change ourselves or change anyone else.

You love your family, so you will really want to learn communication skills, skillful means and wisdom that can enable you to have a better relationship with them. Just by your being available to them exactly the way you truly are, that is a great start. They have known you for a long time, and some of them may be able to see who you have become, so just through that insight the message is getting through. Once in a while there might be a time when you can bridge the gap by weaving a few words together, using words that they are familiar with coupled with new words you can introduce that will be helpful for them. It might open up a little more for them, or it might open up a lot.

How one makes a one hundred percent commitment to open intelligence and harmonizing all relationships is unique in each person's life, but however it may be, we are so fortunate if we have recognized open intelligence and the great benefit of the Four Mainstays lifestyle.

FACING EVERYTHING AND AVOIDING NOTHING

CHAPTER SEVEN

Rather than remaining in a dark hole, we let all data be as they are, and we take responsibility for an open-intelligence lifestyle by relying on the beneficial power of the Four Mainstays. We face everything and avoid nothing; that's the way to go.

In all of the mirage-like appearances of the here-and-now, everything can be easefully left *as it is.* We face everything and avoid nothing, not only in ourselves, but in everybody. This requires being relentless and fearless. We really want to see what is going on and what, if anything, there is that we are afraid to think or feel. We take it all the way in terms of looking within at our own emotional and mental makeup; we go for it completely.

There is a stance of absolute courage that is available to us, one in which we are willing to open ourselves up to absolutely everything, not only in ourselves but to everything that has ever happened to anyone. We allow ourselves to see all data as the purely beneficial expanse of open intelligence. We allow ourselves to really connect to, rather than recoil from, all situations past, present and future. We are willing to admit that if we had had the same data streams as people who have caused great harm, we would have been doing exactly the same thing they did. Through subsuming everything into a comprehensive, beneficial and very beautiful intelligence, the past, present and future become a pool of splendor, and a great equalness and evenness is found.

We decide that we want to be absolutely unafraid in regard to every single thing that comes up for us. "I want to go all the way. I want to fearlessly feel and know absolutely everything about myself and others." A part of becoming totally free is to be very familiar with all the really challenging data streams. It is not easy to take a look at ourselves and to realize how we have hated ourselves, hated other people, and how we have been arrogant, prideful, desirous and fearful.

We could begin a practice of actually writing out the strong thoughts and feelings we are having, being totally honest and brave and willing to go anywhere our inquiry takes us. In our writing we can be as frank and revealing as we need to be. Writing everything down candidly and openly that we are facing isn't some kind of frivolous idea; it is something that has been practiced down through the ages by people who are really serious about this inquiry.

Knowing Ourselves and Every Other Person Intimately

In living for the benefit of all, there are no back doors whatsoever. We have to get to know ourselves and every other person intimately, including the people we may have hated and despised in the past. We do not have to necessarily go over to their house and make friends with them, but we are willing to inquire into their, and our own, essential being. "Who are these people; what is going on with them? Why did they do what they did?"

For example, we could examine our feelings in regard to a person like Hitler, about whom there are many strong feelings. Maybe he is loved by some and hated by many others, but whatever the opinion may be, what is being described here is the capacity to be in relationship with every single individual on earth by knowing them exactly and completely as they truly are. And what they truly are is nothing other than open intelligence.

If we can put ourselves in the place of the perpetrator of a crime or a violent act—even thinking the thoughts that a perpetrator might think or envisioning ourselves doing the things that a perpetrator might do—what occurs is an incredible broadening, releasing and relaxing of all the conventional push-back against those kinds of situations. There is a release into indivisibility with all of that. If we are able to take these extreme data streams and subsume them in open intelligence, that is a very, very powerful form of practice.

Rather than simply condemning a perpetrator, we can see that what they have done is a form of anxiety relief for them; it is an attempt by the person to get relief from extremely intense unease. To simplify it down to what it really is—anxiety relief—is really important. It is true compassion and understanding to say, "Well, this person is trying to relieve their intense suffering and anxiety, and they don't know how to do it. What they did was absolutely horrible, but what they wanted was to relieve their extreme anxiety."

To let data be *as it is* means to open up the great spread of perfect knowledge and to see what is there in that radiant spread of knowledge that is beyond conventional thinking. If we have been involved in a horrific event as either a victim or a perpetrator, it is really important to let everything be exactly *as it is*. By letting everything be *as it is* and by putting ourselves in the person's place—what they think, what they feel, what they do when they do what they do—this brings great heartfelt-ness to the practice of open intelligence. That is a moment of tremendous opening, where we are freed of our need to hate, condemn and disdain.

ENCOUNTERING ALL THOUGHTS AND EMOTIONS

There is a lot of power in seeing that, whatever it is that is on your mind, if that is what you are focusing on, that is what reality will be for you. Whether you try to avoid it, change it, replace it, indulge it or do whatever you do, in holding on to it that is what reality is for you in that moment. There is a choice as to where you will put your attention: on all the data streams that are constantly flowing on by, or on open intelligence.

All the button-pushers that come up are great teachers for us, if we just allow the data streams to be as they are. After all, they are all the shining forth of open intelligence, so it is great to see them as a play of open intelligence with itself. To encounter extremely negative thoughts and feelings as open intelligence is freedom in immediate perception, which could also be termed complete perceptual openness in all experience. For people with great afflictions from their past or present, those afflictions too are free in immediate perception.

We might see these sorts of afflictive thoughts and feelings as kind of scary. "Whoa, stand back, these things are no fun." But then once we are introduced to open intelligence, there is the possibility to clarify the affliction. We come to see that the affliction never was an affliction; rather, that it has always been a beneficial display. We could come to first see the affliction as an old and dear friend; second, we see that it is self-releasing and that there is nothing we need to do about it; lastly, we see that the affliction is outshone by its beneficial reality.

When we are for whatever reason stuck in an afflictive state and unable to let it be, a key bit of advice would be to contact the trainer, involve yourself in as many trainings as possible, read and write out texts and engage in service. No matter what happens, do not pick up an antidote, such as indulging, avoiding or replacing the data with something else.

The affliction is here to show us that there is no affliction. We directly encounter affliction as it self-releases in open intelligence, and this is complete perceptual openness in all experience. Instead of automatically flipping to avoiding, indulging or replacing data, we simply allow the data streams to be as they are. Afflictive states are faced in direct encounter. We test in our own experience what these afflictive states really are. When we face them in direct encounter, what we see is that they come and go. They come and go, they come and go, they come and go.

We test in our own experience what is exactly happening with the data, and we see that a thought arises and it stays but a second. Even though we may think, "Oh, I was angry all day," if we really look, we see that it is not possible to be angry *all day*. We have a period of anger, which then self-releases. Then we have another moment of anger with all sorts of feelings that come up, and it too self-releases. This can be going on throughout the day, and if we are not watchful we may conclude that the anger is present without interruption.

But, again, it is a data stream which arises, remains and departs, to be followed by subsequent data streams which arise, remain and depart. The suffering that we seem to be stuck in is an idea, an idea that we might often share with others who are stuck in the same data stream! We may have friendships based on mutual suffering, and we may form groups to share our suffering and to alert others to our suffering.

The suffering we have been so wrapped up in is itself open intelligence; that is the point. Non-recognition of open intelligence *is itself* open intelligence! So, in a tremendously beneficial way, that completely destroys all of our ideas about our suffering. All our beliefs about who we are and have been are relaxed, and when these beliefs appear for us again, we understand them newly and freshly.

When we take responsibility for our data streams, the afflictive states are outshone. Present for us is the tremendous power of open intelligence in which the people of the world can stand up and claim their own identity. We can see how important it is to be a participant in the end of all suffering through the instinctive realization of open intelligence.

Let's say that all of a sudden we are completely taken over by an afflictive emotion and we decide, "Well, short moments, that is what I am going to choose, and it is not going to be any other action." So, we take a short moment, and just that short moment can give relief with that particular affliction, or it can even provide relief with a memory that has been haunting us for all of our lives. A difficult memory may have been coming up again and again, but with each of these short moments, there is an enormous expansion of wisdom and benefit, because all of that energy and attention that had been placed on reification is now freed up into open intelligence.

A key practice is to not elaborate or proliferate the affliction when it comes up. When you feel anger, instead of going with the emotion, it is a great time for a short moment, in whatever form that short moment may take. The result of resting with afflictive states is not that you become more self-centered; rather, a greater devotion to the benefit of all becomes evident, which encourages very deep listening and caring. If other people are sharing something, you can be completely present for everything that is coming up for them and be available to support them. Feeling the power of benefit within ourselves ensures that we see the power of benefit in others.

When a thought comes up and we are willing to sit with it and directly encounter it and see what is actually happening, rather than merely believing in what we have been told about all these things, we are testing the letting-everything-be-as-it-is practice in our own experience. We apply the scientific method of direct observation to our own experience, and we see that all is well. Yes, in fact, all *is* well. This is freedom in immediate perception and complete perceptual openness in all experience. We can't predict what the next moment will bring, so that is another area where it is really easy to have a lot of humility, but the more we rely on open intelligence, the more assurance we have and the more evident the solutions are for whatever is arising.

Most of us have adopted a lifestyle of lack of education in the nature of intelligence, or maybe we have adopted a lifestyle of seeking, but now all of that can come to an end, because we have found what we were looking for. It is a huge relief to seal open all data streams forever in what they are: the equalness and evenness of great benefit.

DESIRE, FEAR, ANGER

When we look at a very powerful data stream such as desire, we can see that desire can often run wild if it is not left *as it is*. It runs through so many expressions—money, power, prestige, sex, relationships, getting things and wanting more things—but when desire is left to rest in the great power we each have to benefit all, it is an inconceivable treasure. All our desire is always really only the desire to benefit. It might seem like we want all these other things that were mentioned, but if we let them be as they are no matter what they are, we come to the conclusion in our own experience that what is being said here is true: all desire is only the desire to benefit oneself and others. In our own direct experience is where this realization is to be found.

If we expect sexual desire to decrease from the first moment that there is an introduction to open intelligence, that expectation will shortly end, because there may be an increase! Why? Because the desire has often been kept within a little box, but now that we are letting everything be *as it is*, thoughts and emotions are released from being held within that box. As a result, we might be driving down the road and suddenly everyone we see starts to look really attractive! However, it isn't "sexual desire" that we are actually feeling; it is rather a total indivisibility and connection with all people, an indivisibility and connection that was previously interpreted as being sexual desire. None of this is telling us to act on impulse. Rather than giving in to the impulse to indulge the desire, we let things be as they are.

Anger or fear or any other afflictive state has no nature of its own, so to think that any afflictive state has a power to control us is actually quite illogical. "Fear" cannot make us feel afraid and "anger" cannot make us angry. The whole litany of descriptions we have used for so long are only that—descriptions. We are giving up our own empowerment if we think that these descriptions have power over us. One day in the future people will look back on these times and think, "How could they have thought like that and lived that way?"

Any reified ideas we have had that there are things like anger or hatred or sexual desire that have power over us to make us do something is nonsense. We are at the helm in each and every case. Most of us were raised with contrary information; we were told that these urges and surges of anger and hatred and sexual desire have a power and influence of their own that make us do things we do not want to do. That is simply not the case. We always have complete sovereignty over our situation, whatever it may be. We are all-subsuming open intelligence that contains and includes all data streams.

Let's say that the data stream of anger does come up for us. By letting the anger be *as it is* without getting into who has done what to whom, we settle automatically into discernment, clarity, insight and other skillful means, rather than the storyline of the anger. This is very powerful. The first short moment of this clarity provides immediate beneficial potency. The trust in this moment-to-moment beneficial potency grows, because we see how our qualities and activities of mind, speech and body change. We can see how powerful our qualities and activities are becoming.

When we experience anger, we can rely on open intelligence for short moments as the anger appears. That is absolutely essential to seeing the inseparability of the anger from open intelligence. We rely on open intelligence at exactly the same time that all the anger is building. To outshine anger in this way is a novel experience, when compared to simply being overwhelmed by the anger as we may have been in the past. Outshining anger is a platform for also outshining desire, arrogance, pride and jealousy.

The more we feed the description of what is going on with us, the more real it will seem to be. If the anger comes up over and over again, at some point there is the opportunity to rest naturally and to enter into complete relaxation as that, rather than continuing to bring it up and to name it. The treasure is found in outshining all of the ways that we have described ourselves. All of these descriptions need to be left as they are. What is always present as all of these emotions is exalted open intelligence.

INFORMED BY THE SETTLED NATURE OF THE MIND

When a reaction of anger comes up, almost instantaneously the mind starts running a storyline. "Oh, so and so did this to me and I'm really angry about it. This always happens to me." Mind informs speech, so then the next thing we know our speech is also involved. We are either telling someone else about how angry we are, or we are telling the person we are angry with just how wrong they are. Within the storyline of anger, it just spins on and on endlessly like that. Right there we can see how the mind has informed the speech, the body, the qualities and activities within the anger-storyline.

However, by letting the anger be *as it is*, mind settles into the spaciousness and potency of its native condition. We gradually, or sometimes quickly or in quantum leaps, become very familiar with the comprehensive open intelligence at our disposal. Then the thinking that comes about is thinking based on discernment, clarity and insight, rather than a story about anger. The speech is informed by the settled nature of the mind, rather than the story about the anger. All of the qualities and activities of the body follow along as well.

That is much different than going with the story, and there is a much broader range of response. The response comes from a totally settled condition. It does not mean the response will always be a mild one. It could be a wrathful one as well, but skillful wrath is totally distinct from anger, because a skillfully wrathful response always comes from the love of open intelligence and its beneficial intent. Its spontaneous intent is to gather everything into the indivisibility of that love rather than to strike out and hurt or harm.

We gradually become aware that all the things that we thought to be real are nothing other than open intelligence. Along with anger, we could also take as an example the emotion of fear. Fear is something that we are taught is very real, but in fact fear is f.e.a.r.—false-evidence-appearing-real! The thing that appears as fear isn't a real thing, as it has no independent nature. This is the way it is with *everything* that is described; it is false-evidence-appearing-real, seeming to have an origin, power and influence of its own. However, all along false-evidence-appearing-real is always only the supreme benefit of open intelligence.

We begin to realize that we can blow open all these things that we have assumed to be true, such as fear. They are mightily expanded into the reality of what they truly are. The learned descriptions fade away until they are completely outshone, just as the stars at night are outshone by the bright daylight. Then when fear comes up, it is less and less attractive, and its power and influence are realized to be non-existent. What is realized is supreme benefit alone, a vitality that is so real to us. It is not a vitality like that which is gained from physical training or having exciting thoughts or emotions, but the supreme vitality of benefit that is always at the basis of everything.

By granting disturbing emotions an unwarranted influence and magnitude in our lives, we have likely thwarted our naturally beneficial empowerment. Through insight we see that our anxieties and fears are simply the shining forth of data, and in seeing this our capacity to enjoy open intelligence becomes more obvious. We find ourselves gaining assurance in the power of the Four Mainstays to let data streams be as they are—the shining forth of open intelligence.

We feel free to enjoy relationships and tap into our innate open intelligence and its beneficial strengths, gifts and talents of mind, speech, body, qualities and activities. By using the Four Mainstays we can easily live as open intelligence and enjoy each moment of life, no matter what life is bringing us. We experience true life satisfaction and the feeling that everything is complete in every single moment of the here-and-now. People all over the world are now living in this way, and this is really a beautiful way to live.

There is a feeling of total relief when we have been working on something maybe for years, such as jealousy, anger or fear, and we find that the emotion no longer has power over us. We cannot even believe that it could be completely absent, because it has been there for so long, but now it is truly gone. What a great support it is to know that there is something that can deliver the same complete relief, not only in us, but in all human beings. Once having discovered that, well, we naturally want to know more about it and develop as much of a relationship with it as we can.

QUESTION AND ANSWER

Q. I would really like to know more about the practice you described of dealing with the feelings we have about extreme data streams of suffering or abuse. Could you go into that a bit more deeply?

Ziji Rinpoche: In a town where I once lived there was a health food store, and every day the owner of the health food store would be in there grinding carrots to make carrot juice for his customers. People loved to come in and interact with him and drink his delicious carrot juice. However, it later came to be known that this man had sexually assaulted all three of the daughters of the woman he was living with at that time, and that he had also done the same with the daughters from his previous marriage.

I had thought before this came to light that he was such a wonderful man who was going to great lengths to provide organic food to the community. Yet, all the while he had been abusing these girls, and that was very upsetting to find out. These things are not okay anywhere, but when something like this happens in a small town, it becomes an issue for almost everyone in that town.

When I came to know what had been going on, I purposely continued to go to his store, because I wanted to fully see how I felt as a result of this situation and what it brought up in me. I wanted to experience everything fully and deny nothing. So, I would go into his store and I would say hello to him, and I'd see him preparing his carrots, and I just wondered what it was he was thinking. What about him made him feel that he could do what he did with those girls? Did he feel a sense of ownership, like it was his right to do that?

Normally, we might shy away from these difficult situations by saying, "Oh, he's no good; I never liked him anyway." This is the way we avoid relationship; we avoid relationship with ourselves by not knowing how we really feel or think about anything, and we avoid relationship with other people by not really understanding them at all.

I found it painful to directly encounter this man, because I knew one of his daughters, and she was ravaged by what had happened to her. She felt that there was no one to talk to and that no one would actually listen to her. She felt that she was at the mercy of this man and that she had to just let him do whatever he did and that she had no choice. But finally she did speak up, and he was eventually arrested.

I allowed myself to try to think what he thought—things that most people would shy away from—and I allowed myself to feel everything that I thought his daughter might feel. This, by the way, is an example of what it means to really allow data to be *as it is*. In allowing data to be *as it is*, we go beyond all the conventional ways of interpreting data. I think the tendency would generally be to just write the man off or have some kind of contrived compassion for him, but to be able to see him without avoidance or hatred was truly empowering. It is a matter of not being afraid of anything and truly getting real with life in all its many forms. To really know yourself and to know other human beings as they really are, and to really go in and know *deeply*, is an important aspect of being of benefit to all.

I wrote about everything that it made me feel; every single thing that came up I wrote about in a poem called "Carrot Juice." It was not just about me, but everything about him too. Did he feel he was teaching them something? What was there in him that drove him to do that? Was his desire so out of control that he felt that he just couldn't help himself? In writing the poem, there was for me a no-holds-barred attitude: "Look at what is exactly going on and don't hold anything back!" and this clear seeing is really what is required of each of us.

So, everyone in that town either hated the man and wanted him out of town or they were ambivalent about him, but when I had written my poem I could be at ease with my feelings about him. I didn't like what he had done, and I knew that he had to come to terms with the harm he had caused. I also knew that he needed to make direct changes in his life and also make amends with the people he had hurt, but I didn't hate him. The hate was so far away from where I was; it was impossible for me to hate.

Rather than remaining in a dark hole, we let all data be as they are, and we rely on the beneficial power of the Four Mainstays. We face everything and avoid nothing; that's the way to go.

A Relaxed Life of Good Cheer

CHAPTER EIGHT

We have the great power to benefit all, and it is up to us to use it. We must claim our own power to benefit ourselves and to benefit each other. The world may look like it is in a hopeless and helpless state; however, it is only that way if we assume that it is so. In order to correct course, we need to claim our own greatness and our power to benefit ourselves and to benefit each other.

Open intelligence's beneficial potencies are the greatest gift and the greatest life we can ever have. We move forward into our potency one step at a time, and as we do so, we take on a new worldview in which we see that we are exalted and flawless beneficial agents of open intelligence. Instead of being self-obsessed—thinking constantly about ourselves and about all our hopes and fears—we become dedicated to the benefit of all. The question is: are we going to be focusing on our psychological states and the resentment we have for our partner and our need for more money and the pain we have in our foot, *or,* are we going to allow ourselves to rest effortlessly as beneficial potency?

The very least we can do is to give ourselves this gift and to come together as empowered human beings brimming with beneficial potency. The effect of that gift is the natural responsiveness of spontaneous altruism. Instead of being skeptical, doubtful and even indifferent, there is a friendly feeling for everyone and everything. Inseparable from the self-perfected qualities and activities of open intelligence's beneficial potency is the passionate desire to benefit all. The best word for that is bodhicitta, the deep desire in one's life to spontaneously benefit all.

We are learning to give up the grandiose hallucination that we are a special someone if we happen to have education, power, money or other resources. This is a delusion in which we will be constantly struggling with the need to attain and possess more. In a space of total humility, we can join with others who are also giving up this delusion. We are joining together and saying, "No longer do I need to assert myself as a special someone." There can be an end to the struggle for money, power and prestige, and there can also be an end to the suffering of lack of food, clothing and shelter and the destruction of our habitat.

When we use this word "habitat," we actually do not know what our true habitat is. We would conventionally say that Planet Earth is our habitat; however, *open intelligence* is our actual habitat, and this is the habitat we can count on. Once we claim our power to benefit ourselves through short moments of acknowledgment of who we are, we return to that again and again, and as we do so, reality opens up, a reality that has always been available but which had not been acknowledged. Once we acknowledge our reality, then we can live in the ease of primordial benefit in a completely relaxed way. There is no spa, resort or vacation hideaway in the world that can give us the sense of beneficial potency and well-being that is found in open intelligence!

ALIGNED WITH REALITY

No longer do we have to go through all the rigor of having to prove something to ourselves or to others. With any person of any kind that we encounter anywhere, we are connected through the direct acknowledgment of the stainless presence of one and all. We are relaxed, easeful and filled with good cheer. We cherish knowledge that is actually of benefit to all rather than trying to acquire knowledge that will merely promote our own advantage.

We have in fact only made use of a very small part of what we are as human beings, and so we now are beginning to know who we really are and what we are capable of. What we can see is that, as we gain assurance in open intelligence, there is more and more interest in what is of benefit to all. The simple question we begin to ask ourselves at each juncture in our life is, "What will be of most benefit in this situation?" That is a very straightforward and very complete manner in which to make decisions. A beneficial lifestyle that is unlike any other lifestyle opens up.

Due to the fact that this type of education is clearly very important, one would imagine that everyone would be educated in this way; however, as we know, this type of reality-education has in fact been very rarely emphasized in most educational systems. It has not been the emphasis for most of us personally, and it certainly has not been the case for worldwide human culture. This step of alignment with reality through open intelligence is profoundly revolutionary, and many people all over the world are joining in this very important revolution of excellence and exaltation. It is crucial to be aligned with reality in the way that has been described here.

We hold the intelligence of the universe in a usable way, so how are we going to educate ourselves in this way, and what choices are we going to make in our lives based on this education? Are we going to dwell on the faults of our neighbor? Are we going to let greed, anger, hatred, arrogance, pride, envy, jealousy and desire rule us? People are now saying "no" to ignorance of their real nature, and they are not fearful about what is on the other side of that "no." They have the courage to stand up and say, "I will not be demeaned, I will not be marginalized. I'm not going to continue to mistreat myself. I'm going to go to any lengths to fully enliven the nature of my mind, and my whole life is committed to that."

Sometimes people are very ready to hear this message, are open to it and are ready to take it on. Others may have more of a moderate openness, and some are not open to it at all. Often openness can come through seeing the very direct benefits of relying on open intelligence in the lives of others. People see the dramatic changes in family and friends who are relying on open

111

intelligence and they wonder, "Wow, look at that, I wonder if I can do that, too." Other people get the message just by hearing what these empowered people have to say and by seeing how they are, and more and more the lives and relationships of the newly introduced people are enhanced through the benefits of relying on open intelligence.

Many people are making this choice today, so it isn't just a few isolated individuals. If other people do not want to make this choice, then that is up to them; they can certainly go their own way. However, we have a right, even an obligation and a responsibility, to make the choice that says "no" to ignorance. Even though it may feel somewhat foreign and odd in the beginning, we have companions who can share their experience about once having felt the same hesitancy and who have subsequently gone beyond it.

A QUANTUM CHANGE

There is a quantum change that is occurring right now. It is like a great ship that is turning, and all the people on the ship are turning with it. There is no way to predict what will happen as we become more and more accustomed to living with the doors of reality thrown wide open and as we become more and more accustomed to living as an intelligent expanse with no disconnect from each other. We are no longer relying on disempowering and marginalizing ideas that have so diminished us; instead, we are opening up into the complete splendor of the magic of reality. We are then on the right track, and we have made a decision that is really working for us and for other people.

Most often it has been the case that we have not recognized how tremendously filled with exaltation and beneficial potency we are. This is what the community is all about: recognizing exaltation and beneficial potency and wanting to bring that into being in ourselves and in others. When we see that we are in a community where everyone else wants that for us, it is really a tremendous support. We can then carry on in the actuality of reality rather than in some made-up world that always needs to be changed. We carry on in the great treasure, the great fortune and the unimaginable riches that are the very nature of who we are. We experience ourselves as an exalted creature of pure wisdom magic.

When we speak with someone, we do not just throw a lot of memorized jargon at them. Instead, we are totally and completely available, focused on benefitting them in whatever way possible, and ready for whatever comes up. There is a total meeting in complete union with the person. With complete spontaneity and openness we come together with the person, and we are able to be with them as they are. There is no need to have a game plan or a rulebook.

Our mind, speech, body, qualities and activities are those of an intelligent domain so vast that it might be presently inconceivable to us. We *are* that inconceivable domain, and we are just trying to become more familiar with it. We may have had a lifetime of layering on more and more ideas about what a human being is, but these are reified ideas based on a false premise. There is such ignorance of what a human being is capable of. It is up to us to show ourselves and other people what is possible and to hold nothing back.

WE GIVE OURSELVES ENTIRELY

We give ourselves entirely to what we know to be true, and we take action based on that conviction. First there is the introduction to the nature of mind, the introduction which shows us that our basic reality is all-beneficial and accessible to us every moment. Then comes the deepening commitment to open intelligence, and along the way, a growing assurance. The authority and conviction are available to give ourselves entirely to that commitment to open intelligence and to no longer be satisfied with the things that have till now confused us.

It is our good fortune that through relying on open intelligence we are given the knowledge of ourselves as we really are, as compared to what we have been *taught* we are. We have been taught that we are originally flawed in some way and are in need of help. We are also taught that, because we are originally flawed and sinful, we need to aspire to a better way of being. We are taught to conform to some kind of standard that will keep everybody marching along in the ranks. However, in breaking through reified ideas, we are allowed a true lifestyle choice for the first time. There are quite a few lifestyle choices available within the context of the conventional standards of the past, but who would want that when something so much greater is available?

Most of us have trained ourselves to respond to different situations within a range of specific behaviors. However, open intelligence has the capacity to spontaneously respond to each time, place and circumstance in a truly unique and ultra-beneficial manner. Instead of having a set way of being or responding, spontaneity is the basis for responding; we already have everything we need in order to respond with exactly the appropriate skillful means.

It is important to repeat once again that we do not have to effort at all for any of this. The more we relax, the more the immense beneficial energy is available to be of benefit to ourselves and others, and we must instinctively recognize this essential key point. Our beneficial energy becomes more and more obvious, obvious, OBVIOUS! We grow in incredible trust, and this trust is always available, always growing. Often it is in retrospect we see that we have become able to live easily and effortlessly as spontaneous benefit.

POWER-BORN!

We have the great power to benefit all, and it is up to us to use it. We must claim our own power to benefit ourselves and to benefit each other. The world may look like it is in a hopeless and helpless state; however, it is only that way if we assume that it is so. In order to correct course, we need to claim our own greatness and our power to benefit ourselves and to benefit each other.

Even if many of us have been brought up to think that we are defective by nature, we are definitely not defective in any way. We are in fact a powerhouse of innovation and exaltation. We are power-born, filled with so much power that at first it might feel foreign to us and maybe even a little bit scary. "Am I really this powerful? Can I really do what I want to do and not be swayed by what anyone else thinks about it?"

All beings are power-born! Power-born! Being power-born means being willing to go all the way; it means having zero tolerance. "Zero tolerance" means saying "no" to all the untrue things that have been told to us and absolutely not accepting the way things have always been. Zero tolerance means being courageous enough to speak up against ways of being and acting that have caused harm and to not shy away from that commitment.

Reaching the point of zero tolerance is a natural result of profound rest as open intelligence. From the vantage of zero tolerance we have much more clarity about exactly what we want to do and how we want to do it. When we realize that there is another way for human beings to live that brings much more benefit into their lives as individuals and into the collective as well, it is only natural that zero tolerance for what is disempowering and harmful would develop.

Zero tolerance brings a person to the place of right action, so no longer is there any relativism involved in the equation. One of the actual demonstrations of this is the ability to make a decision that does not go along with the norm. We can use discernment, clarity and insight to see what everybody else is up to without necessarily needing to do things in the same way. We are also able to be firm and confident in the face of heavy criticism.

We can share with one another and stand up and speak out about the very real choices we have made. The story we have to tell is the story of our own life and how we came to be empowered human beings and how we came to be able to stand up and speak out with authority and conviction about the nature of what a human being is. Due to our own empowerment we have the authority, conviction and boldness to tell this story. Everyone has a right to be a victim, but now from this vantage of empowerment, wouldn't it be really ludicrous to exercise that right? Why be a victim when we are truly a powerhouse and can accomplish so much?

From the very beginning of our lives, we have wanted to belong and to be accepted and included, and we want a feeling of all-inclusivity to be our actual lived experience. We really want to feel the unity and peace that are naturally existent in the entire world, and it is through empowerment that we are able to feel that. We find that what we are is all-inclusive of the things we might have wanted for ourselves, such as the love of a partner or of our mother and father. We find perfect love and all-powerful knowing, all-open connectivity with everyone—being able to look at everyone and know them completely and know exactly how everyone is at the basis.

Even though we were all born naturally free and beneficially responsive, over the course of our lives we have gradually learned to experience a disempowered way of living. Just as we have learned to live in a disempowered way, through our own direct experience we come to really know profoundly and deeply, totally instinctively and spontaneously that we are empowered with beneficial potencies, and these beneficial potencies can flow freely and spontaneously in each moment of life.

Everything that we say comes out of the nature of our mind, so as our mind becomes more powerful, our speech becomes more powerful. We are less and less likely to speak about things that really do not matter, such as gossip and criticism. Many of the ways that we have been trained through reified intelligence disappear, and we find ourselves living a relaxed life of great care, good cheer and fun. We allow ourselves to have the exaltation of beneficial speech, where every word that is said is completely treasure-filled. That treasure is available because our speech is no longer bounded by limiting definitions. The definition of any word is no longer confined within its reified meaning; instead, its definition has been exalted through seeing that the original definition of all words is "the great spread of beneficial potency."

Our mind is empowered through open intelligence, our speech is empowered, our body is empowered, our qualities and activities are empowered, and we come to see that the same empowerment is innately available to all. The power of our beneficial potencies is inexhaustible, so we do not have to be concerned at all about a destination, as in getting to a state where we are going to feel a certain way. Open intelligence requires no going to a destination and no change of circumstance. Assurance in open intelligence brings complete relaxation beyond seeking. We are taken over by the reality of what we are. Seeking disappears, and relaxation and beneficial potency take over.

INEXHAUSTIBILITY

In short moments of acknowledging open intelligence we instinctively realize an increasing sense of the inexhaustibility of open intelligence. Inexhaustibility is the reality of what human life is. "Inexhaustibility" is not a word we usually hear in relation to who we are or to what reality is; rather, what has been communicated to us was subtle ideas of scarcity and lack. Because of these primitive beliefs, we have become as individuals and as a global human culture very conflicted and confused, and the extremes of conflict and confusion have grown to the point of bursting.

Inexhaustibility is inconceivable and indescribable. It cannot be communicated through any kind of human knowledge we currently have. We must rely on the most comprehensive of all knowledge: the empowered knowledge of open intelligence. No longer need we live a merely human life that is mortal in each of its instants. No longer need we be restricted, constrained or limited by the boundaries of a skin-suit.

We realize that we no longer need to be engaged in trying to puff up an image of self and make it seem better or more special and more unique than other selves. Instead, the idea of the self has gone by the wayside. If we have any idea of the self, it is the "self" of open intelligence's beneficial potency. Rather than being tied to the idea that we are exhaustible human beings who inhabit a body that will drop dead at some point, we find that we truly are inexhaustible. We are in fact the power of the universe endowed with the capacity to benefit all.

Sometimes quickly, sometimes slowly, we come to recognize that our primary capacity to act is through the agency of open intelligence. In this we are inexhaustible. The flesh, organs, bones and the framework of being a person will all eventually slip aside when death comes; however, open intelligence's agency always remains. Whatever happens, the agency platform we have right here continues on.

We are learning that we are inexhaustible beings, and we are discovering what inexhaustibility could mean in each area of life. We are seeing what this new knowledge can provide for people living in a global civilization. We are discovering that by living as open intelligence, we are able to live in a basic harmony unlike any circumstance that we have known before. The harmony is not something that is contrived. It comes from the realization of equalness and evenness. Everything is equal and even, and to know this is the true brilliance of human beings.

It may have taken many years of intensive cognitive training to convince people that they are seeing a world of separate individual things, but it does not take many years to recognize the radiant pool of equalness and evenness. We simply open ourselves to a new way of knowing and being. All is truly a radiant pool of equalness and evenness, and through hearing definitive teachings on equalness and evenness with openness, we come to instinctively comprehend what is truly real, and we realize it on a much deeper level. In open intelligence we do indeed find the spontaneous equality of all our own data streams, and all other equality is based on that. We hear these things over and over again, and then at some point the truth of the teachings strikes us in full.

In any context in which we feel ourselves drawn to emphasize data streams, we rely on open intelligence rather than on emphasizing the data streams. This is similar to spontaneously allowing a heavy load to fall to the ground. We allow the heavy load of data to drop to the ground, and we sail free as inexhaustible open intelligence. Open intelligence is always spontaneously present in data streams, and when open intelligence is experienced as naturally beneficial, all data streams that arise as its virtual display are by necessity also naturally beneficial. All data are naturally beneficial in their great equalness and evenness.

Intelligence is an inexhaustible natural resource, great in the beginning, great in the middle and great in the end. This quality means that training up inexhaustible open intelligence and its beneficial potencies is great all the way through, from the initial step of hearing it, the intermediary step of practicing it to the final step of realizing it. It might look like effort to the uninformed, but it is always a spontaneous display and is never effortful.

QUESTION AND ANSWER

Q. I would be really interested to know how all of this that you are speaking of came about. What were the things that happened in your life that led you to think this way and to start doing the things that you have done?

Ziji Rinpoche: Well, I can start by saying that I was raised as a Catholic in a very devotional home, and there was a lot of prayer. It wasn't prayer lasting for hours; it was just prayers of short moments. All along in my life I adopted ways and means that people had used to discover their human nature. I adopted them in my own way to point directly to what I believed to be true about the world and about human beings.

As I grew older and I became more involved in the world, I could see the power that people had when they came together for change. I also saw the power of community organizing along with the benefit of people gathering together to bring about change. I did that through many of the movements of that time: civil rights, opposition to the war in Vietnam, the domestic violence movement and the international women's political caucus, among others.

But all along I knew that none of these were fully the answer. The problem in all the groups and what made all of them much less effective, was that the individuals in the group did not understand their beneficial potency and the power of their own intelligence. They didn't really understand that intelligence is primary and that the body is secondary to that intelligence.

Through these many experiences I became very interested in education in the nature of mind, and I began a comparative analysis of all of the teachings in the nature of mind. That comparative analysis has been ongoing now for over forty years, and eventually a team developed around this effort. We put together a comprehensive map of what a teaching would look like that would actually draw out these beneficial potencies in people and would also erase all the ideas they had about original sin, bad karma and other such things that make people feel like damaged goods.

From what I had learned in my work in community organizing, I knew early on that our movement needed to come from the grassroots. It couldn't be something that started in an institution. It needed to come from the grassroots, just like other great movements have come from the grassroots. We were interested to find what it was that people wanted from their minds and what they expected from their intelligence and how they could come to really make use of their innate potency. By listening to people, we learned what we human beings are and what we want. Based on listening to the people who continue to come forward, the Teaching is evolving to meet their needs and interests. We make sure that everyone has a voice. We actually have a principle whereby voices can be heard, no matter how unique that voice might be.

Discovering our innate potency can cause the human species to turn around; it is that powerful, and we're in the process of supporting this effort with all our resources. Those of us who live in this particular era are very blessed in a unique way, because we have seen the before and the after: the "before" of reified life and the "after" of a life of potent great benefit. Generations to come will have only seen the "after." They will look back on stories about what it was like before with complete amazement. They will be appalled that anyone could have ever lived a life based on reification of thoughts and emotions.

The greatest gift we can give to ourselves and others is the recognition of inexhaustible open intelligence and its potent great benefit, and the direct lived experience of this potent great benefit in our own lives and in the world. One very specific example of this potent great benefit could be seen in relation to our family and loved ones, with whom we may have previously had quite a fractured relationship. Perhaps they were people we didn't like so much, or maybe we even hated them. But by receiving this great gift of inexhaustible open intelligence, we find that we have a completely new outlook towards them and towards all people.

Maybe earlier we had very upsetting data streams whenever we were with our family, but now we find that we can be quite happy to be with them and that we are even looking for ways to be of service to them. We are learning to live an exalted lifestyle, and we are learning to live the way we were born to live.

Part Three

BENEFICIAL OPEN INTELLIGENCE

THE GREATEST GOOD FORTUNE
CHAPTER NINE

The exaltation of the benefit of all is what human life is about. We hold the knowledge of the universe in a usable way; but we have no access to the exaltation brought about by that knowledge until open intelligence is obvious at all times. That obviousness comes from allowing everything to be as it is—including all our habitual reactions—until there are no more habitual reactions and there is the obviousness of open intelligence at all times.

To receive expert instruction in the profound meaning of open intelligence is the greatest good fortune. It is so marvelous, so incredible and so beyond imagining! And what do we have to do to become aware of open intelligence? Nothing, because open intelligence already is. We relax body and mind completely and see everything at the basis: pure benefit, pure relaxation, pure soothing. It does not matter whether a thought pops up or not; everything, whether thought or no-thought, is fueled by open intelligence.

This profound instruction is like a range of golden mountains stretching back into the distant past and going on and on forever, providing each one of us with innate capacity, endowment, authority and conviction. When we have been trained that we do not have profound meaning and that we do not have good fortune, that is how we will see ourselves. We think we are in this skin-suit of a body and that we are limited to being nothing other than that.

The good news is that there is nothing to be done. Leaving everything *as it is*, every datum resolves itself in its own actuality. In any moment of our life, when we feel any doubt whatsoever, we can show ourselves the pure benefit at the basis. In leaving everything *as it is* we find that the despair and the excessive negativity we have experienced, along with all the joy and laughter in life, are all loaded with profound meaning. It is all power-packed with the punch of beneficial potency that is both soothing and of great power.

Each of us is very potent by nature, and whatever it is that is coming up for us, we have the innate ability to leave it *as it is*. Soon we start to see that our speech is completely empowered by this potency. We have a choice about what comes out of our mouth, and we get to a point where our speech is filled with beneficial intent. Even if it might not immediately sound like it is of benefit, it is having a profound and beneficial impact. Usually the exalted, mighty, flawless, stainless qualities and activities we innately possess are not named or identified for us, and hence we have no knowledge of their presence. But *now* they are being named. One of the wonderful things about receiving an authentic introduction and instruction is that it enables us to recognize the capacities and possibilities of open intelligence.

CLAIMING OUR EXALTATION

We cannot even know who we truly are until we claim our exaltation. Claiming one's exaltation is not something that is new to this present time and circumstance. There are people who have lived throughout human history who have known they are exalted; yet, very few of us in the present time have heard that the great exaltation of open intelligence is our nature. Because exaltation has been held at bay by long-held false assumptions, the actual decisive experience of exaltation has been unavailable for almost everyone.

Due to many different factors, for thousands of years most people have believed certain things that their society and culture told them were true, and one of those things that we have been told is that we are *not* exalted beings. However, by the power of open intelligence we begin to discover our exaltation. Do we now want to take self-responsibility for recognizing our own exaltation?

Again, the knowledge of the exaltation of human beings is not something that is completely unfamiliar; there have been people throughout human history who have known that they are exalted. However, it isn't socially appropriate nowadays to go around talking about how exalted we all are! People have not yet been able to accept their own exaltation, but now the times they are a-changin,' and we can now attest to the exalted nature of human beings.

It is now a matter of facing up to the false things we have been told about ourselves and which we have believed, and to face them directly within ourselves. With every single thing we feel, we let it be *as it is,* and we see it for what it really is. All the things that we have been hiding from, we let them too be as they are. It is a headfirst immersion into which one dives completely, and this also includes diving in completely to the afflictive states and not being afraid of them.

When we allow exaltation to reign, the mind, speech, body, qualities and activities become filled with joy. The exaltation of the benefit of all is what human life is about. We hold the knowledge of the universe in a usable way; but we have no access to the exaltation brought about by that knowledge until open intelligence is obvious at all times. That obviousness comes from allowing everything to be *as it is*—including all our habitual reactions—until there are no more habitual reactions and there is the obviousness of open intelligence at all times.

Look at the beauty of the world we live in and all its inhabitants and all its functions and features; how fortunate and exalted we are! Part of exaltation is the ability to recognize and enjoy these incredible things and to really allow the awe, and to not see awe as just an incidental event. For instance, one could go see a beautiful ocean sunset and be filled with awe and wonder, but then return to a basement apartment in a crowded city and think that the awe and wonder were somehow lost.

True exaltation is to feel natural awe and wonder ongoingly, just more and more awe about what we are and all that is unfolding. This great awe and exaltation is what we have to share with each other, not just the great adulation projected onto a deity or some kind of other theistic conceptual framework, but the great exaltation that we ourselves are.

Open intelligence is inexhaustible, and the awe, wonder and exaltation of open intelligence are also inexhaustible. This is a magical opening to reality that is so ultimately lovely and reliable. Each moment of existence is great exaltation. On an island of gold everything is gold, including you! No matter where one looks on an island of gold, nothing but gold will be found.

Each of us is born to be awesomely beneficial, and we have within us the capacity to use our mind, speech, body, qualities and activities in an extremely exalted way. Open intelligence is our birthright; it is the great exaltation of what it means to be a human being.

There is something really important we each have to contribute, and in order to contribute we have to face the reality that we can in fact contribute in a great way. We have to see that we do have the ability to do what we want to do. If we do not think we have the resources to do it, then we can find the resources. Sometimes we are taught to display a false humility, but false humility is actually just the flipside of arrogance. There isn't anything to be other than to be open intelligence.

There are many stories of what seem like extraordinary, or even miraculous, events, and people may say, "Oh, nothing like that could ever happen." It takes complete openness in order to really understand extraordinary things and to allow oneself the possibility that we are not excluded from these extraordinary things. After being diminished for a lifetime, it might sound strange to hear for the first time, "I'm an exalted manifestation of open intelligence's primordial purity," but why not try it on for size?

Some people slowly and gradually adjust to this, and then for some there is a sudden experience of, "Well, of course this is so! I don't care what anybody thinks; this is who I am, and I'm going forward as that." Unlike reification which seems to be spontaneous but which requires effort and is always very contrived, the potency of beneficial open intelligence becomes obvious at all times without any effort. All responses in the moment are spontaneous and uncontrived, no matter how long we live.

THE BURSTING HEART OF LOVE

One of the things that presently is of great urgency on Planet Earth is the protection of our natural resources, but it is also very important to know what our natural resources actually are. It would be good to begin with the most important natural resource, number one above all others: the bursting heart of pure love! Our number one natural resource is the only one that has the intelligence to take care of all the challenges we face. If we do not encounter that in our direct perception, then it will not be possible to use this enormous gift to help solve the enormous problems in the world.

Many of the conventional concepts of love that have been passed on to us have very little to do with what love actually is. We need to see what "love" and "the heart" really are; they are open intelligence. We no longer need to rely only on the concepts we have had about these things. The love that is so evident in true intimacy, collaboration, transparency, cooperation and instantaneous resolution of any kind of data stream is the sort of love that needs to be spoken about.

In open intelligence we ground ourselves in the reality of pure love. We are able to love ourselves, maybe for the first time, by letting everything be *as it is* within us. We are not indulging, avoiding or replacing the data through labeling. We are opening data up to their beneficial counterpart, which is comprehensive intelligence. This is true love and care for the self. Without this love and care for the self that is all-inclusive and all-encompassing, there can be no understanding of what love really is. So, all discussion of love starts right here, no matter what aspect of it we are talking about.

Relax body and mind completely and open up to your bursting heart of pure love! Open your heart completely, and allow yourself the natural state of being totally in love with everyone and everything. A heart that is always open can never be closed. If you think you have a closed heart, it is just a mistaken belief. To live life with an open heart and to be completely open to feel everything is the greatest gift that you can ever give yourself. We come to be completely in love with everything, and we can say this honestly and straightforwardly, because we have come to see our own data streams as the glorious exaltation of comprehensive intelligence.

We are all familiar with romantic love, and we know how love affairs start. "Oh, wow, I am in love. This is so exciting. There has never been anything like this." But what eventually happens? The euphoric feeling goes away because it is based on something temporary. The true love affair is the love that is based in the ever-present, primordial love of open intelligence, which is where true connection with another person takes place.

For people all over the world who are gaining assurance in open intelligence, love is easy and it is spontaneous and automatic. For them love is no longer a special fall-into-or-out-of state. There is the capacity to love each other openly. This does not mean we go around having sex with everybody; instead, we really open up to one another in a natural way. We are not afraid of sexual feelings;

we can have all the sexual feelings we want to have—more power to 'em!—because we know we do not have to necessarily act on them.

By leaving everything *as it is* in the great heart of love, we are free. This is not a matter of cultivated or developed niceness. It is the beautiful gifted heart that is unstoppable. There is just a space of complete openness and love and the naked, distinct reality that can never be closed or altered in any way.

DEVOTION

There are all kinds of devotional dispositions. Some people come with a naturally devotional tendency, while other people have been in circumstances involving devotion where it has ended up being really crazy, and they are very leery of anything like that happening again. So, in that case, it might take a while to allow devotion to grow.

To have a devotional disposition is just the reality of who we are; the disposition of beneficial potency is a devotional one without trying to be devotional. It is completely uncontrived devotion to the benefit of all. "Devotion" may mean one thing in terms of our relationship with a partner, while devotion to our child takes another form and devotion to a teaching is yet another form. All of these types of devotion nurture each other, and the more devotion there is for one, the more devotion there can be for all. It is not a matter of choosing one object of devotion exclusively.

With devotion, we have nothing at all to do, nothing to seek, nowhere to go—devotion, devotion, D-E-V-O-T-I-O-N. To be devoted is the easiest "doing" that never needs to be done! An instant of heart devotion to the benefit of all goes further than ten thousand words about devotion. First, we are devoted to ourselves, and then we can explore devotion to our community, our trainer and to the training. Every single short moment benefits all, so there is no need to look to some point in the future when there is going to be the devotion in ourselves to benefit all. Right now, this instant of open intelligence is benefitting all beyond anything we could comprehend, and we can have a very deeply devotional relationship to that reality.

Other words can be used instead of "devotion," but if you happen to be a devotional person, feel free to use that word and to exercise it openly and freely. Devotion is the easiest way to instinctively realize open intelligence. The openness in devotion allows for a special type of non-symbolic communication, sometimes called transmission or evocation. In this non-symbolic communication all is said that ever needed to be said. So, devotion is an indestructible vehicle of empowerment. It is an evocation of what is already present.

Devotion to the trainer is seeing the trainer as open intelligence itself. Seeing the trainer as open intelligence is essential to seeing the same thing in *yourself*! You have found at least one other person in the world who you can say is exemplifying open intelligence, and you decide that you are going to do everything you can to support that person, and yourself.

There may be a natural tendency towards devotion in someone who just cannot see the devotion that exists in themselves. Devotion is natural for them and has been with them ever since they were born, but they have as yet not pinpointed it as being something particular to them. Devotion, whether identified in oneself or not, is the quality that draws many people into very dedicated and committed forms of service.

As an example of this, I once met a particularly sweet and kindhearted doctor, and I wondered how he handled all the challenging aspects of his job. On a daily basis he was dealing with life and death situations, and so I asked him, "How do you handle telling people that they are going to die?" and he said, "Well, I am a very logical person, so I just look at all the facts, and then I go into the room with the people and I am totally present with them in every way, and I tell them clearly and honestly what the facts are. Then when we are finished, I walk into the next room and do the same thing once again with full attention and care. Then when I go home, I find myself crying during sentimental movies." This man has lived his whole life with a devotional disposition towards everyone, but yet devotion was not necessarily something he could name or say that he had.

When we enter a truly devotional relationship with others, we develop the capacity to benefit all, and just by that devotion we *are* benefitting all. Devotion allows us to enter the world of the unimaginable and the unbelievable.

WHAT ENLIGHTENMENT TRULY IS

Enlightenment is described in many, many ways and increasingly so with the wide reach of the internet and the very large number of books on the topic; however, what has been described as enlightenment has been tarnished by so many misinterpretations. One way that the term has been understood is that enlightenment only belonged to certain historical figures, time periods, countries or cultures. Enlightenment has also been considered to be a thing, a destination or a place to go, and that one would look a certain way and have certain marks once one is enlightened. However, now the word "enlightenment" needs to be brought into a commonplace nomenclature, which is much better than dressing it up in old garments that are ready to fall apart anyway!

Enlightenment is not a destination, and illuminated intelligence doesn't look any particular way. Enlightenment doesn't need to be grasped. There's no place to get to, for a balanced view has no destination. Everyone is already always arrived.

There are a number of different types of enlightenment, so to speak, and many of them have to do with self-focused enlightenment, which is enlightenment for a seeming self. However, in reality the urge towards enlightenment is not a self-focused pursuit. There will eventually be a realization that there's no self to be realized or enlightened. True enlightenment is the enlightenment of illuminated intelligence, where illuminated intelligence benefits all. The idea, "I am going to get enlightened for myself," is not only fallacious in the end but also a very small space to live from.

There are many qualities and activities of what could be called enlightenment that are very much needed in this world, and many people around the world are saying, "I want a new way to look at enlightenment that is not self-focused."

ENLIGHTENMENT FOR ALL

The internal preoccupation with "I, me and mine" can come to an end. "I, me and mine" may be present in a certain sense, because first we have to say, "I really am interested in enlightenment, and I want the best means of enlightenment available." When we no longer hold realization to be purely for ourselves, we reach a crucial juncture where we don't even think about "my realization" anymore.

This is the Dzogchen attitude: enlightenment of all being, or, said in another way, the enlightenment of all *beings*, if the emphasis is on individual beings. The enlightenment of all beings is at the forefront, and whatever we do to ensure the enlightenment of all beings, we are ensuring the enlightenment of ourselves, because after all, we are already one of those beings that we are striving to enlighten! "All beings" would include us, and that's a very profound realization in itself.

The all-penetrating, unimpeded vast expanse of great bliss seeing emptiness is the key point of inexpressible and naturally inherent mind, beyond all extremes such as rising and ceasing, existing and non-existing. It is so beyond words and out of reach of mental inquiry; it is fresh, pure, sudden and beyond description.

Whether it is a Dzogchen master or lama, or it is anyone else, the mind of great bliss seeing emptiness is the same. The mind of great bliss seeing emptiness is not unique to individuals; it simply is *as it is*. Everyone is the mind of great bliss seeing emptiness, and no one is left out. In resting as the mind of great bliss seeing emptiness, it doesn't mean thoughts or data streams have stopped; it just means that they are not given priority. Reification is not given priority, and more and more data are seen simply as the dynamic energy of the mind of great bliss seeing emptiness.

In resting and fully relying on open intelligence, we naturally see so much more about who we are, and that allows us to really see who everyone is. The more we accept our own data *as it is*, the more we can understand and relate to what's going on with others, even with those who may have a completely opposite point of view to ours.

The strength of our spontaneous wisdom provides the power for us to take in all suffering of any kind we can imagine and to give out great bliss. This is a very, very ancient practice and is one of the most powerful practices anyone can have. It emphasizes that, despite our ideas about being an isolated individual self, we are not isolated at all. We are joined in collective great bliss. We can share that great bliss right here and now, taking in all suffering of every kind we can imagine and giving out the great bliss that ensures the enlightenment of all beings.

Giving one's life entirely to the enlightenment of all and caring about each and every being is a way of life that includes incredible miracles. This life brings more miracles and more of the truth of what enlightenment is than any kind of conceptual ideas about enlightenment.

One can stop for a moment and consider how many other people may seek enlightenment, and realize that, "I am not the only one.

There are many people who desire enlightenment." This is very important and significant. We come to realize that our enlightenment is found in the desire to enlighten all beings. There is this beautiful, beautiful word bodhicitta, and this is what bodhicitta is: supporting the enlightenment of all beings. In supporting the enlightenment of all beings, we find our own.

This is the beginning of what is called "seeing the divinity of all," which really is enlightenment. It's not having a certain individual experience. It is naturally and spontaneously seeking the benefit of all. Bodhicitta is the heart of the enlightened mind's inexhaustibly opening intelligence. Arousing bodhicitta is to commit to the attainment of complete enlightenment for all beings in forever shining brightness.

Everything is equal and even. When we pray for the enlightenment of all beings or pray for the benefit of all, we are praying for ourselves too, because we are included in "all." We are not a separate creature over here observing all. We are the equalness and evenness, the indivisibility of all.

COLLECTIVE SPONTANEOUS WISDOM

There is a collective spontaneous wisdom that is ever-growing in its strength, an instantaneous enlightenment of the collective. Any moment of open intelligence's beneficial energy that is spontaneously affirmed is the instantaneous enlightenment of the collective. What then does enlightenment actually mean? It means the demonstration of profound beneficial energy in mind, speech, body, qualities and activities. The open, enlightened view is committed to and devoted to the benefit of all.

Everything is enlightened after all! That's why there is the saying, "Everything is buddha and everyone is buddha." Nothing has to be done. We are born enlightened, but this recognition slips away due to our conceptual training from the very beginning of life. To

135

hear that we're completely relaxed already, to hear that we don't have to strive, and to know that a teacher will confirm who we are rather than trying to keep us dependent and limited is extremely important. There is a vast change occurring in the way that enlightenment teachings are presented, and in this Teaching, enlightenment is presented as being the natural state of everyone already. There is no one who isn't in the *in*-group! Everyone is equally enlightened.

To see the goodness in others, to exalt everyone as they are, to make sure everyone has the natural enlightenment that is the reality of human nature is so important. We don't use or misuse each other; we care about each other and we care about giving to each other. "I really care about your ultimate good fortune, and I will do anything to support that." That is how we come to feel about each other.

QUESTION AND ANSWER

Q. I would so love to hear more about the joy and exaltation that you are describing. Can you point out more specifically how that might look in real life?

Ziji Rinpoche: When I was a young girl growing up in Bermuda, I found a magical place that I just fell in love with. I could never get enough of that place. There were these caves down by the sea, and they were easy to get to from our house. The caves were like crystal caves for me with stalagmites and stalactites, and there was light at the end of the cave so you knew the ocean was nearby. There was an aquamarine stream of water that was absolutely clear that came into the cave. I could see all the pink coral sand underneath, and so I often walked along the stream into the mouth of the cave which met the ocean. I could see lobster, octopus, whales and so many other sea creatures. This place inspired such awe and wonder in me.

I remember going to my school which was on a hillside overlooking the ocean. At recess I would sit on the hill and look out at the ocean where one could sometimes see whales going by, and because I was so absorbed in this I often didn't hear the bell ring to end recess. So, I was constantly getting into trouble for not returning to class on time! One day I was far down the hill and I did hear the bell ring, and I started running up the hill, but I fell and injured my leg quite badly. However, even in my early years there had always been some sort of recognition of short moments, and the injury did not stop me from taking those short moments.

I already knew by then that there was a way to be that would protect me from everything that I didn't like, that I feared or that I thought was wrong or bad. I also knew that I wasn't going to find my way to that in the school, but that I was more likely going to find it by watching the whales and exploring the caves.

Just like the magical quality of these crystal caves or the enchantment of the whales, life has always held for me an incredible magical quality. Despite what I may have heard or learned to the contrary from others, I knew that this magical quality really is reality. I could see beneficial potency shining in people, and I could see that everything is essentially pure benefit.

I and so many others have decided that we will not settle for living a miserable life. We have so much more to offer, and we won't settle any longer for misery. We're not going to victimize ourselves anymore; we're going to look for an outcome that we can depend on, and then we're going to live from that outcome and help others to find the same.

I just couldn't say "no" to the exaltation of open intelligence's purely beneficial nature and to the inherent benefits of a Four Mainstays lifestyle! How could one say "no" to, "I will care for you for the rest of your life. I will care for you in whatever way is needed for you to know that you are an incredibly beautiful creature. I will do whatever is needed for you. If you're crying, I will hold you. If you need a hug, I'll give you a hug. If you need a pat on the back, I'll give you a pat on the back. If you need a good scolding, I'll give you a good scolding, but it will be a scolding where you will feel loved; you won't feel disempowered and trashed."

So, knowing what I did, once I became an adult I couldn't just sit in my home thinking beautiful thoughts about how wonderful the world might be. I actually had to do something. When I first began giving public talks, someone gave me an old car to use, and I took that old car and drove over the mountain to the city from my house three nights a week in order to give talks, and then I drove back home over the mountain at eleven o'clock at night. I just got out there; I went everywhere anyone wanted to hear what I had to say.

I invite you to do the same thing. Get out there, talk to the ones who want to hear what you have to say. There are many ways of reaching people, but primarily people are influenced by your own living example. Even some of the ones who at first may be the most critical of your lifestyle and who may be totally entrenched in their lifestyle of reification will soften over time and go from arm's length relationship with you to warm hugs in generous quantities!

I am simply another person just like you, and if I can live with full devotion to these stainless qualities and activities, then so can you. That is what it boils down to. There isn't anything about me that is any different from you. I have a great deal of perseverance, and so do you. I have the willingness to look into things to see whether they are true or not, and so do you. We no longer need to go along with things that we have been told are true that really aren't true. People are exhausted from being constantly disempowered, and they long for something different. Many, many people are ready to hear about a life of exaltation, joy and empowerment, and each of us in our own way can contribute to that devotion to the benefit of all.

THE AUTHENTIC "I"

CHAPTER TEN

The idea that our identity has become something solid and fixed is just another data stream, and even if we have learned to speak and to think about ourselves in derogatory ways, these descriptions are not the truth of who we are. We are all-pervasive of everything, and when we claim our right to open intelligence's beneficial potency, we claim our true identity. The one and only true identity of all—past, present, future or timeless—is pristine open intelligence, the pure benefit of all.

We have been relying on data to give us some kind of intellectual understanding of what our identity is; however, once we have actually been introduced in an authentic way to open intelligence, the short moments practice will acquaint us with the reality of what we truly are. We really take on our significance and importance by taking responsibility for the authentic "I."

Disempowering conceptual frameworks have stripped human beings of their natural goodness and cheer and have left them searching for an individual identity that cannot be achieved. The plight then for most of us has been one of confusion, turmoil and competition, and it has involved a lifelong fight to nail down an identity and then keep that identity in place. Nailing down an identity is impossible, unless you know that your identity is open intelligence! Then identity is sealed open forever, and there is no more confusion.

How has human culture developed this disempowering way of seeing things, and how could it have remained in place for so long? It is because so many of us have trained up our minds in exactly the same way people have trained up their minds for thousands of years. We would never consider adopting the same biases or engaging in the same primitive practices from so long ago, so why do we continue to hold on to outdated modes of thinking?

Throughout the course of history, humans have seen themselves in many different ways, and it is at this time in human history that we must see ourselves in a new way: in recognition of open intelligence as being unending and all-pervasive. It is now a period of transition where many people are choosing to move from one view of reality to another. There is a paradigm shift from the paradigm we were born into—of subjects and objects living in a world and of the many disempowering conceptual frameworks handed down from the past—to inexhaustible open intelligence.

FREE OF REFERENCE POINTS

If we are steadfast in the belief of having an independent identity, we are guaranteed confusion. If we maintain that, "I am so-and-so and I have this history and I am this and that," then we are involved in the very difficult work of having a past to base a background on, creating a present through what has gone on in the past, and forming a future in anticipation of what will happen later. To live only from this vantage involves seeking something and never finding it. What a burden to carry! How different our life is in the easefulness of the Mainstays lifestyle in which there is no one trying to manufacture an identity, and there is so much strength and vitality when all of that manufacturing is completely released.

What is required is to recognize yourself again and again as open intelligence. For short moments many times you are recognizing yourself for who you truly are, in the same way that down through life you learned to identify yourself as an individual and call yourself by a particular name, over and over again. You caught on to the name at an early age by being called that name repeatedly by parents and caregivers, and eventually you took on that name as your identity. Before that, in infancy, they were calling you by that name, but you didn't yet recognize yourself as the name they were calling you or as the person that the name referred to.

So, what are all the things that came into being because of belief and repetition of that belief over many years? It is such a key question in the Dzogchen practice: what were you before you came to be named, identified and confirmed as a separate individual? In Dzogchen practice, you return yourself to yourself, the "yourself" that you always are, apart from the naming and identifying. This is what Dzogchen is: the return of oneself to oneself.

We come to see that everything we have considered to be a fixed physical reality, including our own physical bodies, really can't be captured. No totalizing concept can ever describe who we are. It's impossible, because knowledge is fresh in each moment; the data that bring us the power of knowledge are fresh in each moment. Through open intelligence we become highly skilled at using the dynamic energy of data. All this happens in a snap, and our knowledge is spontaneous; we know exactly what to do and how to act to further social benefit. This is the reality of Dzogchen experience and Dzogchen realization.

The idea that our identity has become something solid and fixed is just another data stream, and even if we have learned to think about ourselves in derogatory ways, these descriptions are not the truth of who we are. We are all-pervasive of everything, and when we claim our right to open intelligence's beneficial potency, we claim our true identity. The one and only true identity of all, past, present, future or timeless, is pristine open intelligence, the pure benefit of all. Freed of the reference points of reification, including bondage to a self-identity, our boldness, immense energy and beneficial power are set free.

We instinctively recognize and realize the essence of spontaneous existence in every single moment. When compared to reified intelligence, a life as open intelligence is completely uplifting and exalting. We do not have to think about exalting ourselves; we experience everything as exalted through allowing all of our data streams to be as they are. We exalt each data stream and we thereby exalt ourselves. As we gain more confidence in open intelligence, we can look in the mirror and even see a change in the way we look. Our subtle physical appearance may change, and other people may notice this before we do. The change can also be quite dramatic. "Oh, what happened to you? You look so much different now."

It is a real hamster-wheel ride to try to keep an identity in place. The moment of birth as open intelligence comes in taking the first step: to rest body and mind naturally without seeking anything. Open intelligence's beneficial potencies are then what is obvious at all times without even thinking about it. It is a special dynamic energy or fluidity that one decisively experiences without it being an experience at all. At the same time, open intelligence is inclusive of all experience, so we are not trying to kick any experience to the side. The more we are living as open intelligence's beneficial potencies, the more obvious it is to us that the limited world we saw when we were reifying data is nothing other than the vast expanse of open intelligence.

Likely we can all remember when we learned to write as a child, and we practiced making little circles over and over again with our pencil in order to learn to form the letters. Just as we learned the alphabet through constant repetition, in the same way we have learned to reify data streams, and reification came to be a habit. We saw it performed, we heard about it, we read about it and it was repeated until the belief in reification, and in a personal identity, was firmly in place.

When we have the great fortune of being introduced to the reality of who we are, a similar process of repetition takes place, but instead of it being in terms of reification, it is in terms of open intelligence. We see this open-intelligence reality being lived by others, we hear about it, we read about it, we write about it and we live as it, and through repetition the familiarity with open intelligence grows.

As the familiarity with open intelligence grows, instead of living a life based on belief in data streams, we now live in a state of total release, total openness and complete relaxation, bringing about the full impact of beneficial potency in our life without any effort. Complete relaxation is not some sort of temporary state of the body, mind and heart. We are the stainless, flawless, exalted space that subsumes all. As the all-of-all, we encompass everything.

The only way to realize this is through complete relaxation, and not through trying to improve a reified existence or getting into some sort of contrived state. We relax repeatedly for short moments many times, immersing ourselves in this repetition that is so different from the repetition of reifying data streams. In doing so, the gift we give is not only to ourselves, but to all beings in all worlds.

We are introduced to a new world that is entirely distinct from the world that most of us were trained up in. This new world is one of good cheer. That is what everyone is: a space of exaltation and good cheer, a space wherein anything is possible. Most of us have had joyous states that would come and go, but we find that in the always-on beneficial potency of open intelligence, bliss does not come and go. What is more, it isn't at all like what we defined "bliss" to be prior to coming to know true bliss. Real bliss is already present, so this is what we want to pronounce and announce as "I"—the real bliss that brings a smile, whether the smile is evident on the face or not—within every time, place and circumstance.

As nothing can be found to exist independent of open intelligence's beneficial potency, open intelligence's beneficial potency is what is always already the case. It isn't something that we need to accomplish or achieve. It is always already present as "I." The clearest pronouncement of the speaker of "I" is "I am open intelligence's beneficial potency."

AN IDENTITY LIKE SPACE

Our reality is open-intelligence-pervading-everything. The costume of the body-mind-heart complex is relevant only in the moment of its noticing. We have the golden opportunity to outshine everything we ever thought the body-mind-heart complex is or isn't. Our identity need not be limited any longer. Like the sky, we are vast and all-expansive. Planet Earth could blow up, but space would remain unaffected. Our identity is like space; it isn't space and it isn't the sky, but it is more like those than the fixed, restricted and limited understanding of the body-mind-heart complex that is drilled into us from the moment of our birth.

Gone is the belief in the body-mind-heart complex, and obvious is the pure wisdom-body of inexhaustible extent, like the essence of pure space. The heart of love-bliss benefit is the real heart; it is the infinite heart, the inexhaustible heart, the heart that cannot be destroyed or affected by whims of fantasy.

No matter what kind of situation we are in, it is up to us to come from the perfect knowledge of pure benefit and not to resort to reified ideas. We no longer need be in a reified identity of an individual human being that is subject to life, birth and death, cause and effect, subject and object. We are not restricted or limited by that intellectual understanding; we truly live as the complete relaxation of open intelligence, never knowing what is going to be said or done, but knowing that everything is okay. Everything is *as it is*, and all is well, regardless.

145

If we have never been told about our real nature, how could we possibly know what it is? But once we are confirmed in it, that complete confirmation really gets in and the benefit of all is all we see. The beautiful word bodhicitta represents this incredible self-perfected quality of human beings: the passion to be of benefit to all. Again, this is not something to be cultivated, but is completely naturally present. It is already self-perfected, not needing to be worked on, always already present and one-hundred percent always-on and available. We just become more accustomed to the fact that this is the case for us.

OUR VAST BODY IS INEXHAUSTIBLE

We have learned that our body is just within a skin-suit, but our body is instead the vast expanse of open intelligence. It is this body of open intelligence that includes all knowledge ever known—all knowledge of the past, all knowledge of the present, all knowledge of the future and all knowledge that has nothing to do with time. Authentic knowledge is knowledge that is genuine and of undisputed origin. Whether the skin-suit of the body is around or not, authentic knowledge remains inexhaustibly present.

Open intelligence is primordially pure. This means that within open intelligence there are no data streams that are not primordially pure. Every data stream is primordially pure, no matter what it is. All ideas about purity and what it means are completely subsumed in pure open intelligence. Maybe we have learned all kinds of things about what is pure and what is impure, but open intelligence is encompassing and inclusive of the so-called "pure" and the "impure," and it resolves them in its great outshining. Instead of limiting knowledge to the dictionary definitions of reified intelligence, all of these ideas are expanded into comprehensive open intelligence.

This reality can also be partially demonstrated through contemporary science, which tells us that there is no way to get rid of anything. Even "destruction" is just a rearrangement of protons, electrons and neutrons. Every single instant the whole arrangement of what we are considered to be as a human identity is changing, and at some point, *boom*, the component parts totally release. When we live as the total release of open intelligence, there is nothing to be afraid of. We pronounce fearlessness as our true state of being, and this is what "I" is.

When we outshine pride and arrogance, we are comfortable with seeing ourselves as the vast "I" that is all-inclusive of our everyday "I." To know that these two are indivisible is true humility. This is the "I" that is the essence of all—the beneficial liveliness of vast mind, speech, body, qualities and activities. This "I" is always already present as the unfabricated freedom of spontaneous wisdom benefit. Hanging on to self-identity and constructing and performing the idea of an individual self is true lack of humility. True humility is complete relaxation into the vast "I" without knowing what is going to happen next.

Everything is the shining forth of the expansive "I," not the shining forth of an individual. Open intelligence, inclusive and all-encompassing of everything, is "I." That is the permanent body, and that permanent body is *our* body. No matter what we have learned, the wisdom body, the complete enjoyment body, is our real body. Our voice is the voice of all sound; every sound ever made past, present and future is our sound. All thoughts, emotions, sensations ever had by anyone anywhere past, present and future are encompassed by our wisdom-body shining forth as wisdom light.

We do not have to think our way into this in the same way that we thought our way into a reified existence. There is no thinking required; that is why the instruction is one of complete relaxation. That relaxation gives us a hint of who we are, and any destination disappears.

Always and forever the reality of what we are is open intelligence, subsuming all that comes and goes, meets and departs. There isn't a time of open intelligence coming and going; there isn't meeting with open intelligence then parting from it. We always live as open intelligence, whether we recognize that or not. We live as the profound meaning of unborn, radical reality. There is no need to any longer be wrapped up in ourselves.

When we recognize that our true nature is unborn space, we recognize that everything is unborn space, primordially pure and spontaneously beneficial. The primordially pure and spontaneously beneficial unborn space is not the space of dimensionality at all. It is the space of space, the pure essence of space itself. That is the essence of what we are. Everything we have learned or think we know about time, dimensionality, causality, subject and object is subsumed in the superior comprehensive knowing that is the root of all. This is what we are seeing through our eyes right now.

Our single identity is ever-expansive, totally potent and totally beneficial to all. The ever-essence is the nuance of everything; it is like the essence of the diamond's shine. This ever-essence is what fuels up the skin-costume, and to know this truth is the greatest gift we can ever give ourselves. Conversely, it is no gift to ourselves to hold on to ideas that are totally untrue.

OUR PRIMARY IDENTITY

Open intelligence does not avoid, replace or get rid of anything. Everything is allowed to be exactly *as it is,* the dynamic energy of open intelligence. Subsuming reified identity into open intelligence is the doorway to entering reality. By the power of open intelligence, less and less do we feel like we are compacted and limited by all these ideas that have been presented to us about what life is, ideas like being these little flesh units with our own little operating system called a brain. That idea is not true! Our primary identity is not the body-stuff, no matter the nonsense that has been pounded into us. We can now give up our right to be a victim of this persistent training in reification that has been presented to us.

We are taught that the body is our primary identity, but before the body is, while the body is and after the body is, open intelligence is. It is primary to the body; the body is secondary. We have learned that our mind is located in the body. When we identify with open intelligence as our primary identity, we outshine the body-mind identity, while including mind and body fully at the same time. This is truly an "open" intelligence; it isn't a closed intelligence inside a skin-suit. It is this open intelligence that is inseparable from our own intelligence.

Just very naturally, as a society we are becoming more and more open-intelligence oriented. We can see it in the ways we have extended what we thought was our closed intelligence trapped inside our body. For example, we have extended our intelligence into all kinds of devices, and we can extend our intelligence all around the world. That shows us that our mind couldn't possibly be locked inside a skin-suit, not when we can spread our mind all around the world and back in time many years and ahead many years.

We are intelligent agents of open intelligence, and as intelligent agents our agency is endlessly expansive and inexhaustible. It is very important not to think of open intelligence as a destination. What is inexhaustible cannot be a destination. There is no destination to get to, so that alone is a great relief.

Everything occurs within our very great body of open intelligence. Our identity is this very great body, and all communication is within that, even though it may seem like it is occurring between two or more people. As we naturally settle into open intelligence, we open up so immensely and vastly that we

149

have relationship of being that is beyond anything that could be understood in reification. Simply by opening up to the relationship beyond all contrived ideas, we have a relationship that is beyond common understanding.

We open up to actually being very present with everyone with whom we are in relationship. When we are introduced to our actual identity, we become immensely skillful in realizing the exact specific import of that. We are not some limited little notion of what identity is, but the vastness that includes all beings, which means we have access to any being. "Open intelligence shining forth many intelligent entities" is another way of thinking about being. Open intelligence shines forth intelligent entities of all kinds that are always inexhaustibly inseparable from open intelligence itself. That means that there is always access to and interoperability between all intelligent entities.

And, there is a spontaneous equalness of all humans that is found to be the case. At the same time there is no contrived moral command saying "everyone is equal" and then an attempt to pretend that this is so through setting up different structures and processes. It is our instinctive recognition that everything is equal that allows us to enter into that true relationship of equalness with everyone on the planet, and with any other beings or intelligences there may be.

QUESTION AND ANSWER

Q. I have had a deep sadness throughout my life, and I have identified myself with this so completely that I sometimes doubt whether I can even relate to the joy you are pointing to.

Ziji Rinpoche: We have been told who we are according to a common terminology of disempowerment and diminishment. No matter how we dress it up in that context, the internalized oppression is still there, and there is no strategy that we can contrive that will completely eliminate its arising. So, we need to finally say, "Okay, I'm just going to rest with all that, and I'm going to see who I really am."

The only place the real feel-good is available is in open intelligence, but not as some fancy wishful thinking. It isn't that at all; it is the opening, the direct realization and the illumination of all affliction as open intelligence, even if that isn't the place we had previously been looking for realization. First of all, there's the introduction to open intelligence, and upon that introduction we can see that through our openness, the resistance we might have felt before is transmuted. That is our first example of the immediate radical benefit of a new reality, and that same process of transmutation occurs again and again as we grow more confident in open intelligence.

Open intelligence is the most comprehensive order of merriment! It isn't a matter of sitting around with a stern, serious look trying to demonstrate open intelligence, or on the contrary, walking around with a smile plastered on our faces. Natural merriment and good cheer are spontaneously aroused when we live as open intelligence. Merriment, good cheer and spontaneous goodness are our natural state. There's an innate merriment that is enlivened, the merriment of the smallest subatomic particle. If all these subatomic particles are merry, then we are too!

No longer do we go through the process of cause-and-effect where we try to cause our happiness through contriving positive circumstances. With short moments of complete relaxation repeated again and again, it becomes obvious that our true identity is open intelligence. The grim despair of the ups-and-downs of moods is outshone. The Four Mainstays are the algorithm to guarantee living as open intelligence, and the Mainstays work together step-by-step. If the steps are followed, the result is obvious, and the steps lead to reality.

We find that biology and psychology are not the primary determinant of our identity; rather, open intelligence is the primary determinant. If we rely on all the reified concepts we have learned throughout life, we end up in a real mess, don't we? When we rely on open intelligence, we get just the opposite. Instead of diminishment, we feel better and better, because we are resting in who we really are. We may have taken a hundred self-esteem workshops in the past, but we find that by relying on our own intelligence, we really do loosen up and lighten up. We're not so stiff anymore; we can relax at last, and life becomes more and more effortless and filled with humor and cheer. It doesn't matter what's going on, and even amidst great sadness and grief, there is humor and cheer at the basis.

When we practice the fullness of intelligence with all of its magnificent beneficial powers and activities, life will be joy-filled regardless of circumstances. That is a real mindblower for most people: that life can be joy-filled regardless of circumstances. From the beginning of our life we have trained ourselves to think that life can only be happy if we have certain kinds of positive circumstances. To all of a sudden hear that we can be happy in life regardless of circumstances may be something new to our experience!

Through letting everything be *as it is*, what we find is that no matter what occurs, life *is* joy-filled, and it is increasingly joy-filled regardless of circumstances. We can go through all kinds of things that at one time would have caused us great trauma and upset, and we find that we are breezing along, resting as our inherent nature of joy.

It is a great relief to allow everything to be *as it is*. It is the greatest boon that could ever come along in life, the greatest gift we give to ourselves and the greatest gift we give to others. We get to cheer up at last. "Hurray, I'm finished with that whole burden!" It is so over! Over! Now, if you are one person saying that, then that is of course wonderful, but if there are *millions* of people

152

saying that and everyone is standing up at once, then there is great strength in those numbers.

OPEN INTELLIGENCE AS THE PRIMARY FOCUS OF LIFE AND DEATH

CHAPTER ELEVEN

Open intelligence's beneficial potencies are the greatest gift—the greatest life—any human being can ever have or give to themselves. It is no gift to ourselves to hold onto ideas that are false and harmful. As we give this greatest gift to ourselves, we give ourselves over to spontaneous altruism, and in that way to the world and all its inhabitants. It is a matter of how we want to live our lives.

All of what we need in order to take care of ourselves is already boundlessly present as open intelligence. We need only to become more familiar with it in order to access the enormous resources that are available to us at every moment. Open intelligence will never fail us. No matter what happens, no matter how old we get, how sick we get, how much happens in life, open intelligence never fails us. Even when we feel like it is failing us, it is not. It is open intelligence itself that is at the basis of any idea of it having failed us! There isn't any thought, feeling, sensation, idea or experience that isn't the shining forth of open intelligence.

Open intelligence's beneficial potency is an infinite wealth, and it is a kind of wealth that can never be taken away. It is a wealth that grows inexhaustibly with no fear of its loss. It cannot be lost and it cannot be found; it is simply spontaneously recognized. Short moments of open intelligence many times results in the obviousness of open intelligence as the fundamental basis of our own intelligence. In each short moment we are bringing the enrichment of all data streams into their full expression beyond reification. The act of generosity that we extend to ourselves in allowing all of our data streams to be as they are is the basis of all generosity.

No matter how young or how old we are, if we have been introduced to open intelligence, we have been introduced to a lifestyle that will allow us to no longer be subject to a life of trial and tribulation. We stop settling for the life of reification that has only brought us confusion and unhappiness. However, in terms of becoming familiar with open intelligence, it does not matter what we *could* do, it matters what we *actually* do. How magnificent can we allow ourselves to be?

No matter what we have learned beforehand, it is really important to prioritize relying on open intelligence as the primary focus of our life. We prioritize open intelligence in everyday life and in all we know and do. Without the most glorious of skillful means contained in instinctive open intelligence, life is confusion's path. With the introduction, prioritization and one hundred percent commitment to open intelligence, assurance grows and never stops growing. We cherish powerful open intelligence through the Four Mainstays, and the influence of open intelligence's beneficial potencies is extended to all. Authentic human nature is completely dignified through the Four Mainstays lifestyle.

There are some very extraordinary people who have gone through the very great hardship of fleeing one country for another under very dangerous circumstances, and over and over again they said that open intelligence saved the day for them. They were being shot at from the ground and the air as they fled and people were dying all along the way, and yet they knew that open intelligence was their support all the way through. This support was the only way they were able to make it to another country and to start a new life where they had nothing.

GRATITUDE

Open intelligence's beneficial potencies are the greatest gift, truly the greatest life, any human being can ever have or give to themselves. It is no gift to ourselves to hold onto ideas that are

155

false and harmful. As we give this greatest gift, we give ourselves over to spontaneous altruism, and in that way to the world and all its inhabitants. A heart that is always open can never be closed. It is the very greatest gift to allow our hearts to be completely open to everything and everyone.

It is a matter of how we want to live our lives. "How do I want to see myself; how do I want to see other people? When I really allow myself to feel what others are feeling, what is it I see? What's going on with other people and what is my relationship with them?" When we are fully clear about the answers to these questions, we can look one another right in the eye without hesitation, because we no longer have anything going on in our minds about them. There is a space of complete openness and love, a natural closeness that can never be infringed upon by anything.

There is a distinct way of being that can never be closed or altered in any way, and this is the basis of empowered relationship. We don't necessarily need to know anything specific about people: where they work, how much money they make, where they are from or what their background or opinions are. No matter what language someone speaks, even one that we do not know, we are comfortable with beings and connected with them. No one is a stranger.

There is nothing more precious in life than the recognition of open intelligence, and that recognition inspires a natural gratitude. When we put this gratitude into words, that is one way of expressing it, but basically the gratitude is inexpressible, as it is so strong, powerful and pure. We have gratitude for open intelligence and for all the Mainstays, and we come to know what true gratitude really means. Gratitude, respect and appreciation of an extraordinary dimension naturally arise. We have now been introduced to these things and to discernment, skillful means and insight, and we are open in gratitude and grounded in gratitude.

As beneficial potency becomes increasingly evident, it is discovered to be an inexhaustible treasure. Endless gratitude and appreciation abound for the ever-ready solutions which pop up everywhere. What a wonder it is to enjoy these riches and to recognize their availability to everyone! As we become engaged in this way of gratitude, we cannot help but influence the lives of others. People see what a human being truly is, and through that example they become attracted to what can also work for them as well.

OUTSHINING NEGATIVITY

One of the things nowadays that is right in everybody's face is the enormous negativity in the world. In the media of the world, and especially in social media, there is a constant barrage of negativity, and this negativity is one of the primary afflictive states for many people. The negativity is not only issuing forth from the media itself, but also from those themes being repeated incessantly by people who have heard or watched that sort of media.

To refuse to participate in that barrage of negativity is a very powerful subversive activity! From open intelligence, everything is seen *as it is*, and there isn't any need to change or modify things to make them appear better. If we no longer try to avoid or modify what is being presented to us, then the hatred, contempt, violence and excessive negativity in the world become even more noticeable, and we really get to see how contemptuous society can be and how hateful the ingrained bigotry can be. But this explosive negativity has a reason.

If we look really closely at human existence over the centuries, one sees that there has been such a tribal way of being which sees one's own group as right and all others as wrong. In addition, there has been the tendency to hold on to negativity to the point where it just inevitably explodes. When our attention is held by all the layers of inherited negativity, it is the power of that negativity that we display. However, if our attention is resting as the powers of great benefit, it is the powers of great benefit that we display.

By seeing how deeply entrenched these kinds of negativity can be and by deeply understanding how these negative data streams can take hold of people and sweep them away in a tsunami of negativity, there can then be a response of beneficial potency that soothes all of this. The beneficial responsiveness of open intelligence does not operate by ordinary laws and is not ever lessened by any shining forth of data. We can see how easy it is for extreme opinions and conflict to develop; yet, when these extremes develop, at exactly the same time, always present within those extremes is the beneficial potency of open intelligence.

So much anger, hatred, misogyny, homophobia and confusion are being drummed up through popular culture, politics and the media, but in actual fact it is great that all of these afflictions are coming forth! Why is it great? Because then people feel more comfortable with affliction, and some may be potentially ready to see affliction as a display of very profound and empowered benefit. We have held so many of our data streams within ourselves, feeling that they are taboo and that we cannot share them and that we are wrong or bad if we have these thoughts. However, now these hidden data streams are all out there for everyone to see and so incredibly evident in social media.

In a pervasive environment of negativity and bigotry, people are marginalized due to religion, race, gender, poverty, lack of education, sexual orientation and so many other factors. In that light, we have become so accustomed to putting others down and being put down ourselves, and we may come to believe all the subtle or not so subtle diminishments. We become our own oppressors by constantly criticizing and blaming ourselves, and one of the aspects of that may be in not allowing ourselves to do what is possible for us to do. If there is something really big that we might dream to do, we could also think of all the reasons why we will not be able to do it. "It would be embarrassing to fail; my family wouldn't like it and they'll say I'm crazy. Look how it never really works for anyone to risk it," on and on and on.

The reality is that it is now time for people to stand up and claim the open intelligence that is their birthright and to actively mobilize that intelligence at the grassroots. The grassroots mobilization of potent benefit will accomplish more for us and our aching world than any other thing that could be done. Just by resting as open intelligence, the change that takes place is so enormous. We begin to see our own value, and it is not a contrived value. When we begin to really value ourselves and we begin to identify value in others, we are able to open up into an entirely new world.

As there are more and more living examples of open intelligence within human society, more and more we can recognize that we are in an era of great benefit. Human society is undergoing a massive change, a paradigm shift in which we, the people of the world, are bringing forth the power of open intelligence to completely transform ourselves and society, and this is the era of great benefit. This era is truly emerging, an era in which humankind is coming together in realization of its own open intelligence as a force of unity, service, potency and peace. With greater certainty in open intelligence, the conviction in its innate power dawns brighter and brighter, and there is the increasing realization of the unavoidable basis that is our indestructible resource and support.

This isn't an era which brings about a number of superficial changes and then exhausts itself and ends. No, this is an inexhaustible era of great benefit, marked by a society committed to the recognition of and reliance on open intelligence to empower our innate potency. Those who are recognizing this and are gaining assurance in their true identity as open intelligence are the pioneers of this new era. Worldwide, people are living daily life in the greatly beneficial place of open intelligence.

Each moment that we rely on the immediate benefit of open intelligence, we create a profound building block for all of human society, a true opening that is so vast that everyone can participate. We simply know in the immediacy of complete perceptual openness in all experience that this alone is opening world peace and unity. It is opening up a perfect love that is totally beyond the comprehension of reified thinking.

Ultimately, we come to see that the excessive negativity is itself just another data stream that we have named and that it is inseparable from open intelligence. We can see all of what is happening in the world as "excessive negativity," or we can see everything as the comprehensive intelligence that all data streams are, including the data stream of excessive negativity. When there is a rush of negativity within us, there is no need to impatiently respond and react to what is going on. The power of these data streams eventually dissipates.

All the ideas we have about the atrocities and negativities that we see played out before us in everyday life and all of the excessive negativity that we are exposed to is outshone in spontaneous benefit. This negativity cannot be outshone until there is a significant force of spontaneous benefit present within the population. We can see that this is actually occurring already. We see that the excessive negativity we fostered within ourselves has markedly changed since we were introduced to open intelligence. We can see that if it is possible for us as individuals and for others in the Four Mainstays community, then we know that it can begin to sweep all populations everywhere.

To speak openly about death has sometimes been a sort of taboo in Western culture, but it is very important to bring it out into the open. The death of the body will come, and it can come at any moment. When we are in the process of dying, there are all kinds of options at that time, so it is really important to think about those different options beforehand, and it is wise to have one's affairs in order. If these things are not thought about in advance, during the course of dying there will be a sort of anxious under-mutter that goes on because these things have been left unattended. Hence, we should have a will or a trust and specific directions written up and have everything taken care of so that we do not leave a big mess of complexity for our loved ones. We want to have it all spelled out clearly and specifically.

These practical and potent skillful means are available in all situations of life and death, skillful means which do not rely on reified data streams. Through the use of these skillful means we are brought into the realization of the type of conduct which will be of the most potent benefit in relation to each and every being, place and thing throughout the entirety of all worlds. Skillful means range from a peaceful to a wrathful expression, depending on what is required to benefit all. The best response is not in either extreme; we respond in terms of whatever is required by the time, place and circumstance. In this way, we can live our life in a skilled way.

We make a choice about how we move through our life and then into our death. Something that is guaranteed for everyone from the moment of birth is degeneration and death. People are usually aware of old age and death, but many may not be so clear about the lengthy process of degeneration, if one's life is not ended prematurely by accident or disease. By practicing these trainings when we are young, we will have a life of total release during the process of old age, extended degeneration and death. With the life expectancy most of us can plan for, even in acknowledging that there can never be any guarantees as to how the degeneration will unfold, through relying on the Mainstays there can be greater and greater ease with the natural degeneration of the body and its eventual death.

Along with the concepts of birth and death, we have all kinds of reified ideas, such as time, space, causality, subjectivity, objectivity, but this human world is just one minuscule world among countless worlds. It could be that these other worlds have no idea of time, causality, subjectivity, objectivity, birth and death, and yet all worlds, no matter where they are or what they are, are entirely illuminated with open intelligence.

An interesting insight in terms of the degeneration of the body is that when looking in the mirror and seeing the results of bodily decay, what's looking never changes! Throughout the course of first being an infant, on through life, and on to becoming old and weathered, what's looking is always the same—never-changing open intelligence, always alive, vital, blissful and content. We have been living with the emphasis on the body that is born, lives and then dies, but the "what's looking" aspect is generally ignored. However, the more we allow ourselves to be as we are, the more we understand the implications of "what's looking."

That the physical body does not govern us is a huge realization, and as open intelligence we realize what the word "body" really means. Our body is so much greater than the flesh, blood, bone and organ-based things within a skin-suit. Our true body is vast and all-inclusive intelligence and is decisively realized in complete relaxation. Through this deepening it becomes easier to see what is really happening while dying. Whatever goes on with the data streams after the death of the body is just more opportunity for the enrichment and empowerment of open intelligence.

The body may die, but we carry on as open intelligence. When the body is shut down completely and the mind and speech are gone completely, primordial benefit is totally at ease. Nothing changes the stainless space of who we are. The more practical experience we have in living as open intelligence, the more unlimited are our possibilities during and after so-called death. What is needed is to deepen the vastness of open intelligence as the lived reality, rather than relating to the body as the primary identity.

Open intelligence itself is a great support in the process of degeneration and death, and in a Four Mainstays lifestyle community we take great responsibility for ourselves and for the benefit of all. We are aware and alert to other people as their bodies are degenerating, and we have a genuine sensitivity to that and can step forward and offer assistance when needed. If we have had a life in which our data streams have been running wild, it may be that our focus has been completely on ourselves and we cannot see anything else. So, this sensitivity to others is a very different vantage.

THE ART OF DYING

All the concepts that we have learned, such as birth, life and death, waking, sleeping and dreaming, are data streams. Birth is a data stream, just as life and death are data streams. Death isn't the end of data or the end of open intelligence. The process of dying is a very powerful data stream that gives us yet another choice among many powerful choices to acknowledge open intelligence. To make this choice not only ensures us a wonderful life but a wonderful death as well.

The Dzogchen Teachings were initially meant to prepare one for death, but what the Teachings really do is *prepare us for the death of our descriptions about ourself*! Through training in Dzogchen, we recognize that death can come at any moment, and the

163

recognition of the inevitability of death is a tremendous motivating factor for the practice of Dzogchen. We hope that somehow we won't die, but we fear the fact that we will. This is a common predicament for human beings. We know that everything is impermanent and that death is coming for all of us. Since the beginning of life, death has been occurring. The cells in our bodies are constantly dying and being replaced. By recognizing intelligence now in the midst of life, open intelligence at death becomes a great relief and a source of comfort and support.

When we die, the last thing we know is that we're still intelligent. Intelligence is present as each of the bodily functions and senses fall away. Our whole story about ourselves is resolved—our idea about our agency, who we are, what we're here to do, *poof*, gone! As we are dying, each of our functions leaves us. Sight, then smell, taste and touch, and then hearing is last to go. But we're there—no thinking, nothing—only intelligence. This is what is.

At the point of death, dying people may want to speak or they may attempt to do things with the body. They may think that they are speaking, when in fact no one is hearing what they are trying to say. The brain stays active in its own way during the process of dying, so there might be all kinds of things that are projected.

One could say that the process of dying is like going to some sort of phantasmagorical theme park; all of a sudden the ordinary pictures change dramatically. However, due to the powerful presence of open intelligence, all of these images of the phantasmagorical theme park are known to be just more flickering of the instantaneous colors of open intelligence. It is recognized that all the fantastic images reside in complete purity—subsuming all color and colorlessness, which simply means "beyond the ability to describe." From open intelligence we have the perspective to see things as they really are, rather than through the eyes of conventional ideas of life and death. In the reality of who we are, we can face anything that comes up in a completely relaxed way.

One of the best ways to help a person who is being seized by the death call is to read them a text from the training or some other equally beautiful text. This will bring comfort to everyone involved. In the moment of death, the instinctive recognition of the vastness of open intelligence is very, very important, because as a result of the practice, the dying person can be rooted in open intelligence when death comes. This is why the trainings are given: to prepare for death and to be very much at home as open intelligence at that time.

QUESTION AND ANSWER

Q. I am not so familiar with this term "skillful means," and I would like to hear more about what that actually implies, and especially as it relates to practical everyday experience.

Ziji Rinpoche: Skillful means aren't something like a rulebook or something you do in a particular situation each and every time. The Four Mainstays provide us the ability to respond skillfully, and the skillful means are completely spontaneous and absolutely spot-on to the time, place, circumstance and result. Skillful means are perfectly suited to the spontaneously self-releasing here-and-now.

Anything could happen in life, and does, because circumstances are ceaseless, endless and unpredictable. What we then do in those unpredictable circumstances is where discerning skillful means come in. Each situation is different, and with everything that is going on, open intelligence is always the doer and the done. By allowing ourselves the great fortune of recognizing that, there is nothing to worry about.

Skillful means are effortless, because they are based in reality. When skillful means are blazing, you simply do what you do, just

165

like the sky does. Whatever it is that comes out of your mouth or a gesture you might make or whatever it is that happens in relation to time, place and circumstance is completely natural and is for the benefit of all. In this case, the urge that arises to do something and then actually taking action can go hand in hand. Just sitting around and thinking about a helpful action or talking to your friends or writing about it online is one thing, but actually taking responsibility and taking action is something entirely different. Solution-orientation is what it is all about, not problem-orientation.

I would like to describe the benefit of skillful means in the context of a situation in business that I was involved in some time ago. There was a legal disagreement that had been going on for years, and at some point the case finally came into mediation. There were maybe fifteen people involved in the case, and fourteen of the people were blaming one person for what had taken place.

There were two judges who were present to help make a decision, and they asked each of the fifteen people what their opinion of the situation was. When each person spoke, they blamed this one man. When all had spoken and it was my turn to speak, I said, "Well, everyone in this room knew this man, and we were all participating, so we need to acknowledge to what degree we were responsible for the outcome and not just blame this one person." I really hadn't thought about what I would say when it came my turn, but I was committed to listening to each and every individual and what they had to say, and when it came to be my turn, that is what I said.

In my response there was no need to implicate or blame someone, and at the same time there was the ability to have a voice that did not have to go along with what everyone else was saying. It is very important to know the level of communication and the impact that is taking place, even if we might not even be saying anything at all. The truth is always very striking to people, and they can often see reality clearly when it is spoken. It touches them deeply and they want more of it. Shooting straight always wins!

That comment about acknowledging our own participation in the difficult situation completely changed the whole tone of the discussion, and rather than drowning in blame and victimization, beneficial potencies took control. The judges decided to do just what was suggested: to see what each person's part in the disagreement was and then to decide for themselves what should be done. Even though I was the last one to speak and the only woman there, none of these conventional things mattered in that moment. What really mattered was the beneficial potency of open intelligence as it applied to that situation.

All the harmful reified data, not only what was harmful to the person who was labeled as the bad guy, but harmful to each person who was blaming that man and to the whole group altogether, was forced open and rendered into the benefit of all. Simply the act of speaking up from what we know is true renders a situation into one of benefit.

When there are strong self-righteous mental and emotional data streams, what is required is a transmuting of the situation into its original power. This is just what happened in the situation I described. There were strong, self-righteous mental and emotional data streams in talking about this man, making him wrong and bad, even making him evil. All of this was happening because no one wanted to look at themselves and their own data streams. What is required is complete assurance of our beneficial potency, not in an intellectual way or emotional way, but in actuality. Skillful means are then the response that comes from complete assurance in our beneficial potency.

Very deep caring is something we are each born with; this is not something that is an add-on or a fringe asset. It is our birthright, and if we do not recognize it as such, that means that we have just been brainwashed into thinking something else. But the truth is that we are really creatures of tremendous benefit.

And because death and dying were discussed earlier, I wanted to look into that important topic as well. It might be helpful to relate my experience of benefit during the death processes of two members of my family—my sister and my mother. When my sister died, she was at home in her big brass bed exactly where she wanted to be, and I was lying close to her and holding her. I had my hand on her pulse and I could notice her breath stop and her heart stop beating. It was a profoundly sad moment, and it was also a moment of astounding and blessed openness in which my sister was more real than she had ever been. I realized that our relationship was forever. She was only ten months younger than I, so we were quite a pair, and we still are. The interoperability and interactivity that I had so enjoyed with her, we still enjoy.

And then with my mother, some years ago I decided to harmonize and empower my relationship with her more than I had previously, so I became very actively involved in my mother's life. Instead of wanting something from her, I wanted to see what I could do for her. One day I phoned my mother and I thanked her for being such an incredible mother. I talked about all of the wonderful attributes that she had shared with me and that through her lifestyle of devotional commitment to her family and to the world I was naturally led to follow her example.

For the last twenty years of her life my mother and I had a relationship based on open intelligence, and this was a very beautiful experience. When my mother died a few years ago, I was with her during the dying process. Her death was one of total dignity and beauty. She said one day, "I am going to die tomorrow, and I am going to go to heaven," and so with great beauty she died. In a very simple and direct way, she went from life, through the death point of view to illumination in the open intelligence body.

SPONTANEOUS KNOWLEDGE AND WISDOM

CHAPTER TWELVE

Real knowledge results in benefit and comes into view spontaneously without any need to study or accumulate it. From real knowledge we can see the reality of everything as it is. It does not have to be a matter of a complex amassing of facts; we see everything simply.

Reification is a form of knowledge, and wisdom is also a form of knowledge, but the knowledge that arises from wisdom is vastly different from the mere gathering of facts that is reified knowledge. Intellectual understanding is one form of reified knowing in which knowledge is seen to be an accumulation of information and data. In this context, the more knowledge we have gained, the more of an understanding we will have. We are trained from birth that intellectual understanding is ultimate, and as a result, other aspects of our being are ignored in favor of intellectual understanding. We generally continue on trying to figure everything out intellectually.

Intellectual understanding is like a hamster wheel; it goes around and around, but it never reaches the point of ultimate satisfaction or fruition. When the intellect is considered paramount, we ignore the great reality that is so simple and already present and which is not encompassed by mere intellectual knowledge. It is so much easier to live as this reality than it is to try to constantly figure out everything intellectually, especially because ultimately there is no such thing as the intellect! So, that will be the first statement: ultimately there is no such thing as the intellect; the intellect is a reified construct.

Wisdom is talked about in many circles, but there is very little understanding or comprehension of what wisdom actually is. Upon introduction to open intelligence, wisdom is recognized and acknowledged, and then from that recognition and acknowledgment there is the natural spontaneous increase of life-satisfaction, flourishing, relaxation and easefulness.

In this day and age there is only limited recognition of the distinction between spontaneous wisdom and contrived wisdom; therefore, it is really important to completely clarify the crucial distinction. Uncontrived wisdom has the pure perfect presence of benefit alone. This is much different from the "wisdom" that is a total philosophical abstraction. Now we are clarifying the distinction between contrived wisdom and uncontrived wisdom, and we are making that distinction by coupling the word "wisdom" with "benefit" and "beneficial potency" to help completely clarify exactly what wisdom is. These words are alive and illuminated and are not an abstraction.

Wisdom is the demonstration of the spontaneous beneficial potency of mind, speech, body, qualities and activities. It is not the avoidance of experience or the replacing of negative experience with positive states. We should be very clear about that. Even though very popular and well-known people may talk about wisdom as a matter of replacing negative states with positive states, they do this only because they do not have a clear idea of what wisdom really is. It isn't that they are purposefully trying to fool anyone; it is just that they are seeing things only from that limited vantage.

Ignorance of what wisdom actually is is epidemic throughout human civilization. What is very important when talking about wisdom or beneficial potency is to be able to see that it is the natural state of everyone. *Everyone and everything* is pure wisdom energy. To cultivate positive states to the exclusion of negative states cannot be equated with wisdom. Know this as fact: positive, neutral and negative states are all equal in wisdom, and everything is the all-pervasive equalness and evenness of wisdom-energy.

We have borrowed descriptions of knowledge and of ourselves from other people, either through the things we are taught or things we read, heard or collectively observed. We do this because we want to belong to the human community, and so it is natural for us to conform and to want to be like others and to share their perspective. However, if we do so in such a way that it twists our entire life into one of confusion and turmoil, then we know that something is not right. The way we have been trying to do things all along has led us to the situation we are in now, a crucial point of either our survival or our extinction.

Sometimes in the past, and even in the present day, there have been things that have kept us from learning from other cultures. Sometimes cultures other than our own have been discounted and marginalized because they follow a different religion or their skin is a different color. It is really important for us as a vast human society to come together and to discover this knowledge that exists within the whole of human society and to completely honor the individuals who are knowledge holders of open intelligence's beneficial potency. We also need to honor that capacity within ourselves, because we too are the precious living embodiment of the knowledge of the universe in a usable way.

INSTINCTIVE KNOWING, INSTINCTIVE RECOGNITION

What is needed is true knowledge of the nature of mind. Instinctive knowing and instinctive recognition of the nature of mind is the beginning, middle and end of knowledge creation. We can write countless books and hold the highest professorship and still not have true knowledge of the nature of mind. We can build a linear particle accelerator that costs billions of dollars and which finally identifies the particles we have been looking for, and still we have found nothing. If, however, we took a little closer look at "nothing" as "no thing," that would be a completely different insight into things!

171

Many times when scientists are talking about reality, they have not applied their science to their own makeup. However, they must change their outdated view of subjects and objects existing in a world and deeply ponder the great gift of "no thing"—that is, no-thing-material—which is what open intelligence is. An intelligence that is no thing is our essential nature, our reality. The real examination of nothing/no thing can begin only with the proper education in mind.

All of us have known people who have had intellectual understanding but who do not have true knowledge, and we have ourselves been included in the group of "people who have had intellectual understanding but who do not have true knowledge"! What is more, the intellectual knowledge we acquired did not lead to life-satisfaction and flourishing. A mind based on speculative thought alone can be one of weariness and pain. Through the pristine, all-beneficial vision of reality, the fogginess of the intellectual view is outshone, and just so, the intensity of wisdom-vision potently increases.

Real knowledge results in benefit and comes into view spontaneously without any need to study or accumulate or create wisdom. From real knowledge we can see the reality of everything *as it is*. It does not have to be a matter of a complex amassing of facts; we see everything simply. Through the pristine, all-beneficial, pure transmission of reality, the intellectual view is outshone and the intensity of wisdom-conduct potently increases. We no longer rely on the reified outlook; we see what our own perfect knowledge will show us in each situation. We continue, no matter what the situation is, to live as the comfort of the great reality of what we are—pure and extensive, like the essence of the diamond's shine.

From the perspective of open intelligence's beneficial potencies, we can draw the distinction between ordinary knowledge that is based on contrivance, as opposed to spontaneous knowledge, wisdom and benefit. As we gain more assurance in open intelligence, we can know whether the knowledge is coming from the perspective of ordinary knowledge or from open intelligence. As our decisive experience of open intelligence increases, this will be clearer and clearer to us.

Through short moments many times and a one hundred percent commitment to the Four Mainstays lifestyle, we come to see how knowledge can be accessed without any learning at all. "Without any learning at all" or "non-learning" sounds completely illogical and unreasonable, and one might think, "How could that ever happen?" Non-learning comes spontaneously from open intelligence. This is absolutely key and is worth repeating again and again: non-learning comes spontaneously from open intelligence. Conventional learning is a form of reification, whereas the non-learning of open intelligence's beneficial potency is perfectly free in its own place. Because open intelligence and its beneficial potencies already are self-evident in all circumstances, they are unmistakably so.

In knowledge beyond learning there are profoundly skillful means that always strike the mark in an unforgettable way. We simply live as we are—power–born! Power-born is how we are born, and this is how we are at all times. In recognizing this, we are neither afraid nor hopeful. We are not hoping for some blissful state to occur, and we do not fear that it will not, because our naturally powerful state is obvious to us as a fact just through being completely natural. Power-born!

Non-learning is for those predisposed to be very open. What does it mean to be "predisposed"? In this case it simply means being open enough to actually show up for a relationship with open intelligence for short moments many times, and "showing up" means being willing to be available with open mind, open speech, open qualities and activities. Even if the willingness is not yet there, one can at least be willing to be willing!

Perfect knowledge includes and encompasses *both* non-learning and learning. A love of knowledge, a passion for reading, a willingness to acquire skills and to become proficient in a field of study or education, none of that is excluded. All of this can go on as before, along with the willingness to be open to a realm of undiscovered knowledge that is not found in study alone. "Perfect knowledge beyond learning" is not a contrived perfection; it is not an attempt to make ourselves perfect through fabricated means. Perfect knowledge is always on, always pure and always full of comprehensive knowledge with no need to learn anything. Perfect knowledge is always appropriate to time, place and circumstance and has the result of benefit.

WISDOM-CONDUCT

When we are first introduced to open intelligence, we instinctively begin to recognize the profound meaning of everything *as it is*. We experience the great relief of total release. It may come upon us quickly or it may come upon us slowly, but we decisively experience relief and release from reified definitions, and in whatever situation in life we find ourselves, we will be able to respond in terms of what could be called wisdom-conduct.

If we are only employing our intellectual understanding in making decisions, we may often have to ponder things for a very long time before we are able to reach a decision. In wisdom-conduct it isn't that way. There is a trust in the availability of skillful means, and decision-making no longer involves lots of head-scratching and pros-and-cons lists! At the same time, the more we trust wisdom-conduct and skillful means, the wilder they may be! That is why wisdom-conduct is sometimes called "crazy wisdom," because it seems crazy to the reified world of intellectual understanding. It may even seem wild and crazy to us when we display it ourselves!

Yes, I've found I make decisions more readily in recent years.

174

Wisdom-conduct is open to everyone; it does not have the confinement of intellectual understanding where the only thing that matters is what is found in a book written by a person who has a certain authority. In wisdom-conduct, everything is open, and an answer can come from anyone, from anywhere and at any time. Wisdom-conduct, pure transmission and beneficial potency allow us to be free of needing to know what to do in any time, place and circumstance, because we know that we are capable of expressing wisdom-conduct wherever we are and in whatever we do. We do not need to have a lot of rules and regulations about how we will function. This is an incredibly great freedom, because it allows us to go anywhere and be with anyone or anything easefully.

Yes, I've been experiencing this. I've not heard it put into words till now.

We have now the possibility of a whole other order of life, and that life begins with our commitment to wisdom-conduct. Wisdom-conduct is not a goal; it is always on, already present. From the first moment of introduction to open intelligence, that introduction is wisdom-conduct. The feeling of comfort and ease that no one can deny is wisdom-conduct. It is not an extraordinary thing; it is the most ordinary of what a human being is, because it is reality. It isn't make-believe or hallucinatory.

For sure, all kinds of things are going to come up in life, and some of them will be expected, but many will be totally unexpected. However, basking in wisdom-conduct we know that we are prepared for whatever will come. The more wisdom-conduct is instinctively present for us, the easier it is for our skillful means to be immediate and of permanent effect. The more settled we are in wisdom-conduct, the less likely we are to act from extreme data.

It gets to the point where everything is outshone, and there are no extremes anywhere. They just are not present in our thinking, our emotions or in any way at all in our life. We see everyone as they actually are, and that is the best way to live, because then it is impossible to go to any extreme in relation to anyone.

There could be constant speculation about the body, mind and heart and how to do something to arrive somewhere and to attain some final feeling of perfection; however, that never actually happens! Any time we think, "Oh I've got it now! I'm just so happy, I'm never going to be unhappy again," *boom*, something unexpected can happen. In knowing this, we see that happiness of this kind isn't anything to rely on, and neither are all the fragile speculative thoughts, feelings, and bodily states.

So many of us have found ourselves involved in the thinking, speaking or doing based on cause and effect, subject and object: "I'm going to do this and then that will happen; I will get this thing or person and then I will be happy." If we really allow everything to shine forth *as it is*, we can see that we are beyond cause and effect, subject and object, and as a result we are no longer grasping at fleeting feelings of happiness. The grand space of open intelligence entirely subsumes cause and effect, subject and object, as well as all other ideas.

Limiting ourselves to reification is a form of suffocation. But in the comfort of the great expanse of all beings and all worlds, we are always open and free, safe and protected. We are the shining forth of the pure open-intelligence expanse, and this expanse is beyond all extremes. It includes time and it includes timelessness, cause and no-cause.

There is no place to set a solid position; there is only the spontaneous self-release of the here-and-now. The vast open-intelligence expanse subsumes all extreme ideas, including the ideas of time and timelessness. It is all-inclusive, all-encompassing and all-pervasive of time and timelessness. Just to make it perfectly clear, the here-and-now isn't really divided into parts called "moments," even if conventionally we may use that language. Everything pools in equalness.

If we look for what it is that knows, can we locate it anywhere? Is it in the brain? Is it in the heart? Where is that knowing? All these are data streams that are subsumed in the all-creating essence. Pervading all ideas about who we are—or about "what knows" or "what looks" or "what sees" or "what senses" or "what emotes"—is open intelligence. No data streams or descriptions have power, force or origin of their own or ability to cause or affect anyone or anything.

The comprehensive knowledge of open intelligence subsumes everything in a knowing that is a category beyond all ordinary ways of looking at things. This is a kind of knowledge that is very rare. The all-comprehensive, all-superior knowledge of open intelligence has not been demonstrated in the mainstream of human society till now in a widespread way, and yet here we are now with the skillful means and methods to demonstrate beneficial potency for everyone throughout the world.

In each moment, there can be reification, *or*, there can be the realization of open intelligence's beneficial energy. Open intelligence's beneficial energy is inseparable from reification; however, if we stay only with reification, it is just like being unaware of an oncoming tsunami.

In any moment we face all kinds of descriptions that could apply, but we can keep it simple by resting as our own immediate great benefit. Every short moment is an opportunity for suffering, or, for comprehensive knowledge—of just resting as love, bliss and benefit. We do not think of any of these terms in the moment when we are instinctively recognizing, experiencing and living as love, bliss and benefit. We just trust more and more and feel very blessed.

That which binds those in unawareness, liberates those with comprehensive knowledge. This is a totally profound statement and is the root of all knowledge. Let me repeat: that which binds those in unawareness, liberates those with comprehensive knowledge

KNOWING ONLY A LITTLE

One needs to be willing to know only a little. In each moment we know only a little, and this is very exciting, because we do not have to be a know-it-all any longer! We do not have anything to prove. By acknowledging, "I know only a little in the vast expanse of inexhaustible open intelligence," then everything is an expression of enhanced knowledge creation. It is really wonderful and very special when we honor and acknowledge this capacity within ourselves and admit very candidly that we could possibly only know a little, and that at the same time all knowledge is available to us in open intelligence. Yes, it seems like a contradiction! It is a joyful disposition of openness and of having the means to know what to do and how to act in each circumstance, while at the same time being willing to know only a little in the moment.

The reality is that knowing everything and knowing only a little are inseparable. Skillfully accessing what we need to know in each moment occurs in the context of recognizing that we only know a little. That is the golden key to knowing what we need to know in inexhaustible knowledge. If we are interested in an area of knowledge and we enter into that from the vantage that we already contain the knowledge of the universe in a usable way— and at the same time that we will always know only a little—that area of knowledge opens up in a way that would not have been possible otherwise.

When we are infants and we begin to notice the world around us, we see new things, we notice gestures from people around us and we hear things, but in the beginning we do not identify them in any way with ourselves or with anyone else. The infant is like a sponge taking in every bit of data that she or he is exposed to.

The child eventually begins to be trained to take the data streams and to build them into names and labels and identify them with subjects and objects living in a world. As an adolescent and then later as an adult we continue on creating more reified structures and thinking that we "know," but this isn't really getting us anywhere.

I can think back to when I was a child and learning all the things that I learned; however, when faced with all the different knowledge that I was supposed to learn, I was always very skeptical, because I never really felt it was getting at what I actually wanted to know. Even though I might have been learning a lot, I felt that this type of learning was not really getting to the real point. There was something else that was at the basis that was so fundamental and foundational that was not being provided by the level of knowledge I was being given.

There were the teachers in school and later on the professors at university, and they were claiming to know, but secretly I thought, "Well, how much do they really know?" Many of the things that we learn in school do not give us fundamental and foundational support. It is up to us in this respect to enter into complete self-governance, you could say, and to develop a healthy skepticism about all of what we have been taught along the way. This is a work in progress for all of human society.

There are very few people who question what happens in life or what they are taught in school. They believe they are learning correct logic and reasoning, and they just take what they have been taught to be true. We do not know where all these ideas, assumptions and beliefs have come from that we are being told, but, at best, they are only secondhand knowledge. Everyone just assumes that this logic and reason is correct, when all along it has not been correct, but we just accepted these things. Now, instead, we need to come to terms with true reality, rather than responding from inherited conceptual frameworks, belief systems and assumptions.

"Intelligence" as we have known it will eventually be surpassed, and our entire conceptual framework of what intelligence is will soon change. What is more, factors such as high IQ, many years of formal education, high status jobs and higher incomes will no longer be the best predictors of life satisfaction and flourishing. It will be fully understood that humans have inexhaustible intelligence, regardless of the countless belief systems and assumptions of the past that say we do not.

Lack of education in the nature of intelligence will come to a stop, and we will come to experience the highest level of intelligence on this planet. We will discover a comprehensive intelligence that had been overlooked in earlier periods of human history. The empowerment of this historical era is one in which there will be a marked expansion of spontaneous comprehensive intelligence, altruism and unselfish concern. Inherent strengths, gifts and talents directed to the benefit of all are able to provide skillful qualities and activities required for this particular time, place, circumstance.

Question and Answer

Q. I really resonate with what you are saying about the limitations of intellectual knowledge alone and also the wish to be of benefit. How would that sort of thing look in a practical way?

Ziji Rinpoche: When I was a child, I was fortunate enough to be born with a very deep sense of connection and love for other people and the ability to see a beneficial potency that was completely lively and thriving within everyone, no matter what a person did to make it seem that that wasn't so. Regardless of who they were or what they did, I could see that this beneficial potency was inherent, that it was always already the case, and that there was nothing whatsoever that could take it away. I saw a beauty singing in every single individual, whether they could see it in themselves or not, and I could see what they were capable of.

Even as a little girl I really felt that someday I would explore that deeply, but I had no idea exactly how or when. It was already present in my mind, and after a while, more and more this passion grew in me, and I knew that this was what I wanted to do. I would have all kinds of things going on in my life—different jobs, marriage, children—but always this passion was alive in me. With everything that happened in my life, I knew that somehow it was happening in order to contribute to the unfolding of things that would take place at some point.

I wanted to find out what people thought about their own intelligence and how they wanted to use their intelligence to live their lives. I felt all along that the purpose of my life was to provide immediate benefit to everyone on earth. I had considered an academic program and getting a PhD, but one morning when I was on a walk it suddenly hit me: I'm not going to do that. I'm going to create my own program, and it's going to have a lot of people from all over the world involved in it. I saw that what I wanted to do could never be done in a university, organizational or corporate setting.

I felt that my greatest desire in life was to be of benefit to all, and that was very, very clear to me. I felt that it was my responsibility to take it on and to do whatever I could to make that happen. Because I knew that this urge to benefit was inherent in me, I knew it must be inherent in everyone. So, I wanted everyone to know that as well, because I could really feel the joyous relief it gave to me. It gave me a sense of what being truly human is, and so I knew that it would give the same relief to other people as well.

I wanted to see something come together throughout the world where all people would be able to recognize their beneficial potency. I could see the beneficial potency in myself, and I could see the beneficial potency in everyone else; yet, I could see that many people did not recognize their beneficial potency, and I wanted everyone to be introduced to that.

I had heard about people in India who were enlightened, and I thought, "Oh wow, I'm going to go over there and meet these enlightened people." Yet, I found out the people there weren't essentially different from the people anywhere else. This was great motivation for the beginning of my teaching in a more public way; I wanted all beings to realize that everyone is enlightened, everything is enlightened and everything whatsoever is bursting with the open heart of pure love. It is not a matter of having any special feeling or mindset or gaining any greater intellectual knowledge; it is a matter of truly realizing what is.

If I look back just for a moment at any expectations I had or outcomes I wanted for whatever philosophy, psychology, spirituality, religion or academic study that I was involved in, and then I look at the way things are now for me, I never could have dreamt these things possible. I can say that I live like the forever youthful sun, and I can say it without cringing in embarrassment! There is so much motivation and aspiration inspired in me to benefit myself, to benefit others and to be of great benefit to all. This is what the forever youthful sun is a metaphor for: the youthful vitality and vigor that goes along with open intelligence, no matter how old and decrepit our bodies might be.

Question #2. Along these lines of benefitting all, I wanted to follow up with another question about the environmental crisis we are facing in the world today. Is there anything in your teaching that can help guide a response to the environmental degradation we see and what a skilled and beneficial response to this disaster might be?

Ziji Rinpoche: How could we have gone on this way for so long and continued on destroying our environment? The first step out of denial is to say, "We are responsible for the condition we're in and for the way the world's environment is." With what has happened to the environment, nobody else did it; *we* did it!

And yet, if we know that we are creatures who hold the knowledge of the universe in a usable way, how could we see ourselves as anything other than totally awesome and exalted beings! We *are* awesome and exalted! We can do things far beyond anything we were trained to do, and we are capable of finding solutions for the problems we have created.

To see open intelligence shining forth as all the circumstances of life is very compelling, because to see things in this way is to see them as they are and to see reality *as it is*. I want to know what will be of immediate benefit; that is the project of my life: to know what will be of immediate and long-term benefit to all. There is no way anything is going to take me away from that purpose.

If we are only utilizing reified data, it's impossible to see what is before us, because we can't really see reality. Only from open intelligence do we see reality. Many of us have done all kinds of personal work where we have looked at our data, *but we have never looked at data as being reified!* We've looked at psychological and psychiatric problems such as, "Mom did this and Dad did that," and this sort of thing. With the limited approach that comes from believing in all data, not only do we make ourselves miserable, but living at that level of knowledge can make the places we live and the overall environment totally miserable.

In certain circles one will hear responses to the question you asked such as, "Well, everything is just a great illusion, and so you don't need to do anything at all," but that is an absurd level of abstraction which could be used as a launching pad for endless levels of further abstraction. Nowhere in a statement like "everything is a grand illusion" is there clarification that can show you exactly what reality is and how to live as that reality.

The polar ice caps are melting away and the beautiful oceans dying, and that is really, really sickening. What we need to do to live in this world is to examine ourselves and to see how powerful we are. It is time for people to stand up, to come out of denial and say, "This is not just about the problems; we're focused on the real solutions to these issues and we have the capacity to implement these solutions."

When we consider data from the vast scope of open intelligence and we delineate it clearly and speak it clearly from the vantage of open intelligence, we see things much differently. No matter how we have described data in the past, we can come to see that all of the data of our life have always been open intelligence and that they never will be anything other than open intelligence. This is an enormous breakthrough. It may take a while to adjust to this way of thinking, or it may not; who knows? It's just a great and enormous relief. All future discovery lies within this area of relying on open intelligence, and all discovery will come from this way of being.

It's very important to begin training up open intelligence as early as we can. To train up open intelligence and to know what reality is from the beginning of life is a real boon, even if no one else we know is interested in this. Even though we may be experiencing pushback and resistance to just about everything we say and do; nevertheless, we are committed to knowing what reality is, and nothing is going to take us away from that.

What is helping to break up the whole unreality-parade is global communication, which is people from one culture speaking directly with people from other cultures. It isn't any longer something like, "Well, in OUR country and culture, blah, blah, blah." Instead, now people are saying, "We are fundamentally the same; we share so very many things—including the world's environment—and we must be alike in a lot of other ways. Together we must face these fundamental world problems." We can see our similarities rather than our dissimilarities, and we want to stop the fighting. We want to take our full capacities as far as they can go. We start to see that we are all very powerful creatures and that we have the capacity to find the solutions for the tremendous problems humankind is facing.

Part Four

THE DZOGCHEN TEACHINGS

DZOGCHEN:
THE TEACHING OF GREAT COMPLETION

CHAPTER THIRTEEN

Everyone who practices Dzogchen is nourished by its fruit. Dzogchen is a very specific how-to Teaching that is the short path to immense beneficial energy. The continual flow of Dzogchen becomes a reality and pervades all of life.

Here we teach Dzogchen, sublime Dzogchen, the pure awareness of being. Dzogchen can be called by any name, but in essence it is a philosophy of mind, a method for building knowledge—the kind of knowledge that permeates all aspects of mind, speech, body, qualities and activities, the kind of knowledge that cannot be found in any book, including in this one.

This is a Teaching without complications or elaborations. The only complication that could come about comes through reification and applying a name to whatever is appearing and giving it a meaning and significance that it does not have. Reification is a belief that data, whatever they are, do not belong in the realm of sublime being, while Dzogchen affirms that *all* is included in the realm of sublime being.

My guru, Wangdor Rimpoche, stated, "Realization does not go into words," meaning that there's no word whatsoever that can encapsulate open intelligence; so, realization is not explainable as a described experience. That's why the term *"direct* realization" is used. All the words written about Dzogchen, whatever they are, support only one realization that is beyond words and descriptions, and that is the decisive realization of lucid open intelligence. The words all promote that, they reinforce it, they affirm it, they evoke it, and the reason that we keep coming back to the Dzogchen texts is that they are filled with precious gems that evoke that decisive realization. There is no other writing anywhere in the world quite like that of Dzogchen.

Dzogchen throughout the ages has adapted itself to various cultures and various ways of teaching. No matter what the tradition—Hinduism, Judaism, Christianity, Buddhism, Islam— they all have mystical Teachings. In each of these belief systems, there is a mystical Teaching of enlightenment, if someone can find it. Those Teachings have been expressed in their music, poetry, art and literature. Whether the basic state is called "open intelligence," "timeless awareness," "strong mind," "clarity," "buddha-nature," "Christ-consciousness" or whatever term may be used, the principles of Dzogchen have remained the same.

Enlightenment Teachings have been given in many parts of the world and throughout many eras, so Teachings of enlightenment aren't anything new. However, they looked different in each culture in which a Teaching appeared.

Radical Dzogchen has no specific origin in any religion or culture. Rather, every religion and culture is home to Dzogchen. Although different labels may identify it in those diverse human contexts, its existential reality is the same.

SHORT MOMENTS: THE CORE TEACHING OF DZOGCHEN

The essence of Dzogchen meditation and practice is "short moments many times become spontaneous and automatic," and all meditation—whatever the duration of the meditation may be—occurs in short moments and in no other way. The short moments practice is an ancient Dzogchen Teaching, and the "engine" of Dzogchen is found in short moments. Through short moments we get to know ourselves as we actually are. We come to understand that we truly are the presence of spontaneous energy and love, which are like the great sun caressing the Earth and calling forth its greatest qualities and activities. Our strength and power of action comes from this short moment. It isn't anywhere else.

Before I was exposed to any Dzogchen Teachings, I was practicing short moments myself. I have no idea where it came from or how it came to me, but that was my practice, and short moments is what I relied on. At the outset I did not rely on long periods of sitting meditation—that came much, much later in my life—but on short moments, moment by moment.

In Dzogchen the fruit—the introduction to ultimate reality—is introduced in the beginning, and then the practice proceeds without doubt, leading towards realization. There isn't a process of working up to the fruit. One knows the fruit from the very beginning, and in short moments the ultimate reality that we share as one open intelligence becomes more and more obvious. The Dzogchen view is not just another point of view in the ordinary philosophical sense. It is the fruition and culmination of the short moments practice, in which everything is illuminated from within. Everything is the pure space of luminous radiance itself, and through short moments, radiance becomes evident without having to be sought.

Through choosing to rest for short moments many times, we develop an all-inclusive and all-encompassing perspective, one that clearly comprehends that open intelligence is always and forever inseparable from data and is all-pervasive of everything; it is like pure space. If we examine space we see that space pervades all that we know and perceive. All thoughts, emotions, sensations and experiences—even the experience of something unimaginable, like many worlds—all of these, whatever they are, are the data-display of open intelligence, pure space.

By relying on open intelligence, instead of reifying data, we see that the entire display is none other than the dynamic energy of open intelligence. It can never be anything else. Everyone and everything abides as open intelligence alone, so to look for open intelligence somewhere else off in the future or in some other circumstance is not going to work. To think that open intelligence is one thing and data another is not going to work either. We're not *going* to open intelligence; we're not going anywhere. The only open intelligence there is is right here and now.

As we practice short moments, the decisive realization unfolds more and more. We can count on this without fail. Even though we may not recognize that it is occurring, it is. That's just the way it is. You could say that it's a law, a Dzogchen law! Everyone who practices Dzogchen is nourished by its fruit. Dzogchen is a very specific how-to Teaching that is the short path to immense beneficial energy. The continual flow of Dzogchen becomes a reality and pervades all of life.

The great Dzogchen lamas (*master, guru*) teach this: "If you do what I have done, you will realize what I have realized." Dzogchen isn't a system of higher-ups and lower-downs, as in a high lama looking down on lowly unenlightened people. No, this "higher-ups and lower-downs" is a misguided Western idea. Where a Westerner might see "up and down," that isn't at all the view in Dzogchen and it never has been. Dzogchen is about harmonious culture, genuine knowledge and enlightenment, and our world today is begging for this kind of knowledge.

We really want to rely on sublime intelligence, but it might seem so scary. "Oh, there are all those big high lamas; I am not like them." Well, every single master has had those thoughts at some time. "I am not like them, they are way better than me; look at all the things they do, I could never do that." Whoever it may be, we can only understand our own Dzogchen realization through experience and realization. The experience needs to lead to permanent realization of already-on intelligence. Permanent realization. Then can be in situations without labeling everything going on. "This is a that, and this is so-and-so, and over there is this thing and that thing and the other thing." Well, as you can see, that is very time consuming!

We have never needed clear-light wisdom and knowledge more than we need it right now. We are faced with so many challenges, including climate change and a global pandemic that have threatened everyone in the world. It is a time of great impermanence, and for many people a time of great fear, depression and anxiety. Many have felt in a sense that they were imprisoned, or at the least that their lives have been extremely limited and restricted. There is so much uncertainty, without a clear notion of where a peaceful refuge might be found. So, where to turn in a time like this?

Short moments of open intelligence, repeated many times, become continuous at all times and our realization becomes clear and secures itself. This is the purpose of the Dzogchen Teaching. Always present, open intelligence subsumes everything into itself. Dzogchen realization does not turn on or off. Whether we doubt or are doubtless, we continue to practice.

This practice is simple, but it is not always easy, but not in a way that infers that it is a grind or that we're frustrated all the time. Even though it may sometimes seem like hard work—especially when we have afflictive emotions that just won't go away and that feel like they are overtaking our entire body and mind—by resting naturally for short moments repeated many times, this big force of sensation or emotion, whatever it may be, will resolve. It may not resolve all at once; however, it will resolve and self-release. The here-and-now always self-releases; this is guaranteed.

Now, this may all sound very repetitive to you, I don't know. However, repetition furthers, repetition furthers, repetition furthers. It furthers open intelligence. This is really the foundation of Dzogchen: to give key points that make it very clear what open intelligence is, and repetition is a skillful means that helps support and clarify. In all Dzogchen texts we see that repetition does indeed further, because basically it's the same instruction over and over again, stated in magnificently different ways.

Try it if you haven't already: short moments, repeated many times, become automatic. I did not invent this practice. No one here invented it. This is thousands of years old and it is the core Dzogchen Teaching. What is more, there is nothing new in these Dzogchen Teachings that are being given. Everything that is written here in the Teachings represents what has existed for thousands of years. When written as they are here, the Teachings are simply a fresh restatement of the key points and pith instructions of Dzogchen that have been taught for millennia. I don't have any original words or original transmission to impart. All transmission is already gotten; it's already had, and so, there is no waiting around for something to happen.

DZOGCHEN AS A GLOBAL TEACHING

This Dzogchen Teaching that has survived and flourished and fortified itself for thousands of years is now coming into a new phase as a global type of knowledge available to everyone. Its ideas are no longer classified as being only "spiritual" or "metaphysical." Dzogchen is a practical—a magical!—philosophy of life, and its principles go far, far back into ancient times. There is no way to fix Dzogchen in place; recognizing and acknowledging it for short moments many times is how we become familiar with it.

The form the Teachings took in the past can be quite impenetrable for most people in this modern age, just because the use of language and symbology was so different. So, here we use a contemporary language to present Dzogchen. We don't use the language from many years ago; we use the language of contemporary society. Dzogchen Teachings that are written for a global audience using contemporary language are unusual, as this has not been done before. The original Tibetan Dzogchen texts had been translated into English, but there hasn't been a direct and modern-day language that is free of a lot of the adornment of Tibetan culture.

In the time that our Short Moments sangha has existed, we have proliferated this new form of Dzogchen. It doesn't mean that the old style of Dzogchen is now defunct. It simply means that one can appreciate the old, and one can appreciate the new, yet in this short moment we have not old, not new, not-not old, not-not new.

Wangdor Rimpoche had a very specific wish, which was the betterment of Dzogchen, also called the furtherance of Dzogchen, and "furtherance" meant making the Teachings available to a global audience. With the furtherance of Dzogchen, new methods are employed to make certain that everyone can have access to the nature of mind, regardless of their level of ability. This form of the Dzogchen Teaching has been tested over a number of years, so now we have the actual evidence of profound realization that goes along with the furtherance. It is important to know how to shape Dzogchen into a simple form that is clear and available to many—simpler, but no simpler than is required. I believe that is what we have done.

ALL IS THE DYNAMIC ENERGY OF OPEN INTELLIGENCE

The practice of Dzogchen is not one of trying to get rid of negativity, afflictive data streams or confusion. It has nothing to do with getting rid of confusion or any other negative impression. Instead, through the practice one comes to see that confusion is itself the dynamic energy of reality and nothing else; "confusion," "negativity," or "afflictive states" are merely reified notions. What is described as negative is subsumed in the most comprehensive order of open intelligence and love, unexcelled wisdom and sublime enlightened energy. In Dzogchen practice, everything possible can appear, and we are invited to let everything be *as it is* in the context of unexcelled wisdom and sublime enlightened energy.

Through decisive recognition of intelligence, it is possible to see that everything is occurring spontaneously within intelligence. Dzogchen practice enriches everything about us as a human being. It enriches our mind, speech, body, qualities and activities, and we are more and more expansive in our being. Avoiding negative data is not what Dzogchen is. Cultivating positive data is not what Dzogchen is. Dzogchen is the incorporation of everything into indivisibility, into unconstructed union. Dzogchen philosophy is not a doing and it's not-not a doing. This triple negation is kind of humorous and fun: not and not-not!

Open intelligence, Dzogchen itself, has the power to outshine negativity and amplify beneficial energy, increasing this beneficial energy into infinite quantity. This is not a binary opposition of the "negative" and the "beneficial." Instead, both are subsumed in the most comprehensive order of open intelligence-and-love, unexcelled-wisdom and sublime enlightened-energy. There's no addition or subtraction that leads to Dzogchen. It would be impossible for what already is to be added to, subtracted from, divided or multiplied.

In our lives, we're either reifying data, or we're recognizing open intelligence. We're either getting all wrapped up in the dynamic energy of the data and describing it, or we are recognizing intelligence and keeping that as our basis. Now, when we are resting naturally and some kind of horrific data stream arises, what to do? Say the data stream arises, "Oh my gosh what's going on in the world; is the world ending, is this doomsday? I can't take it any longer. Will the pandemic ever end?" Or maybe it's, "Oh, this great new thing is solving all the problems and ushering in great world peace," or there could be all sorts of opinions in between. Whatever it is, please rest naturally and recognize open intelligence. I invite you to do this. Please allow yourself to be as strong as you really are.

The indivisibility of what is considered negative and what is considered positive is extremely important to realize, and also the nonduality of both positive and negative. It is essential that we realize that positive and negative are the all-pervasion. They are the all-pervasion and nothing else. They are totally pure, no matter what we've learned about them as being oppositional poles. With the proper introduction to and practice of Dzogchen, we will no longer be rebounding between good and bad, positive and negative, reward and punishment.

There are the oppositional poles of good and bad, positive and negative, and the ideas of, "If I am bad, I will be punished but if I am good I will get a reward." I'm sure that if we examine our own thinking, we can see that throughout our lives it has been filled with ideas about reward and punishment. This is important to reflect on. How have we done things now or in the past based on reward and punishment? "I'm going to get this kind of reward," or "I'll be punished for this."

This is found even in the concepts surrounding enlightenment: "I'm going to work hard and do all the right things and I'll get enlightened; that will be my reward. My punishment for not measuring up will be that I won't get enlightened." However, that's not a very efficacious way to approach the topic of enlightenment!

Through resting as open intelligence, for us equalness and evenness are revealed like the magnificent sun illuminating all, or like the moon reflecting on countless ponds. So too, a short moment shines on all the many things that have made us fearful, depressed and anxious. A short moment of rest doesn't remove the fearful circumstances, the dread or the anxiety or improve them or convert them into happy thoughts. The short moment merely reflects what the fear and anxiety are in their essence: open intelligence. We are intelligence, we are strong mind. Everything that appears to intelligence—including the fear and anxiety and all the rest of it—is intelligence and not separate from it. The thoughts, emotions and sensations we have are the dynamic energy of intelligence. They are not unique, not different, not separated out from open intelligence.

We can be assured that Dzogchen realization is present, and it is *spontaneously present*. Nothing needs to be done to bring it about. Through Dzogchen practice we become more and more assured in our realization. We do not need to change our conduct, thoughts, emotions, sensations, haircut, body type, food, job or anything else. The entire focus of Dzogchen is to introduce and bring to fruition the ever-present beneficial power that is the only nature of open intelligence, which again, is spontaneously present. We meet this power in ourselves and soon we have the insight that open intelligence is all that we are and all that life is.

GREAT COMPLETION

In many cultures, the assumptions within that culture are based on the idea that people are bad and that they need moral and ethical injunctions so that they will be good, when in fact they are innately complete and perfect. Dzogchen means "Great Completion" or "Great Perfection" because it sees individuals as perfect, and always upholds the perfection of beings.

The purpose of the practice of Dzogchen is to show us that we are innately complete and perfect. Great completion isn't something that's going to be reached in the future. Everything is right now; there is no future. In Dzogchen we live as a whole, not as something divided, and not with the notion of becoming some sort of "better" being in the future. What then would great completion look like in our everyday life? It can be seen in the all-pervasive love displayed as spontaneous, instantaneous responsiveness to the benefit of all.

Sometimes Dzogchen is introduced with words or sometimes without any words; it depends on the individual who is wanting instruction. Sometimes Dzogchen is introduced simply by being in the presence of another being with a strong realization. When being in their presence, our own realization is evoked and comes alive. We see a person with a strong realization, and we are attracted to it and inspired by it. Our own inspiration to practice short moments is sparked into life.

We all know the commitment that is required for a close individual relationship with someone else, because I would say virtually all of us relate to others in some way in our personal lives. So, think about the diligence that sustaining a close relationship takes, and then apply that diligence to yourself in relationship with your intelligence. If we wanted to really know another human being, we would try to be with them as much as possible and think of them as much as possible. If we really want to know them and if they really want to know us, we would try to be in relationship as much as possible in this way, and it would be mutual. With Dzogchen it is the same sort of interested, engaged and mutual relationship that is present in a personal friendship. We really want to know Dzogchen, and Dzogchen really wants to know us!

When we say that Dzogchen is the final and ultimate Teaching or the great completion, the profound meaning of this is that Dzogchen infuses its sublime loving energy into the whole landscape of life. No matter what name Dzogchen is called, it is always recognizable as this: it sublimes the lived condition. We are conditioned to believe that we are a certain kind of being— an ordinary being. However, through Dzogchen practice we come to realize that we are in fact sublime beings.

In Dzogchen practice, simply be as you are, however you are. You are perfect as you are. This is the Dzogchen Teaching: "perfect as you are." A strong commitment to Dzogchen practice fosters and enhances this understanding, and Dzogchen is an exact method for building this understanding. Dzogchen traditionally teaches that primordial wisdom is the "as it-ness" of everything. So, if we say, "Leave everything *as it is*," then Dzogchen is the "as it-ness" of everything, perfect *as it is*.

Deep, deep understanding of the Teaching is very important, not on an intellectual level, but on a very profound experiential level. But if we complicate things with lots of thinking, well, that is just because we have been trained to be conceptual thinkers. However, Dzogchen isn't about conceptual thinking; it's about open intelligence pervaded by love. Another word for that is compassion, but in Dzogchen it's called bodhicitta, ultimate bodhicitta. The love realized in Dzogchen is the love for everyone, and the mind in its own essence provides the greatest love and happiness that can ever be known. It also gives us the indestructible dignity and energy to spread that love everywhere.

One could say that Dzogchen realization is the way of living in which there is only spontaneous responsiveness, which is the same as compassion. But the compassion that is spoken of here may not correspond to the typical definitions of "compassion." It can be peaceful or wrathful or anything in-between, and it isn't any one thing. It doesn't need to look any particular way, other than that all data streams are gone beyond in radiant benefit to all.

We bring Dzogchen philosophy to humans, and we make sure that every human who is able to do so has an introduction to Dzogchen philosophy, an understanding of it, an ability to leave everything *as it is*, the capacity for pure perception and sublime wisdom and realization. This is a precise knowledge method that has been freely given to us by Tibetan culture.

Even though Dzogchen might sound esoteric, it's really not. It is reality itself. Everything we experience in a reified way that seems to be so real, is not real. It's not, and it's not-not real. "Not and not-not" isn't something we can ever figure out intellectually!

Dzogchen has not always been called "Dzogchen"; it has also been called by other names. Depending on the era, depending on the culture, the Teachings of Dzogchen are given in a way that is suited to those who are hearing it in their particular time and circumstance.

Dzogchen predates Buddhism but was adopted by Tibetan Buddhism, and thus, Dzogchen became part of the path of Tibetan Vajrayana Buddhism. However, there is a pure Dzogchen that has always been on its own, a Teaching that is unique and singular, and this Teaching has been given over many thousands of years in many different contexts and circumstances. In the same way, now it is being adopted for a global audience.

In certain contexts Dzogchen is still taught within Tibetan Buddhism, but in this Teaching of ours it is taught independently of Tibetan Buddhism. In order to give everyone a sense of context and community, we talk about Dzogchen—because we are part of the greater Dzogchen community—but this is a unique expression, you could say, one that is understandable to a modern audience.

Dzogchen was at one time pretty much locked into Tibet, but now Dzogchen culture can influence and benefit today's modern culture, because it is not merely an ancient Teaching that only belongs to the Tibetan people. It has always been a Teaching for all beings who wish to practice it. In this incredible worldwide display that we have today, we each have the opportunity for Dzogchen knowledge. This is a great boon for the world, the boon of the great fortune of Dzogchen, which trains up open intelligence exactly *as it is*.

Dzogchen appears in order to meet the needs of the current culture, not merely cultures of the past or cultures of the future, but *this* culture. Only through providing the benefit of Dzogchen to this era of global culture can Dzogchen continue to flourish. Dzogchen is for all people, all languages and all cultures. Dzogchen is for everyone and no one is excluded from Dzogchen. Anyone who has a calling and a propensity for Dzogchen, Dzogchen is there for them.

Q. The way that you have explained Dzogchen thus far makes me think that it is a sort of slippery concept to grasp! There isn't a set of rules or descriptions that I can nail it down with and say, "Oh okay, I understand it now." But I am open to all the uncertainty that I am sensing here in this discussion, and I would like to explore the topic more. Can you offer some guidance?

Ziji Rinpoche: The lives of the great Dzogchen masters are important to us because they are our mirror. They show us exactly who we are right now. If we want an actual example of our qualities and activities, we look at the great Dzogchen masters and are inspired by them. We honor them, but at the same time, with insight we know that what is true for them is also true for us. Their wisdom lives in us and it is us. We are not separate or different, but instead equal and even—the equalness and evenness of strong mind. This is what Dzogchen masters teach.

We never know when our circumstances will change, and we never know when we're going to die. By reflecting on these great practitioners of Dzogchen, these great heroes—many of whom experienced great tumult and upheaval in their lives—we can understand through their examples how the radiance lives as us, whatever the circumstances are that we may be facing. That radiance is what we are, and we are never anything distinct or different. We come to this understanding through realizing everything to be *as it is*, based on a fundamental understanding of the Teachings.

Some Dzogchen masters sometimes teach through what could be called "crazy wisdom." Crazy wisdom is a fearless attitude and a willingness to do whatever is needed to be of benefit, no matter what it might look like from the outside. True crazy wisdom is the enlivenment of wisdom energy and the bringing of this energy to every single situation. It can look wildly different depending on what's going on, and there are examples of crazy wisdom in Tibetan culture that could get someone arrested in Western culture!

However, a mere intellectual understanding of crazy wisdom can lead to terrible activity. If someone thinks, "Oh, I have crazy wisdom, I can do whatever I want," and goes out and wildly takes drugs, drinks, has promiscuous sex or causes harm to other beings, that is not crazy wisdom. Crazy wisdom is also not something that one *tries* to perform; it only comes spontaneously through decisive realization.

With crazy wisdom, one never knows what one is going to do or say. At first that might be a little scary, but then there's no way to stop it, and one just says or does anything whatsoever, depending on what is required in the moment. It's a direct response to circumstances, issuing forth from decisive realization. It can be a very challenging display for people to accept if it is only seen in a conventional way.

A great example of this is the story of Patrul Rinpoche and the very great Dzogchen master, Do Khyentse. Patrul Rinpoche felt he had a very high realization, and he very much wanted to make Do Khyentse aware of his high realization. He thought, "I'm going to go show this master just how important my experience and enlightenment are." He had heard that Do Khyentse was circumambulating a certain stupa at the time, so Patrul Rinpoche went to that stupa and saw Do Khyentse up ahead. He went to him to tell him about his fabulous realization in great detail and to demand confirmation.

But on closer examination he could see that Do Khyentse was staggering around drunk. Not only that, he was dressed in dirty clothes and he was shouting curse words. Patrul Rinpoche thought to himself, "I imagined this man to be a great Dzogchen master, but I can see by the way he's behaving that he couldn't possibly be one."

But then something incredible and unexpected happened. As Patrul Rinpoche was standing there confused by the whole situation, Do Khyentse suddenly came over and punched him and knocked him unconscious. Knocked him out cold! But when Patrul Rinpoche woke up, he had full Dzogchen realization, not the sort of realization that he had imagined that he had before, but full undeniable realization, rendered by Do Khyentse's fist!

So yes, when Patrul Rinpoche eventually came to, he actually did have the fabulous realization of radiance, and not the one he thought he had, which was only intellectually constructed. Something like what Do Khyentse did would not be acceptable within the norms of Western culture, but in Tibetan culture at that time it was acceptable, and not only acceptable, but the highest expression of skillful means. You can see from this story that beneficial qualities and activities can appear in any way that is needed in a specific time and circumstance, even if they seem to be questionable or extremely inappropriate. What is important about crazy wisdom is the master's beneficial intent and the practitioner's capacity to respond.

There is another story that I would like to tell you which points to the unexpected way that instruction can occur. Some years ago, I was working on a science experiment, and I needed a novel thought in order to move towards the result I was looking for, but I was completely stuck and could not find the solution I was seeking. I looked online at some information and searched elsewhere, but I couldn't find anything, and so at some point I just went for a walk.

I happened to go downtown, and there were some of the so-called drunks sitting in front of the library, and one of them whom I already knew from before was particularly boisterous. He was flailing his arms around and shouting all sorts of things, but at some point, amongst all the things he was randomly shouting, was exactly the answer I needed for the science experiment! Completely out of the blue and surprising, and coming from a totally unexpected source.

However, if I hadn't been open to him, and if I had been locked down in ideas about him like, "Oh, he's a drunk and not someone worth listening to," I couldn't have connected and heard what I needed to hear. I had had fond feelings for him even prior to this encounter, but then after that I definitely had a smile on my face when I saw him! No matter what he said or did, I always felt so deeply connected to him. He had given me something precious that I had been looking for. I never could have expected it, but there it was.

So, in this mysterious and wonderful world of sounds, lights, colors and rays, I would much rather just rest and take a look around, enjoying everything as the mandala of generosity. That's all I can call it—a mandala of generosity—always giving to me and to us.

THE WISDOM TEACHINGS
OF DZOGCHEN:

IMPERMANENCE, EMPTINESS, DESIRE FOR EXPERIENCE, SUFFERING, NOT AND NOT-NOT

CHAPTER FOURTEEN

By knowing that things arise, we know that they cease. By knowing that they cease, we understand impermanence. By understanding impermanence, we realize genuine emptiness. Knowing that apparent reality is empty of itself, let accomplishing and rejecting dissolve. Knowing that genuine reality is empty of other, let go of fixation on achieving some result. The mind, free of trying to do anything or stop anything is blissful, open, spacious and relaxed.

No matter what appears, that which is appearing will change and eventually vanish naturally. The law of impermanence applies to everything. What hasn't yet appeared will appear, and whatever appears will disappear. The things that were appearing at one time have all vanished, and now there are other things appearing. This is impermanence, and in impermanence there are no definitive conclusions that can be drawn and nothing to totally rely on.

Anything that appears is fleeting and changeable. We cannot keep it in place, no matter what it is. If one looks at something in this instant, there is an appearance, but if one looks at the same thing again a moment later, it is not the same appearance. So how could one say anything definitive about that appearance, other than that it is an expression of open intelligence?

For example, if we know anything about our bodily physiology, we know that everything about us is changing. The hair that is growing out of our heads right now isn't the same hair as what was growing ten minutes ago. The cells in our body are constantly changing, and after some time we have new cells comprising our body. Our thoughts move from one to another ceaselessly, and nothing about us can be held in place.

However, every single thing about the human body and mind, like all other data, is nothing other than open intelligence. Everything is changing—appearing and disappearing—and the whole world could blow itself up in an instant, but indestructible open intelligence would still be. So, why not get familiar with that! No matter what we think about whatever is occurring, we have the choice to rely on open intelligence for short moments many times.

This pandemic that we are facing is not something that is going to go away in a month or two. The only way to approach the entire circumstance is through the recognition of impermanence. In the plainest of terms, we want to recognize the fact that, regardless of the total length of life, in each instant life is running out. I would request that you reflect on impermanence as it relates to birth, life and death—your very own birth, life and death. Impermanence. The recognition of this impermanence is very important. These are the two to be aware of all the time: impermanence and death. When we directly confront impermanence, we loosen the desire for experience, because we understand that death will inevitably come. Initially, the purpose of the Dzogchen Teachings was to train people to die skillfully. To know how to die skillfully is very important. In reflecting on death, we reflect on impermanence.

Practitioners are so fortunate to have been prepared to face a high level of impermanence, and daily increasing impermanence. This is definitely a time for any practitioner to see what a blessing it is to be aware of impermanence and to see that impermanence is simply the energy of open intelligence, of great bliss seeing emptiness. The only energy we have is the mind of great bliss seeing emptiness. Nothing we perceive is anything else other than that, so forget all the labels we have been taught to apply to all the impermanent data.

All data are subject to the law of impermanence. No matter how much positive data we have—we could have all the money in the world, all the houses, all the right circumstances—this would never completely relieve the uncertainty that is subtly present, because deep down we know that there could be a colossal negative circumstance that could come and wipe it all away. The skilled view comes from fully realizing that no positive data can be held in place forever. In the moment that each datum occurs, positive or negative, it resolves and self-releases. It is indeed self-releasing, so really nothing needs to be done about it

As long as someone does not accept the fact that data are impermanent, and as long as one does not give up clinging to data as though they were permanent and real, the mind of great bliss cannot possibly be acknowledged in the active mind of that person. The mind of great bliss seeing emptiness isn't a "thing," nevertheless, it is *obvious,* very, very obvious, but totally unheeded when one is wrapped up in data reification.

If we have just a small run-in with impermanence, we get a small bit of realization; but if we have a big run-in with impermanence, we are presented with the opportunity for a big realization! That's why impermanence can be seen as a friend. All appearances are a soothing friend. We have to be able to adapt to all situations, especially to those which most demonstrate impermanence, and to realize how these are *friends* of practice. If we practice and reflect deeply on impermanence, we come to see that all data are inseparable from enlightened energy.

A lot of this may sound very confusing, but we can't figure any of what has been described here with thinking or intellectual speculation. Through resting in the midst of impermanence, we come to understand impermanence as a significant boon to our practice. Only through acknowledging and resting with impermanence can we have the instinctive recognition that allows us to leave everything *as it is*. The instinctive realization is that everything is *as it is* and is spontaneously self-releasing.

Based on this instinctive realization, which is so important and which reveals the real nature of all being, our diligence, our trust and our faith in Dzogchen knowledge opens up even more, and then it opens to pure perception. Based on pure perception, unexcelled wisdom and sublime enlightened energy become more evident for us.

EMPTINESS

By knowing that things arise, we know that they cease. By knowing that they cease, we understand impermanence. By understanding impermanence, we realize genuine emptiness. Knowing that apparent reality is empty of itself, let accomplishing and rejecting dissolve. Knowing that genuine reality is empty of other, let go of fixation on achieving some result. The mind, free of trying to do anything or stop anything is blissful, open, spacious and relaxed.

How brilliant it is that all reifications are self-liberated! All data self-release, but do they release into oblivion? No, they release— they self-liberate—into emptiness. Everything spontaneously releases into emptiness.

There are all kinds of things that could be said about emptiness and many erroneous descriptions that could be applied, but the most important thing above all else is to be introduced to emptiness and then to practice it. However, in being introduced and then in engaging the practice, one should not expect emptiness to be immediately obvious in every single moment.

207

For most practitioners the recognition is gradual, like a wonderful lotus that slowly emerges from out of the mud and opens up in all its glory.

The oft misunderstood term of "emptiness" is a translation from the Sanskrit word "shunyata." "Shunya-" means "empty" or "zero," and "-ta" means "-ness." So, shunyata means "emptiness, the place of emptiness." When we think of "a place," we usually think of a physical location, but what is being referred to here is not a place located anywhere, but the open, empty space of intelligence. Shunyata, emptiness, is not a void or the negation of anything; it is rather the basic intelligence out of which all apparent data arise. If one uses the phrase "the open empty space of shunyata," "open empty space" is a metaphor for the resplendent fullness that cannot be named or labeled.

In resting as emptiness, we're presented with the reality of what we truly are: open intelligence. Emptiness is not an object or a thing. Emptiness is acausal; it's uncaused, causeless. It simply is. Emptiness is not anything to attain and it can't be fit into any kind of concept at all. Again, emptiness is not a void or nothingness. It is the clear light of knowing; it is lucidity. This is important to recognize.

In some circles, emptiness is equated with non-thought, but non-thought isn't a condition anyone needs to aspire to. Non-thought can be misidentified as being equivalent to emptiness, but this is not true at all. Emptiness is the basis for both thought and non-thought. If we have a habit of trying to get into a meditative state of non-thought, we'll always be tugging on the string of non-thought and trying to hold on to it in order to identify with it to create it as our identity. Rest is best.

Emptiness embraces both ignorance and enlightenment as one. In conventional terms, ignorance and enlightenment are seen as oppositional poles, so how could they possibly be seen as indivisible? The whole idea of oppositional poles, like positive and negative, is a byproduct of reification. We cannot intellectually understand the fact that enlightenment and ignorance are non-different. We must simply rest as the basic pure space that is emptiness and allow the realization to unfold. Emptiness is always pervaded by love. In the Dzogchen Teaching, there is no expression of emptiness that is not pervaded by love.

We don't have to look for emptiness in another place or circumstance other than in this immediate short moment. We don't have to fit emptiness to a certain language or into some imagined exalted place or time, because in fact we have the gift of emptiness in every moment, always already present.

THE INSIGHT OF SHUNYA—ZERO

Interesting!

The philosophical principles of lucid mind, specifically as investigated in ancient India, informed the idea of emptiness. Indian mathematicians wanted to create a character for emptiness so they could bring emptiness into mathematics, because they came to understand that the philosophy of emptiness is related to mathematics. Some of the pundits who taught the philosophy of emptiness were mathematicians as well, or they had a deep interest in math, and they used their power of clear knowing to access the insight of shunya—zero. They came up with the idea of zero as what they called "the empty place" or "placeholder."

Through their contemplation of the relation between zero and the other integers, something novel was seen: that all numbers rest as zero; they rest as the empty place. All of the numbers were created from the perspective of zero, and zero is the foundation for all the integers and any other operation that occurs in mathematics. What is more, zero is an exponentiator, so it makes numbers greater. When we have the number one and then add a zero, it becomes the number ten. Then we add another zero, and it's one hundred, and so on. A new philosophical idea of what

209

zero was took place. Zero was no longer only zero; it was something that could be used together with other mathematical objects to create something exponentially greater.

Zero is representative of open intelligence and its clear light of knowing. Hence, zero represents the essential nature of the world. It was seen that in math everything comes down to zero, and in the same way, it was seen that every existent thing comes down to open intelligence. When zero was invented, it stood for the fact that in deep meditation everything goes to zero. Shunya—zero—is then the basis of shunyata—emptiness. Zero is the expression of great completion. It isn't "nothing." Emptiness is great completion.

When we further consider the origin and eventual significance of zero, we see that everything in the world of computation is based on the programming of zero and one, zero and one, over and over again. Zero and one can be put together in immeasurable ways, and that is why we see what we do in computation. Through this infinite display of zeros and ones we have the miraculous expression of the digital world—all the data, information, shapes, colors, sounds, and whatever else can be conjured. We also have the basis for the telecommunication technology that is changing our world.

DESIRE FOR EXPERIENCE

If one were to ask people, "What is the nature of "being?" there would of course be many different answers. Dzogchen offers what I believe to be the most refined and profound meaning of being, and that is: "Being is the desire for experience." "Human being" means the desire for human experience. All reified phenomena appear due to the desire for experience, whether it's desire for sublime experience or ordinary experience. The greatest openness is to recognize the fact that being is purely and simply the desire for experience.

210

Whatever the desire for experience in a human life might happen to be, that desire can be very strong, and being as strong as it is, the attention is naturally pulled in the direction that the strong desire takes it. Then the conscious mind, the body, the speech, qualities and activities follow. Suddenly the whole world is unfolding as a response to this desire for experience. The consciousness that desires experience gives rise to seeing and hearing, as well as to imagining and verbally thinking. In imagining, sensing, and thinking, mental labels of "this" and "that" are given to the appearances, and the process of reification follows from there.

Regardless of how reified data appear, data are merely imputed to be separate from open intelligence—when never being actually separate—on the basis of desire for experience and the consciousness that propels it. Shapes, colors and sounds, which are nothing other than the dynamic energy of open intelligence, are described as having an existence apart from open intelligence. That is indeed what reification actually is: attributing an independent existence to something that is nothing other than open intelligence. Once the attribution of an independent existence for data is believed in and practiced, desire for the positive and aversion towards the negative emerge.

As long as we have the desire for experience, we can count on mental afflictions. We have been trained to find happiness in experience, so if there is negative experience, we want to change it into positive, or if it is not positive enough, it needs to be more positive. We think that if we have negative emotions, we need to get rid of them through some kind of activity that will bring positive emotions. Even though we never actually do find absolute and final happiness in any reified experience, the attempt is continuously repeated. This is only because we haven't been introduced to the knowledge that places us securely, confidently and assuredly in open intelligence.

The root of our suffering is our desire for experience. The suffering comes from clinging to reification and clinging to the desire for experience. When we examine our desire for experience further, we see that it is also connected to our actions; therefore, it is important to understand the relationship of our actions to our suffering. Our action is fueled by desire, and the result is suffering.

The ability to see the desire for experience in oneself and in the world without being overwhelmed by it comes through proper understanding, determination and strength of heart. When we rest as open intelligence, we are able to see the desire for experience as it unfolds. We rest naturally for short moments, not avoiding anything, whether it is good or bad, whether it is inner or outer. In actual fact, with diligent practice it is extremely easy to be able to recognize the desire for experience for what it is and what it brings about in a life.

Dzogchen is called "great perfection" or "great completion," and nothing in Dzogchen points to getting into a state where all points of view—data—have a positive meaning and are happy. This is just creating another habit, one that does not serve us. In Dzogchen, the goal is not to gain positive experiences. In short moments, the desire for endless novelty and experience resolves and is no longer a motivating force. We rest naturally with whatever is coming up. Whatever it might be that is appearing for us, we come to see it as the all-good, the radiant dynamic energy of open intelligence.

SUFFERING AND THE END OF SUFFERING

Once we have realized the truth of suffering, the question is: what are the causes of this suffering? Dzogchen teaches that our suffering originates as a result of the reified and ignorant beliefs that come from the desire for experience. Because we desire experience, we often don't know that there is any other way to be. We think that the desire for experience is reality, and we bounce around from one experience to the other without even realizing it.

This is all due to reification, the reification that tells us that if we bounce around in the desire for experience and we attain enough experiences, then we'll be all right. If we just have the experiences we want and nothing else, then everything will be all right. Well, of course, when we follow that path, what we find in the end is only confusion and disappointment.

Culturally we have been told that we are suffering from negative thoughts, emotions, sensations surrounding desire and lack, hope and fear, having and not having, being and not being. We are further taught that if we rearrange these things, this rearranging will do away with our suffering. We wander aimlessly and experience suffering year after year because of the tight grip of the reification of experience. There is the suffering of birth, the suffering of old age, the suffering of sickness, the suffering of death, the suffering of separation from loved ones, the suffering of facing unwanted data and the suffering of not getting what one is seeking.

When there is the desire for experience, there is the accompanying desire for more experience and better experience—more novelty, more enhancement, more expansion. True bliss and enlightenment can seem very far away. In brief, if we desire experience, every aspect of data can become one of suffering.

Wisdom and discernment need to be applied: how could simply rearranging suffering lead to its end? That is logically and conclusively impossible. We can't rearrange suffering to end suffering. It doesn't happen that way. The Dzogchen Teachings point to a different way of ending suffering, which is the cessation of the preoccupation with seeing reified data streams as being the description of who we are.

Due to our culture and our miseducation, deep down there is a habit that keeps us from seeing, let alone accepting, the changing, impermanent and dying character of our life. For beings who do not have insight into the true nature of thoughts and emotions, the habit causes unhappiness. This enculturated habit of misperceiving things prevents us from seeing the true nature of the world and our own true nature, which is ultimate peace, love, joy and enlightenment.

Because of the miseducation of reification most all of us have all undergone, this innate peace, love and joy is not known, so we go from one state to another looking for happiness. The desire for experience is propelled by the desire for happiness: wanting to be happy, wanting to be successful, wanting to have a lot of money, whatever may be. In each individual life, how the suffering character of data affects us depends on our own particular way of perceiving and experiencing it.

In addition, because we have been trained in the false idea that we are sinners or that we are bad people or we haven't done everything exactly right in our life, we tend to think of ourselves that way. If we have lived our whole life with this fixed belief, and then we come to be old, we may have remorse and regret for all the ways in which our sin and unworthiness have played out in our life. When ideas come up like, "I'm stuck, I have limitations, I have original sin, I have bad karma, I'm this, that and the other thing," the practice is to rest, rest, rest. Short moments of rest is the meditation, short moments of rest repeated many times become automatic, and with it comes the lessening of desire for experience and the alleviation of suffering.

This desire for experience is the basis for the arising of certain afflictions or destructive emotions called the Five Poisons: desire; anger and hatred; ignorance of the truth of reality; pride and arrogance; and finally envy and jealousy. Doesn't look to be a very happy line-up, does it! However, the core teaching is that all data, no matter what they are, are none other than brilliant open intelligence, and this applies even to these very afflictive emotions. In every single "poison" there's an island of gold in which there is nothing but gold.

I didn't say that these poisons are "good" or "bad." Open intelligence is never obscured. I am just stating the facts, but this is the end of suffering: just the facts, just the truth, but the facts and truth seen in the most discerning and enlightened context. Once it is known that being is the desire for experience, then short moments is the choice. "Do I desire experience, whatever it might be—anger, pride, envy, jealousy, hope, fear—or am I going to rest as open intelligence pervaded by love?" By resting, it becomes more and more obvious that everything is pure love. It doesn't matter what it's called, it is pure love.

When we have discovered the origin of suffering and have outshone its causes, then the way is prepared to be open to Dzogchen wisdom and knowledge. To the extent that we recognize the character of worldly data as suffering—transitory and illusory—the grip of our grasping loosens and the craving and afflictions of mind subside spontaneously. This transformation occurs through the introduction to open intelligence and its practice in short moments. Through it all, we continue to practice. And as we do, all is clarified; all is clarified and outshone through the clear light of emptiness. Open intelligence is always present; it is just that throughout life one had not been properly introduced to it.

There is either desire for experience or resting as open intelligence. When we rest profoundly, the desire for experience opens to a new kind of experience, an experience we may have never imagined. By resting as the open intelligence that subsumes the desire for experience, we come to the proper relationship with who we are. The natural end of suffering is coming about right this instant as ever-present open intelligence. Suffering is the state devoid of compassion, devoid of open intelligence.

215

The end of the desire for experience is the end of suffering. The desire to shape our life in terms of the positive experiences we want to have is left behind. No matter what we might want in the desire for experience, we can't get what is truly beneficial for us if we continue to reify everything and if we continue to bounce around in the experiences. Knowing what suffering is, knowing what impermanence is, reflecting on the profound meaning of these and their importance to very profound Dzogchen practice, decisive realization and pure perception become more evident.

When we feel that we have reached the limit of our grasping and we feel that we no longer know where to turn, this is a great time to rest as what we really are. Through recognizing this reality over and over again for short moments many times over a period of time, greater clarity is ensured. There is the end of the suffering that comes from the belief in opposites—reward and punishment, good and bad, having and not having. The space of suffering is subsumed by open intelligence, as all data are.

We have to find this space of clarity, and then we apply the medicine—the path of practice—and we realize our original good health, which is enlightenment. Just as a physician diagnoses a sickness and finds a way to alleviate its causes and apply the proper medicine, in the same way, the causal reification of data must be deeply remedied, and open intelligence understood, recognized and realized.

NOT AND NOT-NOT

Everything we have thought to be true, no matter what it is, is not and it is not-not. What is the profound meaning of that? Things are not what they seem, nor are they otherwise. They are not, and they are not-not. All that can be said about any data stream or any description is that it is not and it is not-not, just like all of us. We are not; however, we are also not-not. So, that's settled! We could sit around and scrounge up something to discuss, but it would be insignificant and totally irrelevant. There's no way to figure this out intellectually, so we rest.

"Not and not-not" has very profound significance for our practice. We can't say that we're not, because we're all appearing here, but we're also not-not. Said in a slightly different way, we are not—we are an illusion—but we're also not-not, because there is something that exists. Even if this can't be fathomed by the conceptual mind, there is a joy in being able to confidently say that things are not and not-not!

We may want to make something out of emptiness, but we never can. Emptiness is not a feeling of nothingness or nihilism, a void, or any other kind of causal description. Emptiness means not this, not that—or, data not, and data not-not! That's definitely a conundrum for Western philosophers and many others as well. It is a logical dilemma that needles our thinking.

We are trained to manipulate what appears, and using dualistic thinking we see oppositions and definitions—good, bad, reward, punishment, empty, full and so forth. In Dzogchen, however, what is stated is that all of what appears is not, and it is not-not. The realization of this comes about only through practice, and practice has definitive stages.

There is no future and there is no past; these are made-up ideas. There's not time and there's not-not time. We honor the fact that time is not and it's not-not. We recognize what is ultimately true about space and time, and yet our conduct is directly related to the time, place and circumstance that is right here and now.

Short instants are not timeless, and they're not-not timeless; they're not time, they're not-not time. Just rely on short moments without trying to figure it out, and with the support of these very beautiful practices, everything opens up more and more.

Q. Wow, I am so glad that you have spoken about impermanence. I think that with our experience with Covid, climate change, a disastrous world political situation, and with so many other things to fear, many of us are feeling quite hopeless now. I truly do despair sometimes.

Ziji Rinpoche: Everything is impermanent and changing. When the Chinese invaded Tibet, everything immediately changed for the Tibetans, and there were horrible consequences for millions of people, even for the most revered people in Tibetan society. Many people were arrested, and some were imprisoned or even murdered. I can imagine what I would feel like, but only imagine. I can't really know what it would be like.

There were great lamas like Chogyam Trungpa Rinpoche, Wangdor Rimpoche and Minling Trichen Rinpoche who were forced to flee Tibet, and their journey out of Tibet happened for them one step at a time, with extremely negative circumstances almost all the way along. People were being shot by the Chinese, some were falling off the trail into deep mountain gorges and some were starving to death. People were being injured, and since nothing could be done for them, they had to be left behind.

This is likely a degree of severity that we haven't experienced yet and possibly won't experience. But maybe we will! Here we are in our beautiful safe place, but suddenly tomorrow we could need to be somewhere else in order to continue life. There are things that come up in such a situation that are totally unexpected, and they appear in ways that we never could have imagined.

If you have never had something like this occur, well, open your eyes. We are seeing and experiencing things we could have never predicted or thought possible. Human beings all over the world are in intense fear and suffering right now. Fear and suffering are ever-present due to the kind of situation the whole world is in.

Does that mean we collapse into fear? No, it does not mean that at all. The fear can be whatever it is, even hysteria or panic. However, we remain as we are without any need to control what's coming up.

After the Chinese invasion, Wangdor Rimpoche had to carry his guru Thuksey Rinpoche on his back all the way from Tibet to India. Should we think they had good feelings or emotions all the time? Should we think that they were blaming anybody for the condition they were in along the trip? No, that wasn't their state of mind, because they were motivated by faith and trust in the practice. They knew the practice worked, because they had been great practitioners for a long time.

We are extremely blessed to be connected to these very great lamas who were refugees from Tibet. When we look at all of what they so bravely faced, we can see in them a living example of the fruits and benefits of resting, a *living* example. If the great lamas who had to flee Tibet can rest naturally in such a tremendously difficult situation, then we know we can as well.

This is a truly a living example, because they are people just like us. They may look a little different, but they are exactly like us. There is no process or potential that exists in a Tibetan that does not exist in us. We all equally have buddha-nature. We are its presence, and we are its energy in the world. That's the way it is. During the long life that I've been fortunate to live, I have had so many things come up that were extraordinarily painful and things that one would not want to have to deal with. This may continue to happen, but as I go along, I know what to count on, and from that knowledge I will know what actions to take.

We have to realize that we are not powerless in life. No person or circumstance can pull anything over on us, no matter how much power those persons or circumstances appear to have over our life, and no matter how much habitual thinking we've built up about their perceived power over us. We should always feel free to feel, always free to think whatever thought comes up in our mind, and always free to have any sensation or any kind of experience. Always free, we're always free. We can best learn this by being free in the midst of extremely negative experiences.

The great Tibetan lamas are dying off now and they will be no more. That is sad, that is really heartbreaking, and we could stop there with "sad and heartbreaking," but that is not where we want to rest. There will be fewer and fewer gurus who have the Tibetan Dzogchen mastery available, because the old gurus are dying and many of the new gurus aren't from Tibet. There is a special flavor in Tibet, but that flavor carries on to us now. We have a different culture, but Dzogchen adapts to whatever culture it's in. We live in a global culture, so Dzogchen has adapted a way to be expressed in a global culture.

We can see through the brilliant examples of these great ones how just a few people can change the world. They can change the way the world looks at things, just as the great ones had changed Tibetan culture in the distant past. Now Dzogchen will transform the world we inhabit. I am so extremely grateful for this gift.

THE RADIANT GEMS OF DZOGCHEN PRACTICE:

BODHICITTA, TONGLEN AND ENLIGHTENED ENERGY

CHAPTER FIFTEEN

My guru, Wangdor Rimpoche, said that the greatest type of realization is one in which bodhicitta moves to serve the world in some profound way. It could be anything and in any way. It could be in being a recognized teacher, but it could be in being a physician, a janitor, a housewife, a stockbroker. There is nothing excluded. Bodhisattvas and buddhas come in all forms.

Bodhicitta can be a very challenging concept, especially for those who have no previous experience with it. For many, what bodhicitta truly is wouldn't be entirely clear, because it can't fully be put into words or grasped intellectually. What can be said in a simple way is that greater recognition of bodhicitta opens the space of loving qualities and activities more and more. Even if the obviousness of bodhicitta seems to change—to increase and decrease—it never is so. Bodhicitta never comes and goes. The changes that seem to occur are only the flow of the dynamic energy that is inseparable from open intelligence.

Inseparable from the self-perfected qualities and activities of beneficial potency is the passionate desire to benefit all, and the best word for that is bodhicitta. The strong intention of bodhicitta, rooted in natural compassion, is to realize enlightenment in order to benefit all living beings. Bodhicitta is compassionate energy filled with the aim of enlightenment of all beings, *right now.*

In Dzogchen, the motivation is ultimate bodhicitta: ending suffering for all beings through enlightenment immediately. We are first compassionate towards ourselves in that we practice short moments, which is the ultimate form of compassion. What a gift we give ourselves in doing so! With short moments we give ourselves the power to move through all circumstances with ease and grace. So, by being compassionate towards ourselves, we can be compassionate towards others.

We offer a short moment to the pain which is so prevalent in ourselves and in the world today, and we open the door of wisdom-power. The wisdom of compassion enters the pain, and this empowers beneficial energy. When we choose to rest naturally, we are really choosing bodhicitta. We're giving bodhicitta-love and devotion to ourselves, and naturally growing out of that bodhicitta-love and devotion to oneself is the expression of compassion and benefit for all. Bodhicitta is a state of complete vulnerability, the complete vulnerability of everything that is.

The compassion of bodhicitta focuses on total benefit, which supports the resolution of the strong afflictions resulting from complete self-focus. Our motivation is no longer one of trying to find happiness for a separate individual through adjusting data streams. Through practice, the interest in maintaining and enhancing a separate identity gradually lessens.

In enlightenment, there is inherent happiness, and it is due to bodhicitta, this overwhelming compassion that gives itself fully to the benefit of all. With increased resting and greater realization of bodhicitta-love and devotion in our practice, our actions and decisions are informed more and more by bodhicitta, the ultimate ground of being. And yet, bodhicitta is not an action; bodhicitta is innate wisdom, so it requires no action. Again, the ultimate act of bodhicitta is to rest naturally.

THE QUALITIES AND ACTIVITIES OF BODHICITTA

With greater realization of bodhicitta-love, we spontaneously benefit ourselves and others. We have a new way of being, and we can see that this new way of being affects those around us. There is no limit to the inconceivable qualities and activities that come from complete rest. They cannot be enumerated or defined, because each is entirely unique and responsive in the short moment. These skillful qualities and activities aren't cultivated or generated in advance and then hoarded in order to be responsive to the next situation. No, it is rather a spontaneous outpouring of compassionate skillful means in each time, place and circumstance according to what is needed.

In resting as open intelligence, we don't get involved with establishing truth as belonging to one party or another or to one viewpoint or another. At the same time, we can see how contributing circumstances in life relate to each other, and we can act accordingly in a non-harming way—in the way of bodhicitta, the way of exaltation. Bodhicitta is one of non-harm to oneself and to others.

My guru, Wangdor Rimpoche, said that the greatest type of realization is one in which bodhicitta moves to serve the world in some profound way. It could be anything and in any way. It could be in being a recognized teacher, but it could be in being a physician, a janitor, a housewife, a stockbroker. There is nothing excluded. Bodhisattvas and buddhas come in all forms. They could come in the form of a great physicist who makes an incredible breakthrough that changes the very face of the way physics is done, or it could be in the form of something that in conventional society would be seen as unworthy, like a prostitute or a prisoner. No one and nothing is excluded. For each being, their strengths, gifts and talents are their own special flavor, whatever it may be. It is their flavor of enlightened energy, and their flavor doesn't have to be like anybody else's.

Both of my gurus, Wangdor Rimpoche and Minling Trichen Rinpoche, were emanations of graciousness and of ultimate bodhicitta and peacefulness. That was their way. Even if they could both be fiery as well, they engaged through a peaceful discourse.

The great compassion that is the expression of infinite light includes everything that appears. It is the warmth of everything. Ultimate bodhicitta is realized in the radiance of being able to see everyone and everything as open intelligence. There is a softening and a willingness to engage in a way that so wonderfully expresses the profound meaning of human life. We really see that we are both the sun and the sunshine—the sun of awareness shining rays of bodhicitta. We always already are the clear light of bodhicitta; inconceivable brightness is the basis pervaded by bodhicitta. As the clear light of bodhicitta, we contribute enormously to every being; we are joining with every being and knowing them through the language of clear-light bodhicitta

The only purpose of Dzogchen meditation and practice is the enlightenment of all beings, and this is the motivation we set at the beginning: to enlighten all beings and to end suffering immediately through enlightenment. So, dear ones, please embrace bodhicitta. Be diligent in devotion and in asking for enlightened energy. Don't withdraw from bodhicitta toward reification, towards trying to make everything into something it is not.

In conventional terms, the compassion that is very often practiced comes from trying to generate kindness and empathy through intention and effort. Of course, generating compassion and aspiring to serve others is a worthy goal. But at the same time, it is a *practice* of compassion, one of being kind where we could have been other than kind. But *trying* to generate compassion isn't a Dzogchen practice. Especially now when there are political, economic and health disasters affecting all of humankind, this is a perfect opportunity to rest as our ultimate nature and to manifest all-accomplishing activities spontaneously without efforting.

In Dzogchen, "being kind" or "being other than kind" are subsumed by ever-present and all-pervading bodhicitta, which is naturally and abundantly present. It's important to realize that bodhicitta is who we are as beings. The enlightenment of open intelligence is already fully packed; it is pervaded by ultimate bodhicitta already, and through short moments it becomes more obvious. To have enough confidence to show up day after day— while not having any preconceived notions and without knowing exactly what to do, and yet having the trust that there will be an insight to carry out the kind of social benefit we're committed to—is a courageous act of bodhicitta. The motivation of ultimate bodhicitta is not only courageous, it is an inescapable driving force.

As our familiarity with our already-present bodhicitta grows, our healing energy begins to spread out to benefit all. Our strengths, gifts and talents become exalted beyond anything we ever could have imagined, and we dedicate those gifts to the benefit of all. We don't really even have to think about strengths, gifts, and talents, because they are exhibited spontaneously in exactly the right way, at exactly the right time, in exactly the right circumstance.

TONGLEN

Tonglen is a practice of connection, and it's also a practice of sharing. It isn't simply a casual contact with other beings; it is generous sharing. Yes, a practice of connection and sharing, a practice of ultimate bodhicitta. As we are exposed more and more to Dzogchen realization, we cannot help but carry it into everything we do. It isn't something that can be turned on or off. And so, from that first moment of recognition we are really changed, and the practice of tonglen becomes more possible for us.

When we are no longer threatened by our own data streams, we become willing to take in the data streams—the suffering—of others, to understand it deeply and to pour out everything that we have realized. We can give it away to those who are suffering. The beautiful practice of tonglen is that of exchanging oneself for others, which means taking in the suffering of others and giving out the bodhicitta-bliss one has realized. Of all the prayers, sutras, tantras and practices I have had laid at my feet all of my life, to me tonglen is the most exquisite of all practices.

Because we have gone through life having it drilled into us that we are a separate "other" that must be protected and preserved at all costs, the tonglen practice of exchanging self with others, of taking and giving, is extremely important. In this practice, it is not just us; we are not alone any longer. We are sharing the experience with others, *taking in* the suffering and *sending out* to them loving benefit and compassion. It is astounding to realize the connection and to practice taking and giving. We envision taking in someone else's pain and giving out compassion. Taking in and giving out, taking in and giving out.

According to the way that we have been trained up in life, normally what we are doing is the *reverse* of tonglen! We have been seeking relief for ourselves and basically ignoring the similar situations that others are going through. We're taught to hold on to things, and in many ways, we are trained up in a manner that leads us to lack generosity. However, tonglen is uttermost generosity.

In tonglen practice we can take on a particular hardship of others, one we both might share. Perhaps we are ill. We so much feel the pain and suffering of being ill, but rather than retreating into self-focus, we deeply contemplate the millions of other people who are ill. We rest naturally and experience without avoidance or rejection the pain and suffering of that illness, which may come in the way the body feels and how the way the mind is going this way and that way.

Then we imagine all the people in the world who might be suffering from illness. We are certainly not alone; there are many suffering from illnesses around the world, many of them much worse than ours. The sincere recognition of this provides such a tremendous opening. Even a young child can do this; they can be encouraged by their parents to visualize the fact that there are others suffering from an illness, just like they are.

Now, one might secretly think that if we take in the suffering of someone else, it will drain us of our happiness and well-being. This type of thinking is really an idea based on models of scarcity—thinking that we only have so much happiness and well-being and that we've got to hold on to it. Well, essentially, we possess nothing anyway! As all data streams are always resolving into and emerging from open intelligence, it's impossible to gain or lose anything.

In tonglen practice we become accustomed to the ending of suffering. When we give of ourselves and take in the suffering of others, we are moving towards ending our own suffering by refusing to sustain the limiting beliefs about who we are and what constitutes human relationship. Heartfelt human relationship is based on openness, and the openness flourishes in difference—not "indifference," but "in difference"! We learn to empathize with those who are different from us and who may even have opposing values and beliefs. When we can exchange ourselves for others, we start to feel that there is only one beating heart. There is a single beating heart, and we are that beating heart, all of us collectively. No matter how we feel about anyone or what our individual attitudes might be, this attitude of tonglen includes all.

You can practice tonglen if you want to, and I would definitely urge you to consider doing it. However, if you don't feel you have the strength to practice, you do not need to do it. If you do wish to explore this practice but you haven't done it before, you can start with something simple. It's important to start with something manageable and to practice in a small way. But you could also practice in a medium-sized way or a big out-of-the-box way! That is up to you. In any event, to whatever measure, it will be a practice of benefit for all, which is beneficial to you individually and to all beings.

So again, if you haven't practiced before, please begin gently with something simple, instead of something like, "I'm taking in all of the world's suffering and I'm giving away all my happiness." Maybe you don't want to start there. But maybe take one person's suffering. "I'll take that person's suffering and I'll give happiness and well-being to them." Even if that sounds risky or scary, you can proceed with confidence in the practice. From this you develop great, great strength. In giving and taking you connect to the wisdom and love that you are. You expand your thinking about who you are into a vast expanse of equalness and evenness that includes everything. Everything is indeed inseparable and pure.

ENLIGHTENED OPEN INTELLIGENCE

The essential nature of all data, all phenomena, is enlightened open intelligence. The mind of all being is enlightened open intelligence; the life of all being is enlightened open intelligence. Enlightened open intelligence includes and embraces all. Data and enlightenment can't be separated out from each other. The nature of pure wisdom does not involve any kind of separation between data streams and enlightenment. The sublime enlightened energy of data and unexcelled wisdom accompany each other as the essence of decisive realization.

We'll never find open intelligence anywhere other than in the thoughts and emotions and all the other data streams, so that's a relief. We know where open intelligence is to be discovered! We don't have to wait for something to happen, because whatever the thought or emotion is right now, that's where sublime wisdom is happening. At the same time, it is not as if a being who is fully confident in open intelligence has no emotions or feelings; no, not at all. Thoughts and emotions may be there, but they are *not ordinary*. They're all displays and expressions of wisdom in some way, expressions of enlightened energy.

Enlightenment is luminous emptiness infused with bodhicitta, and it is naturally that way; no one needs to make it that way. Enlightened open intelligence outshines focus on emptiness and on non-emptiness. The directions of "existence" and "non-existence" also fall away in unending profound space. Enlightenment can't be attained or created or changed. No one has to do anything to be enlightened, because there's actually no one to do anything!

The prevalent cultural norm throughout the world usually involves beliefs such as original sin, karma and samsara, which is a way of expressing, the conviction that people are born flawed and sinful. Many people think that they couldn't possibly be enlightened because they are too sinful or their karma is too bad. This is all part of a pervasive self-contempt that has been present for many generations. Even if we presently have no aspiration for enlightenment or we feel that we are not worthy to have that aspiration, we can still have the aspiration for the enlightenment of all. Perhaps through that benevolent wish we will come to feel a fondness and a soft spot for ourselves, such that seemingly impossible things become less impossible.

One of the hindrances to realization is feeling that we don't deserve enlightened energy or we've done too many questionable things to ever have enlightened energy. These feelings are quite common. But maybe it isn't "not deserving it" or feeling unworthy; instead, it's "I've got this. I'm already fully realized!" Either way, no problem, it's all good. Any kind of thought or feeling is just more fodder for realization. It's so important to know that there's no kind of blockage; there's nothing in the way and there's really nothing that needs to be done. With the indestructible dignity and humor of the Dzogchen view we relax, free and unrestrained as loving energy.

ALL KNOWLEDGE IS IMMEDIATELY AVAILABLE

When we hear the word "enlightenment," it may sound like a totally distant condition or like a place we have to go to, but what is really being talked about here is our own immense, ever-present enlightened energy. In inexpressible, inconceivable open intelligence there is no grasping, and there is no antidote needed to combat "un-enlightenment." We're not creating knowledge and we are not achieving enlightenment. Within open intelligence, all knowledge is immediately available. Open intelligence is like an indestructible, inexhaustible diamond, and every single brief instant of practice is revealing that rare diamond.

The practice of "short moments, repeated many times, becomes automatic" keys people into the moment, rather than trying to create a specific state in the future or trying to hold onto a good state and avoid anything that's bad. By resting for short moments, it's much more likely that one will stay rooted in enlightenment-right-now, rather than trying to create a contrived situation in the future.

Even though the short moments often might seem bland or result-less at first, if we look back, we can see how this quantity of rested short moments has served us, because each short moment is affirming enlightened open intelligence. As each moment is unique, "enlightenment" doesn't mean that each moment will be of a certain kind. Each moment is whatever it is. It's important to be down to earth, yet deep as the ocean, vast as the sky. Sublime conduct is down to earth; it is spontaneous and not some kind of abstracted or planned-out activity.

At some point our realization grows stronger and stronger until suffering comes to an end. The end of suffering is right here, and it's in a short moment. We get a taste of this; everything is hanging plump with its flavor. Immensely beautiful beneficial energy is what we see coming alive in us. It already *is* fully alive; we are just beginning to recognize it. So simple and direct. This is the complete healing that enlightenment brings to our mind, speech, body, qualities and activities.

When we are able to respond to each situation from wisdom and compassion and from the essence of enlightenment bodhicitta, a profound power comes to the fore spontaneously and naturally. Wisdom-insight and discernment inform skillful means, and the skillful means are a direct result of the profound power and sublime energy of enlightened qualities and activities. Through these skillful means—wisdom-insight and discernment, the profound power of qualities and activities—beings are liberated.

One has to ask oneself, "What does ending suffering really mean? What is its profound meaning?" Its profound meaning is the enlightenment of all being— not all *beings,* but the enlightenment of all *being.* This distinction is so key. Those who have practiced Dzogchen down through the ages have had the aspiration for the enlightenment of all being. So now, in our present context we state further: "the enlightenment of all being, immediately." This is what our commitment is, and this is what we practice, knowing that the knowledge and capacity are always already available.

Then comes the dedication: the dedication of our practice to the benefit of all and to the ending of suffering for all being through enlightenment itself, completely and immediately.

Enlightenment does not know suffering. Enlightenment is the clear light of emptiness, bodhicitta mind, in which suffering has never occurred. Resting as open intelligence allows us to continue on with trust and faith.

Devotion fills intelligence with love. "Devotion" means total dedication to the realization of the enlightened energy of all being. Our field of intent is the end of suffering through unexcelled wisdom, sublime enlightened energy, instinctive recognition and deep understanding. It is the wish that all of us realize this, and that we realize it immediately.

ENLIGHTENMENT OF ALL BEING, RIGHT NOW

Enlightenment of all being, right now is the Dzogchen attitude. Most often, if something like enlightenment is even considered, it would be seen as something way off in the distant future and meant for someone else other than any of us! Enlightened energy is living one's life for the enlightenment of all being; this is the sublime Dzogchen Teaching.

Dzogchen teachers who teach nothing but Dzogchen know there is nothing in the future. The only future that comes about is one short moment at a time, so we can all be reassured about what we have taken to be the future. For very, very few is this realization instantaneous. For most it is a gradual path to recognizing what is already present. It is not instantaneous but rather gradual; and yet as stated in the paragraph above, there is the enlightenment of all being, *right now*. Hmm, not and not-not again!

If we were to speak of any "accomplishment" in this context, it would mean that all characteristics of body, mind, qualities and activities come to be expressions of open intelligence, rather than expressions of reification. So, for example, our speech becomes accomplished speech. We know what to say and when to say it and how to act with insight, discernment and sublime wisdom. We manifest sublime enlightened energy and wisdom exaltation in our qualities and activities.

As Dzogchen practitioners, whatever it is we say carries a lot of power. Each time we speak we invent ourselves anew. Through resting, we know just what to say. In a difficult situation it might require anything possible. It could require at one end of the spectrum a loving embrace with consoling speech, and at the other end, speaking loudly and boldly, taking the person by the shoulders and holding onto them for their own safety. So, one extreme to another and everything in-between, but skillful speech, qualities and activities are what carry the day. With Dzogchen, the response comes from a place of loving benefit. The response will use whatever is necessary to communicate for the enlightenment of being(s).

We're responding to each situation *as it is*. Whatever our response is, it is what is required in that time, place and circumstance. It could be wrathful, it could be peaceful, but whatever its characteristics, it comes from the profound power to know which to express. Maybe we've always been nice, and then suddenly we surprise everyone because we're wrathful in our expression of skillful means. Well, what can be said? That's just the way it is naturally unfolding.

Enlightenment is luminous emptiness endowed with bodhicitta. In meditating on enlightenment, what one can call to attention is that enlightenment is bodhicitta. It is luminous emptiness filled with bodhicitta; that's what it is. It has the power of open intelligence and love inherent in it.

There's a great distinction between "personal enlightenment" and "enlightenment of all being, pervaded by enlightened energy," and that is the distinction that is made clear and evoked by a master of Dzogchen. The enlightened energy is always already present for everyone, but it may take someone with the skillful means to convince us of that. A master can cut right through all the confusion with their words and their presence. They don't really need to say that much. If a Dzogchen master does speak—

even if it is just a few words, those words will carry a lot of weight.

Because we are raised to believe in self—self-protection, self-sustenance, self-doubt—enlightened energy has been very remote in our perceptual field. It just isn't obvious, because we have been taught to reify everything. However, through practice we come to know data as nothing other than the dynamic energy of enlightened open intelligence, and more and more the whole concept of a separate self dissipates. When we examine our sense of self, we can see that the entirety of what we believe ourselves to be is constituted of data streams woven together to create a self.

Enlightened energy is not a subject or an object; it's not a "thing" or "a subject observing a thing." Open intelligence doesn't need to be generated or remade; it's just that with practice its qualities and activities become fully obvious. The more wisdom and blessings—meaning "enlightened energy"—that we discover, the more the realization, and the more we can see what is blatantly true.

As a result of practice enlightened energy opens up inexhaustibly, far beyond the notion of a separate self. There's never a point at which open intelligence occurs and something else does not occur. It is *always* the display of enlightened open intelligence. This is a very important realization. When open intelligence is first introduced, *that* is open intelligence. It does not need to be shaped or made into something else through practice. It's always the fundamental nature that is the profound meaning of every practice. It isn't creating some kind of new reification.

We are opening up our very own reality that is always utterly complete, and its realization is only in each short moment of data occurring. Due to our devotion to reification, we have not been aware that we are enlightened energy, but through the practice of short moments we begin to actually realize and experience enlightened energy. Indestructible dignity and sublime enlightened energy are right here. Like the surging energy of the ocean, they do not stop and start. These are our own natural qualities and activities.

QUESTION AND ANSWER

Q. I appreciate your emphasis on practice and enlightenment and all that, but I have to say that it seems to me to be insufficient when we have so many extreme crises out there in the real-life world that need to be solved. These issues won't be solved with people just sitting around on cushions meditating.

Ziji Rinpoche: The apparent answers we as a human society have come up with thus far for the problems that we face—war, discrimination, poverty, climate change and so many others—have, frankly, not worked. There is no denying the importance of these issues, but in my deep consideration I had to ask myself, "What is the highest level of solution for these things?" I didn't want to work on a solution that is merely transitory and insufficient.

I wanted to look very carefully at solutions that would bring about the results that are truly transformative. It has been stated many times, "The thinking that created the problem cannot solve the problem." The way of reified thinking that we have used until now has caused the problems you mentioned, but has using that reified thinking solved the problems? Far from it. Isn't it time to respond in a way that is revolutionary and unexpected? We need to be humble and open to a way of being that has not been revealed by our previous way of thinking.

That would mean thinking and acting in a way that expresses a wisdom that cannot be encompassed by ordinary thinking. There are stories from the Dzogchen tradition that point to this revolutionary way of seeing, but we have to be open to what is being suggested, because it can look very different to what we have become accustomed.

From Buddhist traditional wisdom comes a story about a ship captain who is guiding a ship with two hundred bodhisattvas (*great compassionate beings*) onboard who are carrying the message of Buddhism around the world. This captain is himself an enlightened being, and he comes to know that there's someone on the ship who is going to murder all the bodhisattvas. So, what does the enlightened captain do? He kills the one who's going to kill all the bodhisattvas. He kills the potential murderer, not with planning or malice, but spontaneously, shocking even himself.

The captain of the ship had the wisdom to know the difference between inaction and taking skilled and compassionate action. He also had the wisdom to be able to exhibit wrathful compassion. Compassion does not always have an outwardly peaceful expression. Compassion means wisdom; it means knowing what to do and how to act in accord with compassion. In sublime loving energy, one knows what to do and how to act skillfully and beneficially. The great gift of enlightened energy is that it brings harmony to all beings; it brings generosity and love to all beings. We have ideas about love that we have been trained in, but that doesn't mean that what we have called "love" is truly love.

These powerful stories don't give us license to do just anything we please. These stories are a form of instruction which supports us in understanding and realizing in our own experience what the Teachings mean in a profound way. Again, this isn't a license to murder or to cause harm to other beings; the sea captain acted in response to time, place and circumstance. It is important for us to be very cautious and careful and to not just spontaneously act in harmful ways if we don't have the realization to back it up. With the sea captain, in the moment and in that particular circumstance, what he spontaneously did was exactly what needed to occur. It is the wisdom and realization that are key here.

In Dzogchen, compassion could be kind, but it can be very wrathful as well. Every Dzogchen master I have met can be wrathful, every single one. It doesn't necessarily mean that they're nasty, mean or going to murder you or somebody else! No, their qualities and activities issue forth from loving bodhicitta and are for the benefit of all. What is more, these great beings have the capacity to push one further than ever conceived possible, so that one's realization goes far beyond anything conceived possible. Wisdom exaltation, sublime enlightened energy—we don't usually hear about these things in our conventional world, but they are who we are, and these masters help us to discover this.

If we steadfastly believe in an independent identity, which is a belief in our own subjectivity, we are guaranteed misery. If we keep revolving in the same thinking that created the problems and believing that this thinking will bring about ultimate solutions, well, what a burden to carry. What a ridiculous mess! Where has all this taken us? Reified ideas have really taken us nowhere. We've destroyed the beauty and the power of what a human being is, and we've destroyed the habitat that we live in. Let's leave that miseducation and misery behind and take on a new way of seeing and a new way of knowing.

Part Five

GREATER COMMITMENT AND ASSURANCE

NO LEARNING, NO TRAVEL, NO DESTINATION

CHAPTER SIXTEEN

No matter what anyone says to us, no one can change who we actually are. What does it matter if this new way of seeing things is not immediately acknowledged in general society? It is reality—and not just acknowledged by some people, but now acknowledged by an entire open-intelligence community.

The reality of open intelligence is the view of this moment, and that view is seamless and indivisible and need not be sought. After an authentic introduction to open intelligence, seeking ceases, because it is seen that there is nothing to seek and no one to seek it. Dzogchen realization begins with a single instant of introduction to open intelligence. We are directly introduced to open intelligence and love, and we grow more familiar with that open intelligence and love.

It is not some vague idea or some kind of soothing, feel-good space we go to because we want everything to be okay. That isn't what Dzogchen is. Sublime love flooding the moment, this is the true introduction of Dzogchen. To rest as the moment initiates the surge of beneficial power. Just as the great Pacific is made up of single droplets, so too sublime open intelligence is both the mighty ocean and the single droplet. Though vast like a great ocean, open intelligence is only and forever the totality of this moment—this data stream, this feeling, this thought, this emotion.

If we have the good fortune to hear about open intelligence, at the outset we may subtly believe that it is a place we have to get to; however, what is always already present requires no effort to achieve. This recognition may take a while to sink in, but that is perfectly okay. In the meantime, there might be all kinds of ideas that come up. "Oh, I've got it now because I feel this way," or "I definitely don't have it now because I feel this other way."

We come to see that feeling one way or feeling the exact opposite way are both equal and even. When learning and non-learning, effort and non-effort, traveling and non-travel, positive and negative are all known to be unborn open intelligence, everything is pervaded by perfect knowledge. All rests in great completion and great perfection. To recognize this equalness and evenness is such a soothing relief and is also intensely empowering.

Some of these crazy-wise ways of being, such as living without travel, destination or learning, may seem a little odd, because we are not accustomed to them, and at first we may be a little bit afraid of this way of being. So, it is very important to just allow ourselves to become accustomed to this unaccustomed vantage. All we have to do is completely relax, free of worry and effort, and we are exposed to the reality and power of who we truly are.

Everything is realized to be totally primordially pure, yet filled with vivid potency and knowledge of everything we need to know, filled with fun, filled with glory, filled with all kinds of things we never imagined or dreamt of. Life is much easier that way. Gone are all the worries, "Oh, what am I going to do? Did I do this right, did I do that right? Am I really going to be a good person? What will people think of me?"

Everything is *as it is*. If a data stream is being reified and given a meaning and an independent nature, it still is *as it is*. It still is primordially pure, spontaneously present, entirely open and indivisible. Even though it is being reified to be a certain way, it never is that way. Each so-called individual already is pure perfect presence. It does not really matter what is thought or what the reified notions are; everyone is already who they are, and no word they say, no thought they think and nothing they do can take away the reality of who they really are.

NO ATTACHMENT TO PATHS, NO RULEBOOKS

In fully relying on open intelligence, one is no longer attached to paths with reified characteristics, and there is no quarrel about the words and categories of paths. In the same way that there is only fatigue from trying to achieve permanent happiness, there is great fatigue produced by trying to travel a path to open intelligence. By freely relaxing in the unfabricated state, one rests as primordial presence and sees that travel on paths to a goal is not necessary.

In complete blissful relaxation, we do not need to have fixed guidelines that everyone has agreed on, and there is no need to have a game plan or a set of rules. To live without rulebooks and game plans is a vastly different way to be, when compared to following conventional social codes and ethical ideals.

We have been told for decades, "What, you're not reaching your goals? Then work harder." If at some point we are fortunate enough to hear about complete blissful relaxation, that will also be the introduction to perfect knowledge beyond learning or efforting. In complete blissful relaxation we acknowledge our own self-nature. We are not requiring someone else to do it for us or waiting for someone to say, "Oh yeah, you've got it now." It is much easier to acknowledge our own true self-nature than it is to figure out whether we have met some societal standard about our worth and well-being.

We let the thinker think as it will; we let the doer do as it will; we let the feeler feel as it will, and we just let the sensations be as they are. All the crazy ideas we have had and all the baggage we have been carrying around about who we are and who we aren't are ideas that are based on reification. They have no power and absolutely no truth value. If we want to know something about ourselves, we want that "something" to have absolute truth value.

In terms of the words we use within the realm of reified thinking, we have a limited dictionary-definition set out for us, and we really do not have discernment, clarity or insight about the true definition of the word. When we allow everything to be *as it is*, we find that, rather than continuing to live within limiting definitions, a vast expanse like pure space emerges. It does not have any limit or restriction to it. It simply is *as it is*, and that vast space is the vast space of beneficial, potent, comprehensive intelligence.

We can see now how we have lived in a reified world, and as a result we can also see how to leave it behind. We know that reification is already always primordially pure, and we can have a big laugh about it, because a reified life isn't what we are living any longer. We might use some tools of reification as needed; however, we no longer live from reification. We do not live from desire, we do not live from hope and fear, we do not live from anger, we do not live from pride and arrogance, and we do not live from envy and jealousy.

HOPE AND FEAR OUTSHONE

Once the introduction to open intelligence takes place, hope and fear begin to be outshone. The endless cycle of hoping for a thing to happen and fearing that it won't—hoping that this person will do something and fearing that they won't, hoping that we can do or get something and fearing that we won't—is outshone in realizing that all our hope is related to the hope for open intelligence and all of the fear is related to not finding open intelligence. There is a complete relaxation when hope and fear are outshone.

Whether we are aware of it or not, we are always looking for the ultimate satisfaction and fulfillment delivered *only* by open intelligence, and even in living a fully reified lifestyle, it is actually open intelligence that we are looking for.

When hope and fear are subsumed in the very nature of who we are, there are no limits. We can respond in any way that is needed, because we are no longer restricted by the limitations, prohibitions and injunctions of conventional society, and yet, this would never be a license to cause harm. Open intelligence is ever beneficial, and a path of "no limitations, prohibitions or injunctions" will never deviate from total benefit for all.

We no longer see ourselves as a fabricated thing made up of parts. The unique unborn essence is right here, and so all thought about getting somewhere completely disappears. Whereas at one time a destination may have seemed so important, now we can know that we no longer need be destination-oriented, and it is the recognition of inexhaustibility that relieves us of all destination-orientation.

Most all of us to some degree or another have picked up the idea from our caregivers and from society in general that we suffer from some original fault or sin. Along with that comes the notion that we have got to get away from that fault or sin and come to some better place. We think that we have to accumulate lots of positive thoughts, emotions, sensations and experiences, and then maybe we will be a good person.

The belief that we will become a good person at some point is another part of the conceptual framework of destination-orientation. Seeking to be a good person through reified means does not reveal the profound meaning of human life and is like shooting an arrow in the dark, whereas ever-radiant open intelligence is the deathless, permanent, sublime reality of everything and everyone, and it always hits the mark.

NO LONGER NEEDING TO BE A "SOMEONE"

We have been taught to avoid and replace negativity while cultivating positive states, because certain things that are seen to be immoral need injunctions against them, while other things are considered acceptable. It is taught that a person should struggle to avoid these immoral things or replace them with something more positive. But why all the work? Who wants to work, work, work in this way all their life?

In this context, we are first taught that we have to be a someone, and along the way we are taught that we have to go to school, get a job and then work, work, work at that job to get money and more money. We earn all the money so that we can retire, then when we retire, we may soon be too old and debilitated to enjoy all the money we have worked for! So, now that we are old we have to work on our ill health. We have to work to keep from degenerating, all the while subtly thinking that we might somehow be able to fend off death. Then when death actually comes, thoughts arise such as, "Oh, I am totally scared and out of control. I have no idea what to do."

Why not just relax and take it easy instead with an easygoing attitude of "nothing left to do" that accomplishes more than all that work and effort. What a relief it is to know that we already are who we are and that no one can change that.

When we hear that nothing need be done about appearances and that there is no learning, no travel and no destination, this does not suggest that we become a couch potato. It does not mean that we should fall into any form of inaction or passivity whatsoever. When we get in touch with the super-intelligence of the natural order of everything, we have immense power, force and super-intelligence in our own lives. The practical application of this power is expressed in the world as skillful means, wisdom and diligent attention to the benefit of all. When we are truly familiar with open intelligence, we have the skillful means to be superbly helpful, and that is accompanied by the wisdom of knowing what to do and how to act in all situations.

Living a life of extremes is completely freed up. Where does that freeing up place us? Right here and now and fully available. The reality of who we are is that we are bliss-born; we are born to be blissful, dynamically bright and intelligent. We are born to solve problems that have previously defied solution. We are born as a creature that has knowledge of the entire universe within and the power to use that in a beneficial way. If we settle for conventional conceptual frameworks, we miss all these incredible things that are there for us.

Traveling the path of reified data is a life that begins with pain and suffering, endures pain and suffering throughout and dies in pain and suffering. So, as we realize the actual meaning of reification, we open our eyes and we see the tremendous existence we have, the tremendous world we live in and the possibilities we have that just weren't noticed before.

If we have been traveling the path of data reification, we should realize that we actually have been fooling ourselves. Even though everyone else is traveling that path, we can stand up and say, "I've found the way of life that is most beneficial for me and others, and that's the way I'm going to live." No matter what anyone says to us, no one can change who we actually are. What does it matter if this new way of seeing things is not immediately acknowledged in general society? It *is* reality—and not just acknowledged by some people, but acknowledged by an entire open-intelligence community.

QUESTION AND ANSWER

Q. I have been doing the short moments practice for some time now, but still I find that strong feelings of anger and depression can come up for me. I see all these people around me with smiling faces who look like they must be free of these feelings, and it seems to me that I must be the only one who still has these sorts of negative emotions.

Ziji Rinpoche: In my own life, it had been driven into me throughout that if I had certain afflictive sensations, thoughts, feelings or physical states, it meant that I was inevitably going to be miserable. But upon introduction to open intelligence, I found that wherever I go, there I am, and that one need never be cut off from complete relaxation. I eventually had the great good fortune to discover that I am perfect just as I am, as we all are. If there is a problem or seems to be a problem, complete blissful relaxation is the answer.

You should know that these feelings of anger and depression you have are shared by many, many people. In fact, a wonderful practice is to acknowledge how very widespread such things are. These afflictive feelings may have been until now a personal matter for you, an individual problem unique to you that you're all wrapped up in and that you've got to figure out. But to suddenly realize that there are millions of other people suffering from exactly the same data stream at exactly the same moment completely changes one's perspective. This pervasive data stream is then no longer something that belongs to you alone. This is the practice of tonglen.

Quite strong thoughts of anger or depression may come up; however, with greater assurance in open intelligence you realize quite clearly that you don't want to live any longer from such a narrow and congested space. Instead, you live from the true "I"— the all-creator, the power-born, the mind of great bliss—and you never settle for anything else. You never settle, no matter how old and decrepit your body may become. It is key to know that nothing needs to be efforted for and there is no destination to be reached; open intelligence is your birthright and is always already present. Truly, there is no travel and no learning necessary here.

The reified thinking that may have become habitual in us isn't who we are. We're given the solution to move from the space of anger and depression to complete relaxation in love-bliss potency and comprehensive truth. The strong feelings that had previously so mastered us now mellow out to the degree that we are no longer under their sway.

Thinking a negative thought doesn't make us bad, wrong, fatally flawed or anything else. It is a data stream that happened to pop up, who knows why. We don't even need to understand where it came from or what caused it. All that is needed is the bright perspective of discernment, clarity and insight. We have to see that all data streams are primordially pure, including the ones that we have seen as negative.

Some of us have learned in the past to apply effort to avoid negative states and to cultivate positive states, some have learned to apply focus on a deity to keep from experiencing negative states, and some have learned to be compassionate as a means to avoid negative states and to develop positive states. However, the reality of what we are is all-pervasive, and there is no need to assume one posture or another, as everything is equal and even.

With more confidence in the beneficial potency of open intelligence, the realizations just keep coming on one after another, and all qualities and activities are seen as spontaneous benefit through blissful relaxation without effort and without learning.

The Four Mainstays allow us to ramp up comprehensive perfect knowledge with no constraints whatsoever. We have a simple practice—short moments—and we have been introduced to open intelligence's beneficial potency. We have a trainer, and we have many texts to read and talks to listen to. We have people all over the world who look at life the same way we do. We do not need to hide out in our afflictions any longer.

GOING TO ANY LENGTHS
CHAPTER SEVENTEEN

We have to say, "I'm not going to live the old way anymore. I am going to go to any lengths to discover what is true, and my whole life is committed to that." Many people are making this choice today, so it isn't just a few isolated individuals. It is up to us to show ourselves and other people what is possible, to hold nothing back and to be willing to go to any lengths.

Open intelligence is the intelligence you have right now, as you sit here reading this, as you are speaking or doing any of the multitudinous things you might be doing in any given day. All of it, every form of it, is open intelligence. There is no other open intelligence located somewhere else. There is not some open intelligence you are going to get to in the future or in which you existed in the past and now you are out of it. Everything, no matter what its name, is included in all-encompassing and all-pervasive open intelligence. Everything pools in the great spread of beneficial potency, the great singularity. Now, that is reality, my friends. My dear, dear friends, yes indeed, that is reality.

To be introduced to open intelligence is so incredible. How lucky we are to come into contact with an open-intelligence training that is genuine, and then to have a simple practice, a trainer and a community of amazing people to love us along! What a grace it is to acknowledge who we are and to know that what is true for oneself is true for all. It truly is a remarkable good fortune.

The title of this chapter is "Going to Any Lengths," but that wording is just a manner of speaking and a way to offer encouragement. In fact, no effort is needed and there is nowhere to go and nothing that needs to be accomplished, because open intelligence is already accomplished. "Already accomplished" means that it is already present and obvious. Open intelligence may not be recognized, but it is already accomplished, present and obvious. Open intelligence is the easiest doing never done! We already have been given everything we are. If one ever hears the phrase "a wish-fulfilling gem," well, this is what the wish-fulfilling gem is.

With open intelligence, there is no getting out of it and no getting into it. All the sobbing and lamenting and self-blame that goes on for people who feel that they are not recognizing open intelligence is completely misplaced, as all of the sobbing, lamentation and self-blame are themselves open intelligence! The worst feelings we have ever had and the greatest elation we have ever experienced, all are equal and even in open intelligence. An instant of instinctive recognition and heart devotion to open intelligence goes further than ten million words about it.

It does, however, come down to each one of us. We have to say, "I'm not going to live the old way anymore. I am going to go to any lengths to discover what is true, and my whole life is committed to that." Many people are making this choice today, so it isn't just a few isolated individuals. It is up to us to show ourselves and other people what is possible, to hold nothing back and to be willing to go to any lengths. Yes, we go to any lengths, even if that involves going against conventional notions and no longer relying on the usual supports of safety, security and familiarity.

Being willing to go to any lengths—turning one's life upside down, taking incredible risks and doing whatever is needed to render benefit—is real practice. This is practice with a punch, a practice with a vow, you could say. We do not have formal vows in this training, because if we did, probably very few would be willing to participate! But the total commitment to short moments could be seen as a sort of vow. We are fully faithful to what is true, and for short moments many times we remain unwaveringly committed to that. We have in the past "taken a vow," as it were, to marry reified data—to love, honor and obey it—but now a different commitment is being made and held to without fail.

Many, many people who came before us have cared enough to go to great lengths so that we can have the opportunity to be instructed in this way. The historical accounts of the people who did so are really extraordinary. They did go to any lengths to carry the message instead of the mess, and now we are benefitting from what they have so generously gifted to us. The word is out and it can never be taken back. It has spread to all parts of the world, and what was once secret and taboo is no longer secret and taboo.

SOME GO QUICKLY, SOME GO SLOWLY

The word "introduction" in its profoundest sense means "to completely confirm." It is not a matter of "pointing out," which is a misinterpretation of the phrase. "Pointing out" and "completely confirming" are entirely distinct. The former is indicating something as a possibility, whereas the latter is completely confirming the reality of what we are. While the introduction is of course very important, it also remains our choice as to whether we accept that introduction. One can either take it or leave it. If the decision is made to accept the invitation, then it is best if that acceptance is endowed with a one hundred percent commitment. With the genuine introduction and the one hundred percent commitment, assurance will grow.

Any teachings that occur prior to, during or after that introduction should never veer in any way from the reality of that pristine introduction. In other words, there are no dualistic concepts that are interjected anywhere. The training should unerringly and completely confirm the primordial purity of open intelligence as the reality of all identity and of all data, and it should point to nothing else other than this.

We are never too young and never too old to be introduced to open intelligence, but at whatever age it may be, it is important to be *properly* introduced. Many people think they have been introduced through this, that or the other thing, only to find that they never have been properly introduced to open intelligence in an authentic manner. Once we have been properly introduced, depending on who we are, we will likely quickly take up the open intelligence lifestyle, or not. Some go quickly, some go slowly; some are quantum leapers and some are not. It really does not matter; it is just a matter of disposition and circumstance and that alone. Regardless of how it might be for us, it is important that we have been properly introduced and that we know the importance of relying on open intelligence above all else.

Once we are introduced to open intelligence, it may take us a little while to get the hang of it, and it may take us even a little longer for it to be obvious at all times. It depends on who we are. Some people are new to the introduction and are still a bit unfamiliar with it, while other people have a vast amount of experience. This isn't some sort of competitive event where we have to compare ourselves to others and gauge our progress in that way. However it may be for us, we want to find the best way to be supported in growing in assurance.

We can learn from each other. For the ones who have been around for a long time, when they hear from the newcomers, they can understand where the newcomer is coming from and can contribute so much benefit to them. For people who are new, there are so many other people with more experience, and seeing their example breeds trust and confidence. We can see in others what is real for ourselves. It is very comforting to know that people all over the world are connecting through the commitment to open intelligence.

Till now we may have been relying solely on data reification, so once open intelligence has actually been introduced in an authentic way, it usually requires short moments of acclimating to the reality of that in order to become accustomed to it. An authentic introduction provides the proper user interface for open intelligence, one could say, and upon introduction we will always have the user interface at our disposal. Short moments can be taken in many ways, but whatever form it takes, it is fine. This is a matter of getting to know oneself in a new way rather than continuing to rely on reified descriptions.

In the genuine introduction to and recognition of open intelligence, everything comes forth exactly as it should. After introduction we might be deluged by strong feelings: for instance, feeling fantastic and on top of the world and that we have understood it all, or feeling that we are the most worthless creature ever and that we will never get it. We have to know that when something like this happens, there is a very powerful reason for it happening. It does not mean that we are going crazy, as we once might have thought. It means that a perfect opportunity has arisen for us to rely on open intelligence and to break away from an old way of thinking.

To no longer deny our right to be who we are is an exquisite act. It is an action of exaltation, and in the moment of the affirmation of our reality, there is the quality and the activity of great exaltation, and because it is so new and unfamiliar, there can be all kinds of responses to that moment. For example, there could be either, "Hurray, this is great; I'm going for this," or "This isn't such a big deal, but I do feel a little better." It could be anything, but certainly perseverance helps support the further commitment and assurance.

The Four Mainstays are the passageway through all afflictions old and new. It is important to rely on short moments and the key points and pivotal instructions given to you by the trainer. The training media itself will reveal to you exactly the advice you need at this time, and the worldwide community will support you to live the lifestyle of open intelligence and its beneficial potencies. The Four Mainstays are so very important in all life circumstances, but especially in extreme and afflictive circumstances. It is really important to prioritize the Four Mainstays lifestyle and to use the resources provided there.

COMMITMENT AND ASSURANCE

At some point we have to make a one hundred percent commitment to the practice of short moments of open intelligence until it becomes obvious at all times. It is only with an authentic introduction initially and then with the one hundred percent commitment that assurance can come. The one hundred percent commitment is the single door to complete assurance in open intelligence and its beneficial potencies, because the commitment is actually a process of confirming that all data are open intelligence. Along with the commitment to open intelligence is a one hundred percent commitment to the Four Mainstays, and the best way to maintain and deepen that commitment is to be actively involved with other community members who are committed to the same thing.

The results of a one hundred percent commitment to open intelligence are not only the assurance that open intelligence actually is, that it does exist and we are it, but also the incredible skillful capacities that come into play. We are suddenly able to handle each situation that occurs, and we have things that come into our mind to do or to say that we know could not have come out of reified intelligence.

Each one of us has so much to contribute, and yet, with greater assurance in open intelligence, we will come to discover that we have so much more we can contribute. It may be that we have concluded that we are facing things that we think are too difficult to solve and are beyond our capabilities. Perfect knowledge is our nature, the nature of open intelligence, giving all of us the opportunity to be and to do exactly what we want to be and do. We are shooting an arrow, which even if shot in the darkness will hit the bull's eye every time. That is the kind of assurance that comes from a one hundred percent commitment to open intelligence. One no longer dwells in hope and fear.

The more we rely on open intelligence, the more assurance we have. It is just like a bird learning to fly. The fledgling bird has wings but has not flown yet, and even though it might see all the other birds flying, it will have no assurance about its own ability until it flies itself. The same is so with recognizing the obviousness of open intelligence in one's life. Just like the bird that has actually flown has the direct experience of flying, we come to have the direct experience of the obviousness of open intelligence. Assurance could also be described as being like cutting off a finger. When one cuts off a finger, it is gone forever; that's it, it is a direct slice. The assurance of open intelligence is a direct slice that severs reified thinking.

Assurance comes about because there is the assurance that data have no independent nature, and from this assurance open intelligence becomes obvious and predominant at all times. With increasing assurance, we come to realize that our intelligence is exponentially more beneficial, potent, open and inexhaustible than we had learned. We gain more and more trust that we can respond accurately to each time, place and circumstance, rather than relying on some rulebook about what we are supposed to do in each situation. Assurance never stops growing, as it is inexhaustible.

Through familiarity with Dzogchen, there springs great confidence and trust. Similarly, sunlight pervades space. Rather than searching for the next experience, one returns to rest as one's nature. There is no urgency in anything, simply strength and love. There is nothing complicated or overwhelming that resting mind will not cure. Rest is best. Short moments, repeated many times, become automatic. Here it is!

Sometimes people may have certain ideas about what it means to be committed to open intelligence, and they may feel compelled to act in certain ways based on what they have seen other people doing in the past or present. Maybe, for instance, people feel the need to wear special clothing that identifies them as being "spiritual" and somehow apart from other "non-spiritual" people, or maybe there is also a tendency to speak in a contrived way or to adhere to certain fixed behaviors. Things like that have been done in the past, but this is a convention that we can very easily leave behind now.

Whoever we are and however our engagement with open intelligence is, spontaneously we can know how to dress, how to act and how to speak, and this comes about naturally and easefully. Each person is unique and has their own unique response to their data streams. Hence, the spontaneous benefit flourishing as those data streams will also be unique. No one needs to be stamped into a single mold. The commitment to open intelligence really is the freeing up of the opportunity to completely be oneself.

What we could call the "costuming" of our mind, speech and body begins at birth, and the manner in which people dress, speak and think could be seen as a sort of performance based on gender, social class and cultural background. When we begin to clarify the miseducation and misinformation that we have been exposed to, we can see this costuming and taking on of roles very clearly in ourselves. Rather than responding from reified thinking and taking on roles based on gender and background, we can now make spontaneous choices from the space of open intelligence that are very powerful and effective. Through our commitment to ourselves as we actually are, rather than as popular culture would have us be, we live as open intelligence, the one and only context for a wholly beneficial life.

THE PRACTICAL BENEFITS OF COMMITMENT AND ASSURANCE

Through the subtle and not so subtle implications of culture and religion, we human beings have been led to believe that we are damaged goods. The people around us and we ourselves reinforce that belief, so eventually that is just the way we come to see ourselves. We have been told who we are throughout our lives using a common terminology of dehumanization, disempowerment and diminishment. We may have tried our best to make ourselves better, but the efforts never really seemed to do the job.

We have learned and taken on these negative notions from society, and maybe we have been convinced that we are damaged, inadequate and worthless. Not only that, we have perpetuated these ideas through our ongoing belief in them and willingness to live according to them. There isn't any intellectual trickery that can simply eliminate these strong data streams, and so instead we can say, "Okay, I'm just going to let all of that be *as it is*. I will be at rest with all of that and rely on short moments to reveal what my innate intelligence is." Some of us in our lifetimes are lucky enough to stumble upon a training that allows us to do just this, and we are able to see ourselves as we really are. Just to reflect on the good fortune of discovering a training like this brings great joy.

If we think we are unworthy, bad, wrong and not the kind of person who could ever have open intelligence, it is so vitally important to take heed of what is being spoken about here. A human being isn't damaged goods; a human being is a stainless, flawless, exalted creature. This is not a prideful, arrogant human being, but one who is exalted and beneficial. Exalted human beings exalt not only themselves but all others. They exalt their habitat and all its inhabitants, and they know how to take care of the habitat. This is a much different understanding of what a human being is than thinking oneself to be damaged goods.

We did not realize that we have an incredible innate intelligence, so how could we know how to access it if we didn't even know that we had it? It is very, very important that we *do* recognize that we have this innate intelligence. This recognition is a revolution of self-understanding, in other words, a revolution in the way we understand ourselves in relation to the world and other subjects and objects in the world. At some point we recognize, "Hey, I am not going anywhere else. I know what works, and I am going to pour myself one hundred percent into this commitment." People want a safe place where they know they are not going to get criticized, made wrong or intimidated. They come because they want to find a place where they can be of benefit to themselves and to others and where they will only be supported and exalted.

In open intelligence we have great freedom in deciding how we will be. We naturally want to be what is of greatest benefit to all, and through introduction, commitment and assurance it is easy for us to create new ways of being for ourselves. We do not live inside the box of conceptual frameworks anymore, and we begin to see all kinds of innovative ways of proceeding.

QUESTION AND ANSWER

Q. I so love this expression "going to any lengths." I think I understand what it means, but could you explain further what it means for you?

Ziji Rinpoche: Yes, I would be glad to, and as is often the case, a story can best illustrate what is being spoken about, because an illustrative story can allow an abstract idea to come alive. What I am about to tell you is a true story that comes from one very extraordinary person's direct experience. A story like this can really hit home and demonstrate in a simple and natural way what "going to any lengths" could mean. So, that having been said, I would like to tell the story of a life event from a person very dear to me that truly demonstrates that trait.

This person, my guru Wangdor Rimpoche, is a Tibetan lama who had to flee Tibet many years ago when the Chinese invaded. There had been special signs that accompanied his conception and birth, and his parents knew through these special signs that this little baby did not belong to them, but that he belonged to the benefit of all. And so, he was brought to a monastery when he was a small child, and he lived there with his guru for many years. By the time he was sixteen he had received transmissions for all the pinnacle Teachings in Tibetan Buddhism.

As he got a little older, the circumstances in Tibet started getting very dangerous because the Chinese had come, and there was a rumor that many Tibetans had been attacked and killed. Wangdor Rimpoche and many of the people around him decided that they needed to flee Tibet and go to India. His beloved guru, Thuksey Rinpoche, was quite old and was also a very large person, and it was not immediately obvious how he was going to be transported.

The monks in the monastery tried all sorts of different ways to get Thuksey Rinpoche out of Tibet. They hired some mountain men to carry him, but that didn't work out. Next, they decided to get two or three yaks to carry him, but that attempt also was unsuccessful. Each of these attempts failed, but Wangdor Rimpoche refused to leave Tibet without his guru. There were many people who were also students of the same guru who wanted to save themselves and get out of Tibet, and they went on ahead and left the guru behind.

But Wangdor Rimpoche didn't think that way. He resolved, "I leave when he leaves, or I don't leave at all." Finally, he concluded, "Well, there is no other way to do this, so I'm going to carry my teacher myself, because if I don't carry him, there is no way that he will make it." So, he decided that he was going to carry his guru all the way to India—carry him, on his back, across the Himalayas, all the way to India. That is just so totally unbelievable. The only possible force that could allow something like that to happen is total devotion.

The journey to India was extremely arduous and dangerous. The group that traveled together never knew whether they would have enough food and water, and they had to go over many high passes and cross over dangerous mountain crevasses, and frequent falls claimed the lives of many of the people in the group. In fact, out of all the people who left Tibet with them, only a few would make it all the way to India.

Every single step Rimpoche took, even when he did not think he could make it, was empowered by the dynamic energy of great benefit. He did indeed carry his guru over many mountain passes and through many incredible dangers all the way to India. What in the world motivated him to carry his guru on his back such a distance? He knew that if he did not carry him out of Tibet, there would be teachings that would be lost forever—teachings that he hadn't heard, but more importantly teachings that no one would ever hear unless he did what he did.

With the profundity and strength of great benefit and great compassion, he was able to perform an incredible feat. Without needing to figure things out conceptually, he simply gave all of himself. He was able to demonstrate qualities and activities that he had never known in himself before, things that he might have thought were impossible. The story of his life and who he is as a person are demonstrated by the actions he took to save his guru. Wangdor Rimpoche said that carrying his guru to India was the greatest accomplishment of his life, because he knew that it ensured that many people would be afforded access to the beneficial potencies of these teachings. This incredible accomplishment of his is possibly one of the most brilliant examples of what "going to any lengths" actually means.

COMPLETE FREEDOM

CHAPTER EIGHTEEN

Relying on open intelligence exposes us to our real identity and real condition. We are empowered in ever-new ways, and every way that we are empowered is unique to us. No one needs to be put into a mold; everyone has complete freedom to express their own strengths, gifts and talents in accord with the benefit of all.

Each and every moment shines forth as the power of illuminated knowing. This isn't just abstract philosophical knowing; it is knowing pervaded by luminosity. This knowing which is always inexhaustible and unending is open intelligence beyond conceptual constructs or abstraction. There would be all kinds of ways of intellectualizing and philosophizing an abstract philosophy about this topic, and different philosophies might be a good read now and again, but mere philosophy is not sufficient to provide permanent evocation of beneficial potency.

The images in a mirror are reflected equally and evenly and without bias. We can point a mirror here, there and everywhere, and no matter what appears in the mirror and whether it is described as good, bad or indifferent, it is equal and even in the mirror. So too, in open intelligence all data are an equal and even vast expanse of luminous beneficial potency.

The spontaneous wisdom-benefit of all is always already present as open intelligence. That is your only description, your only reality, and there is no way to get to it or to get away from it. All that shines forth in open intelligence is its own reflection, like the reflections within a crystal ball. All notions such as life, birth and death, past, present and future, waking, dreaming and sleeping are all the shining forth of the wisdom-light of open intelligence.

Just as space pervades everything within it, similarly open intelligence's beneficial potency pervades all and is all. Stainless space, the living reality of wisdom-light illuminates everything; it illuminates the thoughts we think, the emotions, the sensations and all experience. These are all the shining forth of wisdom-light, and by freely relaxing as this unfabricated reality, we set ourselves free.

Dzogchen doesn't parse and nuance data into definitions. Instead, the Dzogchen view is that all data are all-good. How do we intellectually assess something that says that all data are "all-good"? What about things such as war, violence, hatred, suffering and so on, definitions that seem all-bad? They are seen as all-bad due to the way we have been trained in ordinary culture, which is to define data as positive or negative. When we have the introduction to Dzogchen, we are introduced to the Dzogchen view, and our attention is no longer rooted in reified definitions of data. We don't need to cling to any kind of experience. Dzogchen subsumes ordinary thinking and mind altogether. Dzogchen provides the tremendous boon of opening up not only the exquisite beauty of mind—the all-comprehensive, all-pervasive, all-inclusive mind—but also the exquisite beauty of wisdom speech, qualities and activities.

What happens is that we have a soft spot to nurture! Open intelligence and love, that is our soft spot. I say it's "soft" because it's comfortable. We have the solid foundation of a short moment of recognition of the nature of mind, and that is the change of perspective into this softness. Dzogchen is like the best graduate program in the nature of mind. It is something that is proven to work. If a student goes to a great university, they know that they're going to be challenged significantly and possibly pushed into a completely new way of thinking. Same with Dzogchen.

Just as we learned from our birth to be a certain way through repetition—hearing things over and over again, having them driven into us, coming to believe them and then acting these beliefs out in our lives over and over again—in the same way, coming to the reality of who we are deepens with repetition. It deepens with clear communication from those who live this reality, and with this clear communication we can come to completely comprehend and understand who we are. We can completely have trust in who we are. We can know that the spontaneous benefit that pours forth from us is significant, that it is crucially important and that we do not have to struggle for it. We can simply rely on the ease of what comes forth in the moment.

We had learned all along that we had to work hard to cultivate virtues such as mercy or compassion, because we have been told that they are not natural to us. That is what the process of cultivation implies: that something isn't natural to us, so we have to cultivate it. However, in open intelligence we find that these beneficial potencies spontaneously come about in the recognition and realization of open intelligence. Even without recognition or realization of it in an individual or personal way, in the understanding or comprehension of open intelligence these beneficial qualities will come about.

Just as there is a distinction between contrived compassion and spontaneous compassion, there is a distinction between contrived wisdom and uncontrived wisdom. In contrivance of wisdom there is an effort made through avoiding certain negative data streams or replacing negative data streams with positive data streams. Cultivating positive data streams is what cultivated wisdom is, but spontaneous wisdom is crucially distinct from cultivated wisdom. Spontaneous wisdom-benefit comes about naturally without any effort at all, and spontaneous wisdom is synonymous with uncontrived benefit.

Over and over it is emphasized that spontaneous benefit is without effort, without cultivation and without development so that we can subsume all effort into the reality of spontaneous benefit right here. This is emphasized repeatedly in incredible detail to support our fluency in living as spontaneous benefit alone. Repetition of these teachings, over and over again, is a crucial aspect of their communication.

Spontaneous wisdom-benefit is available to us day and night. Through effort we may be able to develop something that looks a little bit like benefit, but it is entirely different from spontaneous and effortless benefit. Even if things come up which could be described as challenging or difficult, nevertheless, within that challenge and difficulty, we spontaneously know what to do and how to act, and so we respond as beneficial potency. The only way to be is to be immersed in open intelligence and to get to know ourselves profoundly in that way. As the thinker, doer, actor and producer of wisdom light, we live purposefully from that space without thinking about it at all. There is then the sheer delight of living life without hope or fear.

REALIZING THE REALITY

In always-on open intelligence, there is no dependence on reified thoughts, emotions, sensations and other experiences. There is no dependence on accumulating positive thoughts and deeds. There is no dependence on life, birth and death. Open intelligence is spontaneous benefit beyond cultivation, so the lifestyle of working, doing and efforting to get things done is left behind. But this does not mean that we become apathetic. It means instead that we have more energy than ever, and now it is an entirely beneficial energy that is not just meant for us or a few close friends or other loved ones, but is for the benefit *of all*.

263

The ever-intelligence of open intelligence sees body, mind, speech, qualities and activities in the same way that it sees all other data streams. In each instance, our own open intelligence clarifies and subsumes everything into itself, including all ideas we have about being a body, speech, mind, qualities and activities. We see clearly that the reality of who we are is open intelligence's beneficial potency. This is what will live on as after the human mind and body are gone.

When we were young children, people said to us, "You're a girl, you're a boy, your name is such and such," or whatever other information it might have been. There was constant exposure to these ideas, and we decided, "Well, they're saying that, so I guess that's who I am." On the other hand, relying on open intelligence exposes us to our real identity and real condition. We are empowered in ever-new ways, and the ways that we are empowered are unique to us. No one needs to be put into a mold; everyone has complete freedom to express their own strengths, gifts and talents in accord with the benefit of all.

Sometimes we seek antidotes to the burden of reification: "If I could only change this partner I'm with," or "When I can go on vacation everything will be better," or "If I can get that promotion, then it will be okay," but in fact there is nothing to obtain. There is complete and total release in the effective reality of who we are. The very great inexhaustible wisdom body is the one and only thinker, speaker and doer, so there is nothing to get rid of.

That which is inexhaustible has no destination. Where would there be a destination in inexhaustibility? All we do is relax in the inevitability of who we are, and as we relax, our intelligence opens up to all of that knowledge that is available in a usable way. Knowledge that is available in a usable way for the benefit of all is wisdom knowledge. The means and power to benefit all, everything that everyone might ever need, is available through open intelligence as the thinker and doer.

In resting as the great benefit of each moment, confidence and strength are generated. Confidence and strength are not something we need to build. So, where are confidence and strength to be found? Right here where we are now. There may be all sorts of concepts about who we are trying to be, but nothing is required, other than utter relaxation, for confidence and strength to be as they are.

The indestructible expanse is always present and ever obvious and can never enter a concept and be stuck there. Open intelligence is in everything and everyone, like wetness is always present in water and heat is always present in fire. There is nothing conceptual to hold on to, nothing at all. In the moment of trying to hold on to it, it is released, so we might as well just enjoy the ride! There is complete release from the need to be quarreling about the meaning of things or fixating on any particular characteristic.

We can experience the extremes we have in our life as being the perpetual revelatory force of inexhaustible open intelligence. Even if we might be writhing in pain and unable to move, all of that energy is open intelligence. We could call that energy all kinds of other things, but it is always nothing other than this.

Even if we feel like we desperately want open intelligence and we are not getting it, we already are it! Even in the pronouncement, "I don't have open intelligence at all," open intelligence is required for that thought to take place. It is kind of a funny little joke that open intelligence plays on itself. We no longer need to feel miserable as a result of thinking, "Oh, I've no longer got it," as there is no way to get away from open intelligence; it is inescapable.

If we are frustrated or feel a little down and cannot see ourselves as open intelligence, we can maybe see the spontaneous benefit reflected in those around us who are relying on open intelligence, so we can borrow their confidence and know that the same kind of spontaneous benefit is true for us as well. Others can share their own experience with us and support us, and through this we can recognize our own potency to enliven spontaneous benefit. This is the power of community.

We can completely leave the life of extremes in which we have tried to get rid of negative things and grab fleeting positive ones. We go completely from that life of extremes to living right here, the supreme way of being as the only thinker, doer and actor. The tiring struggle of belief in the power and influence of data as though data had an independent nature is definitely not the way to go. The struggle to produce a good person, to hang on to positive ideation and emotion and to try to get all those perfect experiences helps contribute to the dis-ease of aging. What a great effort all of that is! It is much easier to just enjoy ongoing relaxation.

In Dzogchen practice; the fruit is introduced immediately, first thing. The Dzogchen Teaching is only "short moments, repeated many times, become automatic," and "rest is best." In short moments, repeated many times, open intelligence becomes obvious at all times. Short moments, many times, is the meditation of Dzogchen.

From the moment of dawn, sunlight increasingly exposes day. Likewise, open intelligence is first introduced and then increasingly revealed. This revealing may be very new to us, but no matter how long we have been around, it is always fresh and profoundly new. Could anything come along that is better than what is right here right now?

PURE PERFECT PRESENCE

In this instant the unmistakably pure presence is already present, already arrived, already here. Even though we may have ideas of all kinds of things like, "I'm a loser," or, "I'm so fantastic," or whatever it might be, all of these are just reified thoughts. They have nothing to do with what we really are. The essence of any word is pure perfect presence; the label that is usually applied to it has nothing to do with its actual essence.

When we are first introduced to pure perfect presence, it seems like a thing, as in, "Oh, well, okay, now I've got a good hold on this blissful feeling," but what we find is that pure perfect presence is absolutely inexhaustible and does not come and go. Everything is all-giving beneficial beauty. By resting completely and naturally, it comes to us that everything is like a perfect gem. No matter what it may seem to be in reified terms, it is outstandingly beautiful.

Part of the beauty is that we instinctively and naturally know how to take care of ourselves and others. We do not do things that have a risk of harming ourselves or other people. We are free to be natural, free to be loving, free to be all-giving beneficial beauty. For most of us this capacity is not recognized overnight, even if sometimes it *is* recognized overnight! Whichever it may be, what is most important of all is to completely relax and let things be as they are.

TRUE SATISFACTION IN OPEN INTELLIGENCE

Only in open intelligence is there true satisfaction. Thus, any kind of seeking for fame, power, money or pleasure through any means whatsoever ends with more seeking for more power, more money, more privilege, more pleasure. All of this leads nowhere ultimately. All power, all money or whatever else people might be seeking will be stripped away at some point, and at death it will surely be stripped away. There is no amount of power or money that can comfort a dying person, none.

Only the perfect love of open intelligence comforts all in all situations. This is the reality. We no longer need be so burdened with data-definitions, and we are no longer going through life dragging a huge bag behind us that is stuffed with all kinds of memories and all the bad things we think we have done or were done to us. Instead, we are freed up completely from the burden of the past.

We are so very much limiting ourselves if we are consumed with self-loathing, self-blame, self-obsession or self-anything, and all the wantings of self. In being consumed in this way, so much of the attention is directed solely at oneself. "I'm thinking this; I'm feeling this; I'm afraid of this. I hate this other thing," and on and on. This is what reified intelligence leads to: a life based on self-focus rather than on the benefit of all. By making the benefit of all primary rather than merely focusing on oneself, we experience a beautifully lived life of all-pervasive, all-consuming great benefit. It is not some kind of stiff, starched life where we have to give up all concern for our own well-being. No, it is a life filled with joy and good cheer in all ways and for all beings, including for ourselves.

We realize that we do not need to be engaged in trying to puff up an image of self and make it seem better or more special and unique than other selves. Instead, the idea of the self has gone by the wayside. If we have any idea of the self, it is the "self" of open intelligence's beneficial potency. Rather than being tied to the idea that we are exhaustible human beings who inhabit a body that will drop dead at some point, we find that we are in fact the power of the universe endowed with the capacity to benefit all.

All the things that we have thought to be true about ourselves can be blown open. The descriptions we have learned fade away until they are completely outshone. Then, when fear or desire or any

268

other strong afflictive state comes up, it is less and less captivating, and eventually the power and influence of these afflictive states are realized to be non-existent. What is realized to be is supreme benefit alone, a vitality that has become so real to us that it outshines all data, just as daylight outshines all the planets and stars that are so visible at night.

Due to the depth and insight that come from complete assurance in open intelligence, the way we have looked at life changes completely. What we thought to be pain and suffering, or the constant seeking of pleasure, is now seen as the dynamic energy of beneficial intent. Pervading all of inexhaustible open intelligence is immediate benefit for all being. All being, all beings, whoever they may be, and all things, whatever they may be, are pervaded by all-beneficial, all-encompassing, all-inclusive inexhaustible open intelligence, and the differentiation that appears to be so is not so. All rests as great completion and great perfection without a single thing left out.

Perhaps there have been people around us, even in our families, whom we did not like so much, or even whom we have hated, and yet through relying on open intelligence we can come to have a completely new disposition towards them. Perhaps our thoughts would run wild whenever we were with them, but now we may find that we are looking for ways to help them and to make them happy. A fundamental change in relationship like this is absolutely marvelous, it really is.

The more we live as open intelligence, the easier it is to see people without bias or judgment. When we look at them, we see something that is familiar to us. And why is that? Because it is like looking in a mirror. We are not just looking at somebody else, we are looking at ourselves. We have come to terms with who _we_ are, and we are entirely comfortable with that. The reason we can be with others as they are is because we have been able to be with ourselves as we are. That is the only way; there is no way to know another person without knowing oneself first. The old adage, "Know thyself," could not be truer. Know thyself—not just certain things—but everything.

QUESTION AND ANSWER

Q. I am getting a lot of pressure from my family. Their expectation is that I should be married and have children and get enough money and security to be comfortable and to lead a normal life. They are quite critical of the way that I am living now and have made their displeasure very clear, and this situation has caused me a lot of distress.

Ziji Rinpoche: Well, for me, I can say that I was born with a defect of character, and that defect was that I did not obey the rules! I cannot tell you how happy I am that I did not obey the rules. There was no way I could buy into the usual expectations. I started raising questions when I was quite young, and in school if I questioned something that one of the teachers said, I would sometimes be rapped on the knuckles with a ruler. I guess that was supposed to stop me from thinking my own thoughts or questioning what the hell was going on, but those actions did not overrule my own discernment, however young I might have been.

My life has involved a lot of going against the grain. I just could not go along with what I was being told to do, and I could not make nice or go for some kind of fakery, when I could see that many things were really not okay. There were so many things I would not be involved with because they were intrinsically opposed to what I knew to be true.

There are all kinds of defined roles for everyone, as there have been for me as a wife, mother and grandmother. I did not live the way that most wives, mothers and grandmothers of my demographic are supposed to be living. People-pleasing was not my main goal! I wanted to radicalize my energy and take it somewhere else other than what had been expected of me. I

270

realized that the best mother and grandmother I could be would be as a person spreading the intense loving energy I have for my sons and grandchildren to as many beings as possible in all reaches, rather than confining my love to a family unit alone.

I have had to make many decisions that did not go along with what other people wanted for me, including what my own parents, my husband, my children and my grandchildren wanted me to do. In each of my decisions I asked, "According to my abilities of mind, speech, body, qualities and activities, what must I do to be of greatest benefit to all?" That was my decision-maker and it still is. I wanted to see in my life and the lives of others the exaltation that human beings are inherently capable of.

I had to decide about the way that I would live my life and what I would focus on. That came very naturally to me, because nothing else but the benefit of all was of interest to me, and that's how I made my choices about what I would do and how I would act. I strongly felt that the greatest legacy I could leave my family would be to take the path that I could see so vividly in front of me. That's the easiest way, I would say. In that light I also had some practical choices to make. No matter what decision we make, whether the decision is for the benefit of all or not, some people won't like what we are doing. Instead of worrying about what other people think, why not have a life filled with satisfaction and flourishing based on your clear insight and discernment?

Open intelligence allows a fierce defiance to all the seeming barriers, and it allows for total care of the self and of others. There has been such rubbish put forward in terms of care of the self, and many have not dared to challenge these strongly held ideas. I was always very clear that there was a new philosophy brewing, and this new philosophy was the philosophy that I wanted to be investigating. I wasn't interested in just going along with the norm.

There is such ignorance of what a human being is capable of, and we have layered on ideas from the past about what a human being should be and should do. We learn so much about ourselves that is just not true, and that's why we need an education in the nature of mind—a real one that can truly support us. It's up to us to ignite the beneficial potency, to show ourselves and other people what's possible, to hold nothing back and to be willing to go to any lengths.

THE OBVIOUSNESS OF OPEN INTELLIGENCE IN DRUGS AND ALCOHOL

CHAPTER NINETEEN

By relying on the obviousness of open intelligence at all times, no matter how much one has drunk or used drugs, the obviousness of open intelligence is what will outshine this strong data. There is nothing quite as powerful for someone who has been addicted as the recognition of open intelligence inseparable from drunkenness or being stoned. The shine of open intelligence is seen to be in the vodka bottle and in the joint. Everything is recognized to be the liveliness of open intelligence.

Let's say that there has been a very strong issue in your life, something such as abuse, abandonment, addiction or whatever it might be, and you have tried everything you can think of. You have bought many self-help books, gone to lots of different workshops and joined as many support groups as you can find, but still that issue lingers on in your life.

However, with greater and greater assurance in open intelligence, you can find that this very issue can disappear completely, like the flight path of a bird in the sky, and all the anguish, torment and sorrow that went along with those learned ways of conducting yourself just are not there anymore. Complete assurance in open intelligence and in its great singularity and exaltation blows away all the conventional expectations and ideas about these sorts of things.

There may have been certain data streams that you think could not be open intelligence because they are just too bad, or they are just too much fun! Yet, by the simple practice of simultaneously practicing open intelligence while engaging in whatever this activity is—sex, drinking alcohol, doing drugs, whatever it is— you will find that open intelligence is equally present in everything and that everything is indeed the dynamic energy of open intelligence. There isn't anything left out; it is all-inclusive and all-encompassing.

This is such a radically new way of approaching things that you had previously considered to be so shameful and unworthy. It is SO radical. In this decisive experience of complete resolution, you are incredibly enriched, potentiated and soothed all at once. Yet, there is no testimony to this that could be greater than your own decisive experience of it. Unless you have the direct experience of these afflictive data streams being completely resolved in open intelligence, what is written here will not mean anything.

Once we are introduced to open intelligence and our intelligence begins opening beyond this notion that everything is independently generated, we find a much more expansive way of looking at things. So, for example, if we are concerned about our "bad habits," this more expansive way of looking at things shows us that what we would typically call bad habits are not excluded from open intelligence. It does not mean that we simply give ourselves license to act out harmful behavior, but now when the thought of a bad habit comes up, we know that the thought and the bad habit are inseparable from open intelligence. From that recognition a skillful response can come.

We see flawless nature in the thought or the emotion or sensation or any other experience we're having right now, and we can really live as the stainless, flawless, exalted nature of whatever it is we are experiencing. By living in this way, an unparalleled vista of completely indescribable great illumination is opened up. The "perfect" and the "un-perfect" are both included.

The essence of the urge to seek relief in drinking or drugs is really the urge to ultimate freedom. When we don't really know where to look or what to look for, it comes out in other ways, such as, "Oh, I feel so miserable and I want some relief, so I am going to have a drink or smoke a joint." There are all kinds of things available today. All of these things, if they are troublesome in any way and they are things that you have wanted to change in any way, you have probably already tried to change them. But maybe you haven't been able to do so.

Recovery is very difficult if the person is being marginalized and seen as someone who does not fit in because they are doing such things as drinking excessive amounts of alcohol or using drugs. It is not going to work to put people down and to have them obsessively examine and then avoid all their shortcomings. By relying on the obviousness of open intelligence at all times, no matter how much one has drunk or used drugs, the obviousness of open intelligence is what will outshine this strong data. There is nothing quite as powerful for someone who has been addicted as the recognition of open intelligence inseparable from drunkenness or being stoned. The shine of open intelligence is seen to be in the vodka bottle and in the joint. *Everything* is recognized to be the liveliness of open intelligence.

No matter what is going on, the immediate benefit of open intelligence is already present. If we do not know what to say, if we do not know what to do, if we do not know what our next action will be, we can rely on that immediate benefit to inform it. Even if we need to take a few moments to decide what to say or how to act, that is perfectly okay. What is most important is that it is coming from the great benefit of open intelligence. It is complete dedication with every bit of ourselves, outshining, outshining, outshining all data streams

As the assurance in open intelligence grows and as open intelligence becomes more and more obvious in our lives, these strong afflictions will have less and less hold on us. The data streams that are still present become fainter, like planets and stars that are so evident at night becoming fainter after the rising of the morning sun. Soon too these lifelong issues are faint, and then gone. They are completely outshone by the light of open intelligence.

These days alcohol and other drugs are a great challenge for many people. When I was quite a bit younger, I overindulged in alcohol for a few years, and I can remember one particular example from that time. I was in my twenties, and I was a very active mother in the lives of my two sons. I was with them all the time or in some way guiding them, even if I was away from them. In this circumstance that I am describing, I happened to not be with them for a few weeks, and I was very sad. I was so sad in my heart, and I think I had never been that sad. I was in such pain and I did not know what to do.

Suddenly I thought, "There is a bottle of vodka in the liquor cabinet. Why not have some vodka?" So, I went and I had some vodka, and before long I was sound asleep. Well, you know what? A couple weeks later, it wasn't just one shot of vodka, it was like an automatic hand throwing back the drinks. Clearly I was attempting to forget. But I could see that it was leading me nowhere at all. So you see, I am not talking about alcoholism as something I have not experienced myself. In those times when I drank, I *really* liked to drink, and I *really* went after it. But did anything change? No. Was it a real remedy for anything? No. Did it cause physical and emotional upset? Yes.

I was never very much into drugs because I really wasn't in the crowd that was doing that sort of thing, but drinking I did. If I just think about alcohol for an instant now, it's so physically and mentally sickening for me.

And all along, an atmosphere of great cheer is right here! Cheer is our native language, and we all already have native fluency in the language of cheer through repeatedly returning to short moments. Then our native cheerfulness becomes increasingly obvious to us. I don't know about you, but I do know that I couldn't escape cheerfulness even though I tried! I have tried many things to be cheerless, such as drinking massive amounts of alcohol. Massive amounts of alcohol—what a cheerless endeavor that was!

When I decided that this was not a lifestyle that I wanted for myself, what I had to do was to rely on the sovereign authority of open intelligence. In that way, through relying on the sovereign authority, I could see that drinking alcohol was just of no interest to me. I could see that it was really open intelligence that was of interest to me. No matter what it is that is being outshone, it is in open intelligence that we realize the inseparability of the alcohol or the pot or the drugs from open intelligence.

I had to ask myself, "What is of the greatest benefit to all? Is it that I rely on open intelligence and that I will continue on with that course into the unimaginable future I see?" I didn't know quite what was to come, but I knew that it was something really great and that it had to do with communicating the spontaneous presence of open intelligence as the great reality of what we are. That completely outshone my impulse to drink alcohol, and I knew that I would never pick up again.

That decision for the benefit of all completely changed my life, because I suddenly was living in a new world in which I wanted to fully contribute to the benefit of all. That was my only interest and is my only interest now on a moment-to-moment basis. At some point, I could see that the shine of open intelligence was also in the vodka bottle. Everything shone forth as open intelligence in a way I cannot even describe. Open intelligence shone forth so dramatically, so radically and with such revolutionary zeal that my complete system of intelligence changed. The way I looked at everything completely changed, including the way I looked at alcohol. After that I never drank again. Never.

MAINTAINING OPEN INTELLIGENCE
WHILE TAKING THE NEXT DRINK

If you choose to drink, you can take a drink while taking short moments. Take a drink while taking short moments, and pretty soon you see that short moments is a lot more powerful than any antidote you could bring up to combat the drinking. You can be supported in exploring areas that you may have learned to be ashamed of or afraid of. Everything is equal and even; however, you may not yet deeply believe that. So, it's important, in a safe way, a way that will not harm you or anyone else, to really experientially and instinctively recognize that all is equal and even.

During the time that I over-enjoyed alcohol, whether I drank all day and all night, it didn't do anything to divide me out from open intelligence. However, it was just an incredible intrusion on my own energy and it was causing upset for myself and others, so I actively chose not to drink alcohol any longer. The alcohol wasn't something that was "bad" or something to be avoided in order to ramp up open intelligence's beneficial potency. In my own life, I needed to find out how I could be of greatest benefit to all. I needed to see how I could take the experience of over-enjoying alcohol and make it beneficial, not only to me, but to others. How could I use the empowerment of open intelligence to outshine resorting to alcohol?

No matter what it has been in my life, I would always look at that situation in terms of how it could be of benefit to all. Benefit orientation was the only way that I could keep from swinging on the gates of insanity and death. I found a short moment of open intelligence to be the greatest prayer, the greatest meditation and the greatest benefit-orientation for me and for everyone. If I was in a situation that required great resilience and fortitude, a short moment of open intelligence always gave me more beneficial potency with which to address the situation.

Open intelligence's beneficial potency continues to be of increasing profundity in my life, to the degree that I do not have a thought and emotion-based life anymore. In other words, I don't have thoughts and emotions that are plaguing me or that are cheering me up. That has all been outshone. I knew it was possible for me because I had seen it in others.

THE BEST TREATMENT PROGRAM

There are so many things today that are sold on the street that can kill people. Alcohol also can kill, and probably almost everyone knows a person who has died from alcoholism. Usually the cause of death is not the alcoholism itself; it is listed as something like cirrhosis of the liver, but cirrhosis of the liver is the last stage of alcoholism. Of course, there are other ways to die of drinking and using, and one of those ways is driving under the influence, or even walking under the influence. While walking under the influence the person might be much more likely to step in front of a car or do something else that is dangerous.

Alcohol abuse is an issue for many, many people around the world, and tens of millions of people, possibly hundreds of millions, face this challenge. In short moments we have a skillful means of treating alcoholism that has worked very effectively. Number one, alcoholism is normalized; it is seen to be just another data stream and not as a special shameful thing that needs to be separated out. In exaltation there is complete sobriety. What's going to work better, exaltation or shame?

Sobriety means soundness of mind, but in this case, it truly means *real* soundness of mind, which means no fear of drinking or using. Again, it doesn't mean not drinking or not using substances; it means soundness of mind. I know a lot of people, including myself, who have no fear of drinking or using, because we know what the true healing is, the final healing. We have gotten out of the kindergarten of trying to *not* drink, but then after having drunk or used, blaming and hating ourselves. It is no longer a matter of going in and out of situations thinking that we have to stay clean and sober the rest of our lives, but never being able to do it.

I've seen many people go in and out, and what matters more than anything else is that they are treated with loving-kindness. If we're lucky enough to be in a Teaching like this one, we could say that the greatest healing that can ever take place is in short moments, and the drug or alcohol that is desired is outshone by the short moments. There is no thinking about it, and if someone wants to take a drink or smoke a doobie occasionally, that can be done without doing it addictively. This is possible for anyone involved in the Teaching, and not only that, there are many examples in this community of people who have healed completely through these means.

If you are already in treatment or treatment centers—AA, NA and all the other programs based on the Twelve Steps—all these are the perfect match for the person who needs those things. If people are in this Teaching, it doesn't mean that they can't go to AA, NA, Al-Anon, Nar-Anon or any of the others. It just means that if you are using those forms of treatment, when it comes to things like belief in a higher power, you know what your higher power is. You can find your higher power in short moments. When it comes to ideas like healing shortcomings and asking a higher power to heal your shortcoming, you've found your higher power, and you're it! The short moments are more powerful than any drink or drug, and short moments of open intelligence are with you, whether you know it or not. Open intelligence *is* you, whether you know it or not.

PSYCHIATRIC MEDICATION

I've seen true miracles happen where people have had very severe psychiatric difficulties. It could be something like, for instance, severe bipolar disorder. Very often these are things that are inherited. We may also grow up in a family where bipolar disorder is the case. Today there are medications for bipolar disorder, for example, that can control the chemical imbalance, and if some kind of medication is needed, of course that's included too. So, it might be reassuring for some people to make that absolutely clear. Sometimes the person who has a psychiatric illness feels marginalized and left out of society. It's up to all of us to make everyone feel part of society, no matter who they are.

About twenty years ago there was an article in the respected Buddhist magazine, *Tricycle*. The magazine interviewed five Buddhist teachers and asked them about participants or disciples using psycho-active drugs, in other words, psychiatric medication and healing drugs that would balance the chemistry in the mind and body. This would be done so that the participants could pay attention in the Teachings and really take the Teachings in and bring them to reality within themselves.

Every single Buddhist teacher said that, yes, taking medication is appropriate. They said that if a person has a chemical imbalance, giving these medications is a form of skilful means. They're a viable method; they are wisdom essence. If the participants take the psychiatric medication, they have an opportunity that they wouldn't otherwise have. Different types of psychiatric medication can be a grounding or settling place for people and sometimes are the only way a person can be open to the Teachings. Especially the new medications are really profoundly able to support people, not only in having a normal life, but in not feeling drugged. Many people are able to feel real cheer for the first time in their lives, and they know that the effect will be ongoing and that it isn't going to suddenly disappear.

A Heart-Devoted Way of Looking at Addiction

There is a story that I have told many times before about looking for a solution to a question that had come up for me. I was downtown in the town in which I live, and there were a lot of inebriated people hanging out there. All of a sudden one of those inebriated men shouted something out spontaneously, and it so happened that what he said was exactly the answer to this question that I had had!

If I had seen him as someone who couldn't possibly have an answer for me because he was inebriated, I would have not listened. But I really feel a great heart connection with everyone, and I know the people who are inebriated are inebriated because they are searching. They are searching for what we are so lucky to have in this Teaching. That is a simple heart-devoted way of looking at it.

The way to help someone really break through the cycle of drug or alcohol addiction is to connect with the person directly and to not isolate the person out into a place where, if they are sober but still in fear of drinking, they need to constantly be looking at their shortcomings and trying to get rid of them. What is realized in open intelligence is that the easiest way to look at everything is as equal and even. Everything is equal and even. Whether a person is inebriated or sober, at the crucial juncture of both is open intelligence.

There are so many people who have stopped using and drinking because using and drinking have been seen as just another data stream. All the data whatsoever are equal and even, and to be able to see this is an incredible gift, and it is unwrapped and ready to go!

Instead of going off on your own roller coaster ride of affliction, stay close to what will really support you. Whatever is done, stay close, stay close, stay very, very close. Keep the lines of communication open. Everything is beautiful and free, but if it's hidden from view, it becomes emotional pollution.

SOMETIMES TROUBLE IS NEEDED!

For me, resting naturally and making a firm decision to commit to open intelligence wasn't just a matter of carrying on as before. It was a matter of going through some very challenging experiences, including the drinking that I have discussed at length. If someone refuses to see who they are and they are constantly putting themselves down and they can't see anything but what's wrong, not only with themselves but with all of life, maybe what they need is a nice shaking, and sometimes trouble is needed! Maybe what they need to hear is, "Wait, stop! Look at this! You're absolutely perfect as you already are. There's no need for you to act this way."

This reminds me of a story. I was living in a garage that had been converted into an art studio, and in the middle of this room was a large piece of plywood placed on sawhorses. This was my work table, and I was working on three-dimensional paintings that required a different approach than working on canvases that hang on a wall. I had laid out on the table all of these sculptures and paintings that I had been working on.

A woman came into my studio who was very, very upset and angry, and she went over to the table and with her arm extended she swept everything from my table onto the floor, and then she walked out into the yard. I walked out after her and gently took her by the shoulders and said, "Please don't do this to yourself!"

In seeing the absolute perfection, we are no longer able to do this to ourselves; we no longer put ourselves down in any way. We are able to totally thrive and get on with it. So, yes, sometimes trouble is needed. Circumstances just spontaneously happen, like the woman coming in and throwing all this stuff on the floor and me taking her and saying, "Don't do this to yourself." It was done without ever thinking about what I was going to say at all. I could go on and on with endless examples of this. Sometimes trouble needs to take place for the person in order to get the point across.

I know in my own situation that there was so much pressure on me to live a certain kind of lifestyle. I had everything that most people would want at a very early age—plenty of money, beautiful homes, acclaim, all of these things. Early on in my adult life I realized, "Wow, I've accomplished everything I hoped to accomplish in my whole life and I'm only in my twenties!" I went into a spiraling state of despair. I was seeing that all these things that I thought were going to be a source of life satisfaction and fulfillment weren't going to give me that at all. Then, many coincidences happened, some of which were extremely negative; yet, all of these were the power of great benefit in action.

All my life I had been taking short moments, but I had related them more to negative data streams, so that if a negative data stream came up, then I would take a short moment. One of my most profound realizations, out of the millions of realizations that I've had since then, was that this power of beneficial potency is present not only in negative data streams, but it is the essence and the only reality of *all* data streams, whether they're negative, positive or neutral.

To me that was a huge opening and a great relief, because I had been subtly counting on these positive data streams to hold me up. If I felt positive about my direction and life circumstance, then I felt better about things. But I reached the point where I saw that this was fallacious. It was completely untrue, and it really wasn't aligned with my core beliefs. In order to create complete alignment with my core beliefs, I had to be certain that the short moments were obvious in all circumstances.

This power of great benefit that I experienced in myself was also in everyone else I met, read about, envisioned or thought about.

Everyone I knew was the power of great benefit, so that was very clear to me. This opening within each of us, including me, has to be something that is wanted above all else. If I had anything to communicate to you, it would be that: it is that we must be committed to open intelligence above all else. That commitment must encompass all else.

QUESTION AND ANSWER

Q. You have spoken about the fact that many people come to a teaching like this one because of previous problems with drugs and alcohol. Well, here I am! I so very much appreciate your discussion of this in such an open and compassionate way, so thank you so much for that. I would so much appreciate anything else you could contribute on this very important subject for me.

Ziji Rinpoche: One of the great stories from Tibetan history is the story of Milarepa, who was a very powerful human being who had been a black magician. He had all these relatives he hated, thirty-eight of them, and they had been invited to come to a celebration at a house. They all went and through his powers of black magic he made the house collapse, which killed all the people in it. All of his hated relatives were gone, but then he thought, "Oh no, what have I done?"

Even though he was very learned and knew all the Teachings, he went to a very great teacher and said, "I've done all these things. I want you to give me Teachings so I'll never do anything like that again." His teacher said nothing, absolutely nothing. Why? Because Milarepa had to make direct changes in his way of being before he could get any Teachings. It was years before the teacher, Marpa, ever uttered a word to him other than having him do things that seemed totally crazy.

His teacher had him build many buildings and then tear them down. Then the teacher had him build even more buildings and tear them down, and later build more buildings and tear them down. This occurred after about twenty years of knowing his teacher, and then the teacher finally began to give Milarepa the Teachings, even though in a way the teacher had been giving him instruction all along. But Milarepa was a difficult case, because he felt he wasn't getting enough, so he would go to his teacher's wife and say, "Give me some key points, give me some pith instructions," and she would say, "Go back to Marpa. You're not getting anything from me."

With the skillful guidance of Marpa, Milarepa did in fact come to the highest realization, and in doing so he could see that the horrific hell that he seemed to have created through his powers of black magic was in fact the bright expanse of spontaneous reality. Through that recognition he became one of the greatest wisdom masters to ever live. Thus the adage: "The greater the affliction, the greater the wisdom." The greater the affliction, the greater is the beneficial potency. Did that give him a license to go out again and murder anyone he wanted to? No, not at all. He was rendered into spontaneous humility.

If you end up in this Teaching somehow and you have been a drug addict or an alcoholic, and if alcohol and drugs are the fallback way of making negative states into positive states for you, then I'll give you a quick little lesson here. I know for sure that there are quite a few who like to toke up or have a few drinks or whatever else it may be. If your point in doing so is to avoid any kind of data stream that seems to be pouring down all over you, please don't start thinking, "Oh yikes. I know what I'm doing is wrong. This is bad. I shouldn't be doing it. This doesn't have anything to do with beneficial potency, so I'm automatically out of the in-group of beneficial potency."

So, here are a few tips and instructions. While imbibing or throwing a few drinks back, maintain beneficial potency as the only reality there is, and what is discovered is that there is no distinction to be found. Even Milarepa, the murderer of thirty-eight of his relatives, found that there is no distinction, and he became one of the greatest Rinpoches to ever live. Dzogchen is all-inclusive. Pure Dzogchen has no comment about conduct. Conduct arises as it does and it self-releases. In this self-release, we feel deeper and more increasing loving energy. This is just so beautiful and so perfect.

Many people who like to use drugs or alcohol as a fallback have come to cease using them as fallbacks naturally and gradually, while others have continued on. However it may be for you, I'm just recommending the pith instruction of living as spontaneous reality while doing whatever it is you're doing.

It may be that whatever it is you're doing, you've been into it for a long time, and it seems like it's impossible to recognize complete relaxation in doing it. Well, you don't have to think of it in terms of it being a lifetime task. Think about it as complete relaxation just for a moment, one moment at a time. Please just try one moment at a time. Others have reported to me, and I also find it in my own experience, that one moment at a time of spontaneous reality is much more attractive than trying to create some kind of contrived reality. I want to emphasize the absolute futility in trying to make up reality. Trying to create positive states, trying to avoid negative states, trying to be in any certain kind of way, all of this is futile.

It can be stated quite simply: everything whatsoever is spontaneous vibrancy of total reality amped up to its highest degree of beneficial potency. It is that and nothing else. By entering into and living as that, it becomes obvious that there is indivisibility. This recognition only happens through our own decisive lived experience, here-and-now. It's not really even an experience; it's the living of reality *as it is*.

RESTING AS THE
POWERS OF GREAT BENEFIT

CHAPTER TWENTY

When we meet someone who shows evidence of this immense energy and beneficial power and is not bound by self-identification, we can see a blazing example of what we ourselves truly are. At the same time, we may project our own beneficial potency onto that person and think, "Wow! That person is really something great. When I'm around them I really feel wide open, and these elevated feelings are caused by them." However, this is really only a recognition in another of something we have always been in ourselves.

When we are introduced to open intelligence, it is realized that the mind has completely opened up to its inexhaustible nature. Even if we realize this only for an instant, regardless, we have gone in that instant from thinking that our mind is locked inside a skin-suit to a mind that has opened up into a vast expanse that we cannot really name or grasp. The way that we perceive things changes; we can no longer trace the source of our seeing to organs like the eyes or the brain, and we cannot trace our thoughts and sensations to supposed sources like a "thinker." We know then who we are, and the thinker ain't it!

open spaciousness / emptiness / awareness

Phrases such as "vast expanse" or "inexhaustible nature" may seem remote and not relevant to us at this moment, but our decisive experience and instinctive recognition of the inexhaustibility of our beneficial potencies will grow and grow. The first moment of immediate benefit can clear up all kinds of data streams we have been running. The more familiar we are with the instinctive recognition of open intelligence, the more all kinds of data streams that were troublesome and conflictual become less interesting for us, which includes the data stream that we are not recognizing open intelligence! It is important to know that whether there is recognition or non-recognition of open intelligence, both the recognition and the non-recognition are sourced in open intelligence, and it is always a big laugh when that is seen!

We can release ourselves from the perception of being trapped inside a skin line and the need to be captured by data streams. We let the data streams be as they will; we let the senses be as they will; we let the bodily sensations be as they will. All these are data streams within open intelligence's beneficial potency and are not the reality of who we are. We could give open intelligence lots of names, even if it is in fact something unspeakable, but if we were to give it one name, that name would be "benefit." Open intelligence is always and immediately beneficial.

THE DIRECT REALIZATION WITHIN OURSELVES

Everything rests in the blissful relaxation of open intelligence. Initially in this process there may be a sort of artificial focus: "Oh, there's a thought, and here comes a space between thoughts, and now there's another thought," but even that little bit of insight gives some hint of the complete shining forth within open intelligence. That fixed attentiveness eventually moves into complete perceptual openness and freedom in immediate perception—the simultaneous release upon inception in the great wisdom-light outshining everything.

We are being introduced to the reality of our identity. Our identity is always already in place; it is always already concluded and is just something we have not recognized. But now we are starting to comprehend, recognize and realize open intelligence as our only identity. Radical reality—open intelligence—is like a mirror reflecting images. All images positive, negative and neutral are an indivisible vast expanse of equalness and evenness, just as the surface of a mirror is indivisible. In that sense, we too are a mirror

289

which shines forth all the images, no matter what they are. The immense energy and beneficial power that are our reality are set free.

When we meet someone who shows evidence of this immense energy and beneficial power and is not bound by self-identification, we can see a blazing example of what we ourselves truly are. At the same time, we may project our own beneficial potency onto that person and think, "Wow! That person is really something great. When I'm around them I really feel wide open, and these elevated feelings are caused by them." However, this is really only a recognition in another person of something we have always been in ourselves. Ultimately, the way that we recognize open intelligence is through the direct realization *within ourselves*. Through this direct realization within ourselves, we provide ourselves immediate benefit, and we do so by doing nothing.

There is a sweet, soft spot of immediate benefit that we find within ourselves that is always present, always available and always on. It is here that we begin to feel dignity and esteem, and when we begin to feel dignity and esteem, we become very powerful decision-makers. It is very easy then for us to choose where we want to be, who we want to be with and why we want to be there, and we know all these things spontaneously and instantaneously.

This is the beginning of the flourishing of our strengths, gifts and talents. No matter how talented we have been in the past and no matter what our strengths and gifts have been, their expression increases beyond anything that could have been imagined before. We come to instinctively comprehend that the expanse of mind is in reality our true identity. The vastness of mind is beginningless beginning and endless end, and this is the way it actually is. We rest naturally in the great expanse of mind without seeking anything.

THE BENEFIT OF ALL BECOMES A PRIORITY

Through the introduction to open intelligence, the benefit of all will naturally and spontaneously become a priority without cultivating it or doing anything. There is no other way to be aware of others than to first be aware of ourselves as we truly are, and to be purely beneficial requires first being purely beneficial to ourselves.

In the beginning it may start out as, "Well, to be honest, I am really only interested in my own benefit," yet, very naturally, it can be that an impulse to be of benefit to all will gradually emerge. We test in our own experience to see whether or not open intelligence has something to offer us, and as we gain more confidence in it, we become really aware of ourselves as we really are. By virtue of being aware of ourselves, we become aware of others.

We give ourselves the great gift of not avoiding or excluding anything and of welcoming any thought, feeling, experience into our lives and being willing to be with it completely. This is the easy way. Through giving ourselves the right not to be a victim of our data, more and more we have a glowing sense of immediate benefit. We see ourselves as immediately beneficial, no matter where we are. We do not have to do anything to be immediately beneficial, because we already are immediately beneficial.

As bearers of beneficial potency, our attention is no longer wrapped up in, "Oh, my aches and pains, my emotional drama, my broken heart." Instead, these thoughts and emotions are seen to be aflame with the reality of beneficial potency. They burst forth as they really are with beneficial reality and spontaneous wisdom to spread this treasured ancient message that is alive in all cultures and which is ready to become obvious.

Through the power of the Four Mainstays we come to see that the reality of everyone, even if they are using a reified intelligence operating system, is at the basis still pure benefit. It does not mean that it isn't pure benefit because they are choosing reified intelligence; in fact, the only reality anyone has is pure benefit. Anyone who practices open intelligence knows that everyone has some kind of worldview. In Dzogchen, we have the open-intelligence view, and part of that is to do no harm to others who do not want to participate in Dzogchen.

Many of us have lacked an education in the nature of mind, body, speech, qualities and activities, and we have been disempowered by things that have been said to us or done to us. We have taken these on in certain ways in describing a reality that does not exist; however, that in no way lessens the fact that we have always been pure benefit just as we are.

Beneficial potency is intrinsic in all people, no matter who they are or what they are doing. So, they could be doing something really wonderful for the world or they could be desolate, isolated, disenfranchised, marginalized and harmful; nevertheless, everyone and everything shines from within with great benefit and exaltation. We do not have to *try* to be beneficial; as open intelligence we are naturally beneficial.

Mind, speech and body are expressions of open intelligence's beneficial potencies; thus, we carry the message of open intelligence. The demonstration of open intelligence is great benefit. There is no way to get around it; it just is the reality in every moment. When we realize this for ourselves, we want to share with other people that the immediate benefit we have always sought is found right here within ourselves, no matter what we are thinking, saying or doing. It is the fuel and fire of the thinking, saying and doing.

We could really try hard to cultivate positive traits, such as compassion, but when immediate benefit is already-

[Handwritten margin notes: "I struggle with this, especially in 2023 U.S.A."]

accomplished and completely alive in us, what would be the necessity to cultivate traits like compassion? As benefit is truly already-accomplished, isn't it better to just recognize that? To cultivate compassion requires a person to have certain data streams at certain times, and so mind, speech, body, qualities and activities become very contrived, rather than being spontaneously appropriate to time, place, circumstance and result.

What a marvel it is to live with the burning desire to benefit all! We know how to have immediate benefit in the moment, and when we find immediate benefit within ourselves, everything we do as a human society collectively is fueled and fired by that immediate benefit. When we have a group of friends all over the world who live with the burning desire to benefit all, we can feel even more confident about choosing to live that way ourselves. It is always nice to have some pals in the neighborhood, no matter how large the neighborhood is!

As the recognition of beneficial potency takes over, the whole world of reification is going to relax into its reality. There are going to be great openings and many, many more people will be reached and forever supported to spread their wisdom wings and fly on high. Just as there was a special way each of us was reached, there are many other ways to reach many more people.

STRENGTHS, GIFTS AND TALENTS

There is no way to measure the extent of the activity for the benefit of all. It is like pure space—without beginning or end, and inexhaustible. With that capability in ourselves, we have the qualities and activities to benefit everyone and everything in accord with the way they need to be benefitted. That is very powerful. Again, it isn't something big out there in the future; it is right here in this moment. We have the power to benefit ourselves, and in that power to benefit ourselves we have the power to benefit others.

Access is gained to perfect knowledge, and abilities not known before become commonplace. As the reality of open intelligence's beneficial potencies become clear, we have inestimable capability and activity. It may at first seem daunting that we have so much power and capability. The fact that it is only carried out in the moment gives a different perspective; it is the intimate reality of the here-and-now, rather than being something so huge that it cannot really be understood. We have capability and beneficial potency in this very moment, and this is demonstrated by our own discernment, insight, clarity and other skillful means in each and every moment.

When we begin to settle into open intelligence, we put on a new pair of glasses, as it were. We have been wearing glasses that have made the world look one way, and now we put on new glasses and the world looks another way. We come to see that in our settled-ness and effortless disposition is tremendous beneficial potency. All of the knowledge we hold is for the benefit of all. Every aspect of us—our mind, speech, body, qualities and activities—is intended and purposed for the benefit of all. We each have particular strengths, gifts and talents, and the more that we are able to offer them in an uncontrived way, the more flourishing and life satisfaction we will have.

One of the ways that our talents manifest is in terms of what we really, really like to do and what we feel very passionate about, and our trainer can help us identify what that is. It is very important to identify what we are most passionate about and to choose which talents to concentrate on; otherwise, there could be all kinds of interests spread out everywhere. It would be like drilling many different wells rather than just drilling one well. The question always has to be, "What is it among my many strengths, gifts and talents that will be of most benefit to all?"

We build trust in the reality of our own open intelligence, and so too we build trust in knowing that we can respond skillfully to each time, place and circumstance without even thinking about it at all. We build great assurance in our capabilities, and we know for certain that no matter what life brings, our responsiveness will be right on target. It is just wonderful to be so very free that everything can be directly encountered effortlessly, and everyone and everything can be openly loved.

We relish the gift of reality which is now freely aroused, and we are in each moment discovering our beneficial potency anew and allowing this gift to be naturally and impartially shared with everyone. We cherish each gesture of benefit, all at once realizing our increasing empowerment and feeling humbled by the actual grandeur of open intelligence displayed in, of, as and through us. The commitment is to offer one hundred percent of our strengths, gifts and talents to benefit. Everything is taken over by the pure transmission of open intelligence. The current moment is a splendid surprise, and we look again and again at everything with the same eye of discerning open intelligence.

OUTSHINING

Very early in the morning just before sunrise we can still see a few planets and stars twinkling in the darkened sky. But eventually with the light of the day, none of those planets and stars can be seen anymore, and everything that was visible during the night disappears from view. It is the same way with the data streams that are outshone by open intelligence. Simply by acknowledging open intelligence over and over again, we experience the outshining of data streams. In relying on open intelligence and in letting everything be *as it is*, we come to a point where everything is outshone. Eventually there is a spontaneous and natural commitment to outshine all data and to illuminate their beneficial potency.

To show up in every moment with openness and with no preconceived notions reveals the profound meaning of supreme benefit, but it is supreme benefit that is present in whatever is appearing. Whatever appears is shining forth in that particular way, and whatever quality and activity that is needed just comes forth. The "outshining of data" means that instead of seeing data as something wrong or negative, we now see data as a bright and shining sun of capacity and capability.

Within the great outshining we see that we have been given a very special key, and it opens the door to skillful means, insight, discernment, flourishing and benefit. We may have never dreamt these things possible, and now they are ours. What is more, they do not stay static; they grow and grow and grow. All kinds of possibilities appear and all kinds of experiences in life come about that one could not ever imagine having, and all of this is due to the unfolding of open intelligence.

You shine forth all the data streams as open intelligence and simultaneously outshine them. You shine yourself forth as open intelligence, and in the very instant that you shine forth, all is outshone. The "you" being spoken about here is not a person. There is no "you" getting open intelligence; rather, it is open intelligence shining forth *as* open intelligence.

BEYOND GOOD AND BAD

All of the descriptions of right and wrong or good and evil and the attempt to attain good in order to overcome evil, where has that gotten us? It has gotten us nowhere, with people fighting within themselves and with each other. It starts with the inner kind of war where we are beating ourselves up because we have negative data in conflict with positive data, and we are trying to accumulate positive data and get rid of the negative data. Then that war is projected outside into families, communities, countries and into the whole world.

There is no solution to be found in attempting to construct systems based on good and evil, right and wrong. What we need is a more comprehensive intelligence that subsumes all the current intelligences that have been utilized, and this more comprehensive intelligence is the beneficial potency of open intelligence. Open intelligence, rather than being based on accumulation of knowledge, is based on beneficial potency in exact and specific response to time, place and circumstance and has as its result the benefit of all.

The power source of illuminated body, speech, mind, and beneficial activities is a purely beneficial power source, so there isn't a "good guy" and a "bad guy." It is really important to know that thinking in terms of opposites like good and evil is an outdated mode of judgment. It may take us a little while to adjust to this; however, concepts like good and evil are irrational and illogical and should be outshone. Even if these concepts have been around for thousands of years, they have never been true. They were not really reality, and what we are interested in here is reality.

MANY REALIZATIONS

We hear words such as "realization" or "wisdom" and we may ask, "Is realization or wisdom something a particular someone like me can have?" Real wisdom isn't a thing, and it isn't something that can be cultivated. Wisdom comes about only through resting as the reality of who we are. Wisdom is spontaneous and is perfectly related to time, place, circumstance and the result of benefit. We can just set aside all the concepts we have about how to realize wisdom, because all we have is this brilliant moment. Yes, this brilliant short moment is all we have.

In always-on open intelligence, there isn't the constant mental activity of self-centered thinking about data streams. Instead, there is a great openness to everything and to the spontaneous natural desire everyone has to be of benefit to all. If one wants to speak about "enlightenment," real enlightenment is the deep desire in every second of one's life to spontaneously benefit all. So, without ever thinking about it, all of one's thoughts, emotions, sensations and experiences are all about the benefit of all. It is not like you are leaving yourself out; you are part of "all," so you are benefitted too!

This is the realization that people are talking about when they talk about enlightenment. The desire for enlightenment is placed in its proper perspective. Sanskrit is a language that has a word for the desire that overcomes all desire, and this word is bodhicitta. This is a word worthy of reflection, because when people talk about enlightenment, most people really have no idea what enlightenment is. Real, true enlightenment is bodhicitta—the deep desire in every second of one's life to spontaneously benefit all.

From the perspective of Dzogchen, the idea "I want to become enlightened for myself" is a very small space to live from. One could say that such an idea of becoming enlightened for oneself is realization–driven, meaning that one wants a certain final realization for oneself and this is what is being aspired to. However, in open intelligence there are many, many realizations. Realizations never come to an end! So, we can let go of this drive for a final realization; we let it be *as it is,* and we don't need to try to hang on to the realizations that come along the way. Rather, we can relax and know that we will have many more to come throughout our life of benefit.

If there is a realization of anything, it is the realization of the spontaneous desire to be of benefit to all. The starting point is recognizing the nature of our own mind, and we see how much that recognition benefits us as a so-called individual. It benefits us so greatly that we naturally want to share it with others. By doing so we become interactive with other intelligences we did not even know about when we were living from an ordinary state of mind. To rely on open intelligence *as it is* as our true body, our true mind and the true source of our speech, qualities and activities allows us to open up and burst forth, not only as individuals, but as a thriving human society and a society of all intelligences everywhere.

QUESTION AND ANSWER

Q. I feel very moved to wholeheartedly and fully contribute to the benefit of all in the way that you have described, but I really feel a lot of fear about leaving what is familiar to me and jumping into this one hundred percent. I would love to get some support in dealing with these fears, and not just hypothetically, but through examples that come from practical experience.

Ziji Rinpoche: I can say that in my own life there were many decisions I had to make along the way in order to be able to speak with confidence about these things. It didn't just all come about by happenstance. In my earlier life as a young woman everything had been set up for me—the money, the prestige and so many other things—if I would just go along with what others were doing. But I said, "No, I will not go that way." I decided I was only going to devote my life to teaching open intelligence and I would not get distracted by anything else, no matter what the prevailing mindset was.

I had many people who discouraged me from making the choices that I made. My own parents, my brothers and sisters and many of my friends encouraged me to go in other ways, but I knew that I could not do what they were suggesting and still live as a sane and happy person. So, I did not take that road.

Nothing was excluded and everything was included. I saw my participation in this Teaching as inclusive of the relationship with family and friends, but in terms of the expenditure of my time, energy and attention, I saw that the shining forth of the Teaching would be the greatest legacy I could leave to my children, my grandchildren, my family in general and to the world. After all, this is the world they and their children will live in long after I'm gone.

I felt that if I went to the end of my life as the only one making the choice to rest as the powers of great benefit, I knew that I could still hold my head high. But I'm really lucky in this way, because there is now a huge group of people who are interested in the same things I am interested in and who are supporting the effort to render benefit to all. The more the merrier; it's easier to feel yourself supported and encouraged when you're among many.

I would invite you to take it all the way in terms of your own passionate interests, despite people saying, "You can't do it. You're wrong. Get a real job, save some money, buy a house, become financially secure, give up on this crazy idea." I know that many people have heard these same things that I used to hear. By "taking it all the way," I mean pushing along no matter what comes up. We identify strengths, gifts and talents in ourselves and allow for the possibility of a dream that was unimaginable before. It may be something that appears impossible to do now because it's so big and world-changing. If anything seems to be an obstacle, you look it right in the face and say, "Nothing is impossible for me," and take it all the way. Yes, that would be the life that I would recommend—taking it all the way!

Part Six

THE FLOURISHING OF RECOGNITION

EDUCATION IN THE NATURE OF MIND

CHAPTER TWENTY-ONE

True education in the nature of mind provides the knowledge that is the basis of all other knowledge. Without fluency in this fundamental knowledge, all other knowledge is inadequate. There is nothing that is needed more at this point in history than education in the nature of mind, and the only way to change the momentum of the way the mind is being used on a global level is through this education.

Throughout human history there have been attempts to instruct people in their true nature, and we could call these attempts to describe and instruct in one's essential nature "education in the nature of mind." Seen in that way, we could say that people have been seeking an education in the nature of mind in many places and over many periods of time, but it has often been within a specific cultural context based on a specific time, place and circumstance. Some cultures have been quite committed to education in the nature of mind, yet there have been greatly disabling factors such as cultural biases or even superstition that kept that education from being used in a fully comprehensive way.

It is due to the *lack* of education that people are not clear about their true nature. Most education has been directed towards disempowering ideas about what human nature is, and we have been suffering from a gross incompetency and lack of fluency in this crucial area of life. We have as a result been placed in a position where we are completely out of alignment with reality. For most of the world's people, the way of being, the "mind" as it were, that is needed for the necessary innovations of this particular time period is not the mind that is being used. There is nothing that is needed more at this point in history than education in the nature of mind, and the only way to change the momentum of the way the mind is being used on a global level is through this education. What a great fortune it is to have the Dzogchen Teaching to help provide this education.

It is very important to realize that "mind" isn't some little closed-up thing inside a body. In addition, we need to see that the things that we thought were true about mind were in fact based on completely false assumptions. Mind is a vast frontier, an open intelligence, pure and illuminated like a cloudless sky. We have been using a very primitive intelligence in assuming that we are only a body and a mind within a skin line, when in fact we are a vast, comprehensive, brilliant and inexhaustible intelligence that is unparalleled.

THE NEED FOR EDUCATION IN THE NATURE OF MIND

It is quite remarkable that education in the nature of mind as a system could remain almost completely uninvestigated or only undertaken in a very abstract way. Training in the nature of mind has often been done on a level of abstraction, meaning that philosophical levels of abstraction have been applied to understanding the nature of mind. To use levels of abstraction that are merely intellectual only leads to more levels of abstraction, and if there is only abstraction, there is no comprehensive map for fostering a true education in open-ended knowledge and benefit creation.

Until some decades ago there was no mass transportation around the world and no telecommunications or other extensive communication systems. Distinct ethnic cultures were divided or isolated from the other, and the circumstances were not conducive to education in the nature of mind for a global audience. However, we do not live in the same kind of culture that was present long ago.

Society has now changed in so many incredible ways, and due in large measure to the worldwide reach of the internet and telecommunications, cultural barriers are dissolving. More and more we truly see ourselves as one global community, and the same cultural barriers no longer apply. In this way, the Dzogchen Teachings are now being presented to a global audience that is reachable through these new telecommunication technologies.

We have lacked true education in this crucial area for so long. There isn't anything amiss with anybody and no one did anything wrong; it is just that up until now we did not know of any possibility for this education. But now the opportunity *is* available. Humans have been denied an education in this way due to a multitude of factors, but rather than getting caught up in the reasons, it is best to simply start with the admission that we have little or no education in the nature of mind. Then we carry on from there as we develop and refine the education that is needed.

True education in the nature of mind provides the knowledge that is the basis of all other knowledge. Without fluency in this fundamental knowledge, all other knowledge is inadequate. We need to become very humble; we need to admit to our lack of education here. We need to admit that our lives have been driven by hope and fear and that we have harbored deep anger, hatred, desire, pride, arrogance, and jealousy and envy. We have to see that we have believed in data streams and that we have refused to let go of them. However, even if we have had a lifetime of being trained up to believe in the value of these things, with a true education we can easily train ourselves to no longer believe in them.

We have taken a trip on a very long road, and at the beginning of the trip there were two roads to choose, and we chose the road of reification that took us to where we are presently. So now we can choose another road. We are so fortunate that we have now been introduced to the nature of intelligence and to Dzogchen, and we can make the change from reified intelligence to full reliance on open intelligence. In the near future there will be people who will never have known what it was like to have lived lives based on reified intelligence. In this present generation, we are the privileged group to have "before and after reification"!

THE INTRODUCTION TO THE NATURE OF MIND

When we are introduced to open intelligence, mind is opened up to its inexhaustible and blissful nature. To be introduced to the nature of mind is very easy, because there is only one open intelligence and there is only one mind. If we stop thinking just for an instant and have no thought at all, there is only alertness, clarity and cognizance with no need to name it anything. That is open intelligence—alert, clear cognizance—the nature of mind. Open intelligence is wild and free, and we are inexhaustible intelligent agents of open intelligence.

Each of us can see how we were educated to think about ourselves, as being basically flawed and needing to change, whether it related to ideas we learned in school, in our family or in society at large. These ideas have been a part of human culture for thousands of years, and not only that, they have become pervasive. These ideas that have been passed down to us are implemented through us over and over again, without our even knowing most of the time that we actually have a choice about the way our mind thinks, acts and works. However, we *do* have a choice, a choice that is an imperative for each one of us to take up.

When we let everything be *as it is*, we find out what the mind really is. We come to see that we are exalted and flawless exactly as we are. We see as well that we are pure benefit and that we hold the knowledge of the universe in a usable way. Education in this way is a profound gift to everyone, young and old. The younger we are, the less we will have of a lifetime of believing in data. Regardless of age, we all have the potency of mind, speech, body, qualities and activities to create an entirely beneficial world. Through empowering the nature of mind, our whole life changes completely.

This education is the greatest natural resource. The greatest of all freedoms, the most basic of all human rights and the most civil right is in the education in mind. It is a way for people to come together in the benefit of all. It does not say one cannot be a Catholic, a Jew, a Muslim or whatever it may be. Education in the nature of mind is based on unity for the benefit of all, and this vantage completely takes away the basis for all the conflicts occurring today that are fueled and flamed by religious differences.

Whatever the state of the body or of the psychological entity generally called "mind," we can always count on the mind—open intelligence—that is the source of everything. We can rely on this mind for full potency, no matter what our situation is. The body and mind as generally perceived are very fleeting, and as our open-intelligence power increases we see how impermanent the body-mind is. The body-mind does not have a nature independent of open intelligence, and in leaving mirage-like reified existence *as it is* while realizing the vast expanse of mind, we come to instinctively comprehend that the vast mind of open intelligence is in reality our true essence. Only through the instinctive recognition that our true mind, speech, body qualities and activities belong to open intelligence are we able to really see things as they truly are.

A STANDARDIZED SOLUTION

A very important point is that education in the nature of mind is a standardized solution for the world's people, with no one excluded. There could be all kinds of approaches, cultural traditions and teachings, but now is the time where everyone can come together in a standardized education in the nature of mind.

306

The confusion and debate over terms and methods is put to rest in a very easy and straightforward way. The standardized education is obviously necessary for our species, both in an educational and an evolutionary way.

Why need it be a "standardized" education? "Standardized" may seem to imply stiff, inflexible or unyielding to change, but that is not what is meant here. An education that is standardized is one that is ever evolving and responsive, and at the same time one that includes a universalized language that is not derived from a language and culture separate from other cultures. Standardized education really means giving everyone in the world a common language with which to speak about open intelligence.

Prior to this time, teachings had different approaches and ways of speaking because they had different cultural reference points, but more and more the lines setting nations and cultures apart are being blurred. National, cultural and racial distinctions are disappearing. As a result, we are going through a radical and profound change in the world. This is an enormous turning point for human society, like a great ship turning at sea. When the ship turns, everyone on the ship also turns, whether they are ready or not. This is what is occurring right now.

If everyone had to have their own unique or original language, there would be no easy and understandable way to communicate things. In important fields of study such as physics, chemistry, music, medicine and so many others, there is a standardized language and approach that is used, and this allows people who are engaged in that field to have a common terminology and understanding so that they can talk to each other in a clear and specific way.

In a similar way, to have a standardized education with its precise language is pivotal and absolutely essential. A standardized education in the nature of mind needs to be the foundation, the infrastructure and the framework for all knowledge and all fields.

A universalized form of language is used, and due to that, when people speak with one other, they actually have a basis for understanding. We can relate to one another in a clear way, rather than through all kinds of conceptual frameworks and filters that might blur our vision. Once the nature of mind is directly addressed, human society spontaneously changes in and of itself.

There have been certain things that were not obvious at first but which later became obvious, such as the discovery of gravity or that the Earth is round and that it revolves around the sun. Once they were pointed out, they were so totally obvious that they could not be missed. We are at a point where the same thing is true with the standardized solution to education. It is such an obvious realization which was somehow missed before, just like these other things were missed at first, but now that it has been identified so evidently, its necessity is obvious and clear.

THE NATURAL RESULTS OF EDUCATION IN THE NATURE OF MIND

It is time to get out there and speak up about the need for this education. With the furtherance of Dzogchen, the educational tools that are needed are in place, and we will continue to upgrade and update as we go along. We as a human community have entered into a global collaboration of people everywhere who want to understand the nature of mind and want to do so through a common terminology.

Early adopters and innovators have emerged around the world, and this creates a strong base, but now it is time to go into the mainstream. Between the time of the adoption by innovators and early adopters until it is adopted by the mainstream, there is a sort of gap to be crossed. The growth in this education may at first track along a traditional bell curve: first are the early adopters and innovators, then the mainstream forms a big part of the bell curve, and then the other part is the people who have not yet seen the evidence.

[handwritten: 100th Monkey time]

[handwritten: ← ie, the folks who aren't ready for the ship to turn.]

308

Once they have been introduced to it, many of the world's people will be willing to adopt the education, and the shape of the bell curve is going to change. It will be shaped more like a hockey stick, with the line of increased participation moving up and up and up on the curve. There will be many included because it will be so obvious.

In science and technology and in other areas of advancement, we have many questions we cannot answer and places we cannot go because the people involved there have reached the limit of what they know. They have bumped up against a glass ceiling because they are looking outside at a world made up only of subjects and objects. It has not occurred to many of them to turn to themselves and fully and completely educate themselves in the nature of their own mind and to train it up to full beneficial potency.

Their intelligence is limited to putting together different data sets in order to create knowledge, and they do not know about open-ended knowledge creation and open-ended benefit creation. They may be expounding prolifically on all kinds of fantastic ideas and writing incredible scholarly papers; however, the point has come where this approach has reached its limit. Until we understand our own intelligence to be open intelligence, and until we have an instinctive recognition of the power and beneficial potency of open intelligence, and understand that instinctively in relation to our own experience rather than merely intellectually, we will not be able to go beyond where we are right now. We need to become pioneers of an inexhaustible frontier.

There are many people exemplifying the effects of this Teaching, and they are like shining beacons, the ready and willing evidence of education in the nature of mind. The best example of the benefits of relying on open intelligence is the results in all the people who are practicing it! These people are evidence of the results, and other people come and see that result and become interested through that example. If people can be shown an educational methodology that actually has a result, then they will be very interested.

A MASSIVE SPREAD

Many of us may have tried many different approaches before we find one that really works, and what we have been looking for is an approach that has definitive results. We want to see the actual benefits; we want to see people who are recognizing their strengths, gifts and talents and who are able to demonstrate them. This is key, because when we see other people demonstrating the immensity of all-accomplishing activity, we know that it is possible for us too. This is a profound basis for the actual introduction to the nature of mind to take place.

This educational training cannot be suppressed. It has a massive spread, even in countries that have internet censorship. It isn't as though the proverbial "they" can go and round up everyone who is practicing education in the nature of mind; that would be impossible to do. The other part of it is that no one can ever deny us the right to this education, because it is the most basic of all human rights and can never be taken away.

One of the important factors is that people can see much more clearly what they want in their life and why they want it. It does not need to be a big confused mess any longer, where life is ruled by data streams that are out of control. It is a whole new way of life. With a comprehensive scope of mind, we are empowered and enabled to do things that could never be done otherwise. This applies to everything, whether it is buying a house, taking a job, educating a child or whatever it might be. Once the introduction to the nature of mind is made, there is no way to escape it, because we know who we are.

We are empowered in ever new ways, and the ways that we are empowered are unique to each of us. The full engagement of our talents is so wonderfully immense when we are able to see them flourish. We come to see that we are able to create at a level we never dreamt possible and with an empowerment we never dreamt possible. Whatever we feel most moved to contribute in terms of our strengths, gifts and talents, we honor that. We honor that as the great revelation and discovery of open intelligence in our own life and how it can be of most benefit.

QUESTION AND ANSWER

Q. I have studied many philosophies and read many philosophers, and now I am here learning from you. In what way, would you say, is your philosophy the same or different from other philosophies one might study?

Ziji Rinpoche: I grew up as a Catholic, and when I read all the stories of the saints lying on a bed of nails or wearing sack cloth and ashes, I knew that wasn't my idea of what a loving Creator required. That isn't what perfect love is; it's just impossible that perfect love would ask such things of anyone. I didn't really feel at that time or later that I had a choice about adopting a conventional lifestyle versus a lifestyle of benefit to all. I felt that if I adopted a conventional lifestyle I would go crazy, and that I really needed to go to any lengths to keep open intelligence in place, even though I had no idea what it was, other than love. I thought of God or open intelligence as love, and I found that love only in complete relaxation.

I was very interested in philosophy, and it was natural to me because I had grown up being very familiar with the philosophy of the Catholic Church. As I got older I wanted to hear philosophies from all kinds of different countries. When I was young I had ideas about benefit, love and knowledge, and I was particularly interested in the sort of knowledge that centered around the question, "How can I be of greatest benefit to all through this that I'm interested in doing?"

When I began writing when I was young, I had started out with wanting my philosophical writing to be original, and I was original at the very early age of seventeen or eighteen. However, when I saw that my writings would be just for a small elite group and were no different than any of these other books that I was reading, it became clear that this wasn't the kind of philosophy I wanted to represent or be involved in.

I began this other path, one that involved simplifying things, through which I knew that I would have an opportunity to reach many people. I set out on a sort of mission. I read a lot of the ancient texts that had been read by many, many people, and I saw that often these books were based only on the writer's point of view. Very often the writer of the book was considered to be a person of prestige and renown, but even in reading their books and doing all the practices they recommended, still one would fall short of knowing one's true nature as open intelligence.

What I noticed in reading the philosophies from all the different countries is that there would be a golden nugget somewhere in them and the perfect words would be spoken, and I knew that those few words came from the reality of open intelligence. Eventually I started reflecting more on it and I thought, "Why can't there be books filled *only* with whatever evokes open intelligence, and nothing else? Why can't this kind of book be available to all people?"

This book has had many golden nuggets for me.

It's like when we begin to learn a new language; we need to sit down with someone who knows the language. It's exactly the same with becoming familiar with open intelligence, except that we don't have to learn. We just have to completely relax and be more and more comfortable with who we are. It is important to know that, no matter who we are, we will never *understand* open intelligence. This would be a good time to just let go of the attempt to understand open intelligence. Let it be *as it is,* because no one will ever understand open intelligence. Understanding is the booby prize, the lowest prize you could possibly get, and the booby prize isn't what we want.

From very early on in my life, what I saw in everyone I knew was the gift of benefit, the same kind of benefit that I felt in myself. I saw that everyone had special gifts, strengths and talents wherein the question could be asked, "What will be of benefit to all?" If it is philosophy you are asking about, that is the philosophy I am interested in.

LIKE THE SKY AND THE COLOR BLUE: THE INSEPARABILITY OF OPEN INTELLIGENCE AND DATA

CHAPTER TWENTY-TWO

Data cannot be found to have a nature independent of open intelligence. In the final analysis, all words describe open intelligence. The body and the mind are data within primary open intelligence, and it is realized that even the universe, sky, planet and stars are the dynamic energy of open intelligence. Throughout the entirety of open intelligence, all data that manifest are the dynamic energy of that open intelligence.

Open intelligence is the inexhaustible expanse comprising all data from which it is inseparable, like the color blue is inseparable from the sky. The expanse of open intelligence has no periphery or center. It has no reference and is uninterrupted. Since the true nature of all data is equalness and evenness, there is not a single thing that is not within the expanse of that equalness.

Open intelligence is not a void or a state of nothingness; it is vivid, alert, clear and always cognizant at the highest level of being. This uncreated space is entirely wide open and free of developmental effort. The infinite equalness and evenness of open intelligence, like space and pure by nature, is beyond any time frame. It is unchanging, unceasing and has no substance or characteristics. It neither comes nor goes and cannot be found to exist as some independently generated thing.

Open intelligence is the intelligence we have right now. There is not some open intelligence we are going to get to in the future or which we had in the past. There is only one indivisible intelligence. Even though it may be given another name in order to provoke understanding, always it is only open intelligence.

Supreme, naturally occurring open intelligence is timelessly and spontaneously present.

Since there never has been non-recognition of open intelligence, is no non-recognition of open intelligence and never will be non-recognition of open intelligence, "non-recognition" of open intelligence is just a label, and there is no one who has ever not recognized open intelligence. As there is no confusion at all, nothing exists as some confused state. So, in essence, no one has ever been confused at all in the past, no one is confused at present, and no one will be confused later. This is the wholly positive nature of the original purity of past, present and future presented in open intelligence.

If these words are completely new and confusing to you, just let them settle in and do not try to think about them. In fact, merely *thinking* about them is maybe the worst thing you can do! However confusing or unfamiliar the words may appear to be, they do not need to be figured out or understood. "Figuring it out" is not the tool that is needed here. Just let the words settle in naturally, and then after some time it may be that they will make perfect sense, even if they make almost no sense now!

DATA AS THE DYNAMIC ENERGY OF OPEN INTELLIGENCE

In the final analysis, all words describe open intelligence. The body and the mind are data within primary open intelligence, and it is realized that even the universe, sky, planet and stars are the dynamic energy of open intelligence. Throughout the entirety of open intelligence, all data that manifest are the dynamic energy of that open intelligence.

Data shine forth as open intelligence just as a mirage does, distinct and clear, yet without an independent nature. Like the openness of the sky, the basic space of open intelligence is unwavering and free of elaboration. This great, pure and beneficial space shines forth everything without exception. It is pure due to being free of anything of a different type or kind.

When data are reified, immediately they are given a power and influence of their own. Reification of data is the belief system or assumption that data are somehow independent of open intelligence and have a nature or power of their own. However, all data simultaneously appear and resolve in, of, as and through open intelligence, like a line drawn in water. If there is an orientation of reification, then in giving data an independent nature, the data are seemingly separated from open intelligence.

Whatever shines forth as the dynamic energy of the display of data has never known actual existence, just as whatever arises as a dream image is the dynamic energy of sleep and cannot be found to exist independent of sleep. There is only expansive open intelligence extending infinitely as the spacious reality of natural equalness and evenness. This demonstrates that data do not stray from open intelligence.

Data streams are spontaneously present and can be likened to a rainbow in the sky of the inexhaustible pure space of open intelligence. A rainbow in the sky is pervaded by pure space, and in just the same way, all data streams that shine forth are pervaded by pure open intelligence.

We have used some metaphors here, and all of the universal metaphors used in Dzogchen refer to things that are not made by human beings, like space, like lucid open intelligence, like rainbows, like the ocean, like rivers. None of these were created by humans. And so, when lucid open intelligence is introduced, it's clear that it is not any human being who has created open intelligence. It wasn't invented; it's the natural reality of everything that is, and in that way, it is spontaneously present and pure.

Through allowing a data stream to be *as it is* and by not remaining fixed on the definition, the data stream remains *as it is*—the stoppage-less flow of primordially pure benefit. We come to realize complete fearlessness in the face of all data, and we are able to rely on open intelligence and to face everything and avoid nothing.

The dynamically beneficial displays of data, completely indeterminate and not subject to any restrictions whatsoever, cannot be characterized as "things," for they cannot be found to have an independent substance or characteristics. In that their nature is like the panoramic vista of space, they are naturally present and free of any time frame. What a marvel it is!

Through gaining greater assurance in open intelligence, we instinctively come to realize what our principle reified data are. "Instinctively" means that we know without thinking about it. We just can now know what the principle reified data are that we have learned throughout our life. The data eventually come to be unimportant to us, and we no longer even pay attention to them.

TRUTH VALUE

Open intelligence's beneficial potency is alignment with reality, and in aligning with reality, the doors of the magic of reality swing open. We have been trained to look at data as threatening and that we have to defend ourselves against data or we have to gather and accumulate better kinds of data. When we just come to a stop in the recognition of what our intelligence is, we see that we really do not need to do anything about what is coming up. Data spontaneously self-release upon arising, with nothing needing to be done. We find in the freedom of that spontaneous self-release that all the definitions we have held so dear are outshone by a greater discernment, intelligence and insight.

All data are primordially pure, blessed and blissful like unborn space. Pure, pure, pure, inescapably pure and powerful. Before we decide anything about anything, we must know its basis, and "primordially pure and blissful like unborn space" is its basis! Data are the basis of information and knowledge, and if data are primordially pure, then all information and knowledge are fundamentally primordially pure. This is the correct logic and reason necessary for addressing any problem or to get at any solution. This is the core that must be instinctively realized more and more.

All data have absolute truth value, because their one and only source is singular open intelligence. Contemporary philosophy states that data do not have truth value, but what is being said here is exactly the opposite. No data stream is independent of open intelligence; thus, all data have truth value. The truth value of data is that open intelligence subsumes all data into beneficial intelligence.

We have to really know and understand the truth value of data, not in an intellectual, abstract way, but in a way that has an effect on how we live our lives. Rather than being something memorized from a book, this needs to become our own lived experience. We have to first teach ourselves what correct logic and reasoning are by understanding what data truly are. In doing so, we come to see an entirely different world, a world in which data have absolute truth value.

Data can mean anything at all according to time, place, circumstance and result, and data may mean something in one situation and something entirely different in another. However, by examining data in one's own experience and allowing data to be as they are, we open up a vast space of comprehensive open-ended knowledge. Again, the starting point for this is the knowledge that all data equally and evenly have a singular truth value.

When we see the immediate benefit that is available to us through our own intelligence, we become very willing to make a one hundred percent commitment to that. We see that we have a choice in each moment and that we can make that choice. Whereas before we may have waded around in data, now we increasingly choose to go to open intelligence. The one hundred percent commitment is like driving a stake in the ground: "This is where I stand. This is who I am."

Based upon that commitment, assurance comes about, an assurance that comes from knowing that data have no independent nature. With more and more assurance in this practice, instinctive recognition of open intelligence takes hold short moment by short moment, until open intelligence is always obviously on.

We do not need to stockpile positive data streams or push away negative data streams. All data streams are exactly as they are in the great equalness and evenness of open intelligence. In allowing everything to simply be *as it is,* we outshine all data, and then living according to reified data is not a lifestyle practice any longer. Practically speaking, that is what outshining is: we do not go to reified data any longer. Data are no longer our go-to; our go-to is now open intelligence.

This does not mean that data are just thrown out the window and never used again. Instead, it means that data are *no longer reified*; they are not seen as having an independent nature. That is the beginning of correct logic and reason, an instinctive logic and reason that is completely unlike the logic and reason of reification.

Maybe for all of our lives the data streams have been getting attention; however, if our energy and attention are directed to open intelligence and its immediate beneficial potency, rather than to the habitual process of referring just to the data-definition, we find immediate readiness, total potency and easefulness right at hand.

It is important to understand that once the presence of open intelligence is completely obvious, the emphasis on reifying data comes to an end. At some point, all of a sudden without doing anything and without noticing anything, open intelligence is obvious at all times. When open intelligence is obvious at all times, the short moments practice isn't needed any longer, as all data are outshone in open intelligence. Everything disappears into its basic space; appearances disappear like a rainbow vanishing into the sky. This is the powerful benefit of open intelligence, where there is no longer even the possibility of data drawing attention or notice.

CLARITY AND NOT CONFUSION

We might have lingering data streams that have caused us a lot of pain and suffering in the past, for example, feelings of being rejected or abandoned or feeling lesser than other people or greater than others or whatever it might be. We find through the practice of relying on open intelligence that these challenging afflictions that we once had now begin to slip away. By relying on open intelligence rather than believing in the affliction, that affliction or problem is actually known to be the energy of beneficial potency.

Very confusing data streams are cleared up, and many, many people throughout the world have experienced the end of confusion. "End of confusion" is the natural state in which we live. When we are educated in this way, we are no longer merely trying to sort out confusion and turmoil, but we are living an enjoyable life where we can benefit ourselves and each other and live in a prosperous, natural and generous way.

Open intelligence is always the go–to, no matter how loudly the other thing might be screaming, "Come to me. Come to me." It is always open intelligence that will be inexhaustibly sovereign. Open intelligence is secure in its own place as the dynamic energy of that datum. Maybe a thousand different data streams can be resolved by recognizing just one data stream as being open intelligence and nothing else.

We do not have to get into all kinds of classifications and categories and definitions: "This means this and that means that. If you look at me the wrong way it means that you do not like me. If you look at someone else, it means that you're going to abandon me and go be with them." All these sorts of things that we have dreamed up about our life are seen as the nonsense they are. Whatever datum appears, it is no problem. At all times and in all circumstances, the thoughts, emotions, sensations and other experiences are seen to be open intelligence alone. There is recognition of open intelligence shining very, very brightly in all moments.

All-inclusive, all-encompassing discernment and insight are brought to everything. There is no way to develop a rulebook for how this should look or take place, like for example, if you eat this way or if you move your body that way, then this or that will happen. It may or may not happen, who knows? Each person is fully empowered to take care of themselves and to know exactly what to do in any given situation.

Regardless of the duration of a reflection within a perfect crystal ball, the perfection remains flawless, pervasive and sovereign throughout the crystal. Thus, regardless of the duration of any data stream, open intelligence remains flawless, pervasive and sovereign. We are open intelligence burning away all data of the here-and-now. There is no way to keep the current here-and-now in place, and there is no special state to get into. There is only the self-release of the here-and-now.

DATA ARE FREE IN THEIR OWN PLACE

To let data run free in their own place and to not have them be seen as our own data, which means freedom in the immediacy of perception, is very different from just believing in the data. We come to see the data as free in their own place, and in doing so we reach a vast space of complete understanding that is due to our own direct experience. It is our own decisive experience of the world and not anyone else's. We are not trying to be someone else. It is self-understanding based on a true idea of self.

The potency of open intelligence is a relaxed, alert potency, and there isn't anything that needs to be done to make it that way. When data are seen as having an independent nature, all of their beautiful, magnificent, wondrous, treasure-like qualities are distorted. No matter what the data streams are, they just are what they are, and we allow them to be as they are. That doesn't mean that we "surrender to" or "accept" them; rather, we allow the data streams to be as they are, whatever they are.

Because we have had a worldview that suggests subjects and objects living in a world, we tend to look at everything that way: "There are subjects and objects, and we are in a world of time and space," and there isn't any mention of any other kind of reality. In that case, there would be the subject-data stream seeing the object-data stream. If, however, we rest totally and potently as open intelligence, the data streams of subject and object resolve, because we are in our own place of open intelligence, which is not a subject or an object. The whole body-mind idea of an individual is seen to be a data stream of open intelligence.

We have thought that we were relying on a subjective individual identity to perceive things, but there is no individual. It is open intelligence that is shining forth the whole data stream of the individual subject watching another data stream identified as an object. Instead of the data-definitions based on the subject-object perception being the basis for all of our experience, our experience is based in the fundamental reality, the pure spread of open intelligence itself. The only way to realize this is to have the realization of it in our own direct experience. That realization will put a smile on anybody's face!

QUESTION AND ANSWER

Q. I find myself at times giving in to great fits of anger that just seem to suddenly take me over. I can sort of understand what you are saying about the equalness and evenness of all data, but I feel so defeated when this intense anger comes up yet again.

Ziji Rinpoche: Once we have seen the inseparability of data and open intelligence and the outshining of all data occurs, we're left with great benefit and with living as great benefit and demonstrating great benefit. When we are living as great benefit, we are challenging everything that has ever been seen, known or done. What I'm pointing to here is the value of the power of resting continuously as the power of great benefit and relying on the trainer, the training and the community.

Moments of great challenge can be devastating—or glorious! It is hoped that glory would be found in the devastation; that is what is ideal. In that case, glory shines forth in the devastation, and that is the actual purpose of devastating times in our life. That is their purpose, whether we handle these things only internally or whether they are affecting the lives of others.

I have a story, and I'm sharing this story because it has many levels of meaning, from the obvious to the profound. I was once on the beach with my little seventeen-pound Boston terrier, Rudy Kazootie, and there was a man walking his dog on the beach. Rudy wasn't a fighter and he didn't go after the man or his dog, but at some point the man kicked Rudy right in the stomach. This man is someone who has a spiritual practice and a teacher, but sometimes something all of a sudden can just snap in a person.

In that moment, what I hoped for was that, having kicked the dog, the man could recognize the deeper implications of what had happened. Harming an animal, whether it's a human animal or another animal, is disconcerting. His was such a public display. I had known this man for twenty years, and when this happened to Rudy, all I did was give the man a look. That was all I needed to do in response, and he got it instantly. I don't believe that he is kicking dogs anymore. It was obvious then to him that it was not just a matter of his action harming others, but also that the action harmed himself—the person performing the action.

This kind of incident can happen for any of us. This man didn't plan to be mean to the dog, and he didn't plan to completely collapse out of his spiritual practice in that intense moment. When there is any kind of collapse into acting on afflictive states, then it is absolutely essential to return to resting as open intelligence as quickly as possible, so that the knot that leads to the snap decision to harm another being in a compulsive way is untied. The incident represented a whole area of this man's life that needed to be outshone. It wasn't just about the spontaneous harm to the dog, but also the ways in which he had been harming himself and others.

Only through the instinctive recognition that our true mind, speech, body, qualities and activities belong to open intelligence are we able to make the direct crossing into seeing things as they really are, and only then can we truly access the incredible knowledge and capacities that are available to us. We must take responsibility for the fact that we house the intelligence of the universe in a usable way, and we take responsibility by showing up for open intelligence, by speaking out about who we really are, and by not collapsing into reification.

Through instinctive recognition we are coming to be what human beings have always been meant to be. We have a lot of power that we do not yet know that we possess, and we need to gain access to the educational tools and technologies that will open up the power to use all this knowledge in a way that benefits all. Open intelligence is that power. We must become more familiar with who we really are and take an evolutionary leap unlike any leap that has been taken before. The only way this can take place is for individuals to decide to make this leap themselves and for them to come together with other people who have decided the same thing, and then from that basis to forge ahead.

THE UNIVERSAL LANGUAGE

CHAPTER TWENTY-THREE

Beneficial speech that comes spontaneously and automatically is the highest form of speech. We come to realize that what we are thinking and what we are doing with our thinking in terms of data streams directly influences our speech. The opening of our intelligence sets everything else free, so that our speech goes along with what is real rather than what is not.

When we have a common language rooted in the universal language of open intelligence, we can speak effortlessly with each other. We can share openly, normalizing all ideas, so that everything we share shines forth as wisdom. This is an aspect of the universal language of pure and perfect devotion to the benefit of all, and this language has spread far and wide. All of those dispersed throughout the world who are recognizing the universal language of open intelligence are deeply influencing human society, whether they recognize that they are doing so or not.

The universal language is used as a systematic means for communicating the beneficial potency of mind, speech, body, qualities and activities. It is not a matter of employing a lot of different vocabularies; it is the same language everywhere, a language that points to and confirms the reality of who we are as human beings, even if the language vehicle—English, German, Chinese, Spanish, Hindi—is different.

It may take us a while to get accustomed to speaking in a way that is completely uncontrived and which does not have any forethought, or to become comfortable with our own discernment, clarity and insight and how that expresses itself; however, in a relatively short time it can become a spontaneous and natural expression of our own beneficial intent. Even though we might feel tentative about it at first, it is so engaging and so fun when we see how much we can hit the mark when we are communicating with others.

When we are introduced to a foreign language, at first there isn't really an on-the-fly ability to utilize the language in everyday life, but with growing familiarity we eventually do find that we have that skill. This is the case as well with the universal language of open intelligence. We are first introduced to it, and then as we become more familiar with it, we gradually become accustomed to its use, and eventually we become really adept at using the no-longer-so-foreign language on the fly.

If we want to have fluency in any language that we are learning, we need to look for a teacher who has fluency, and we also look for a teaching, a practice and a community in order to enhance that fluency. It is the same for the universal language of open intelligence. "Fluency in the universal language" means ready and effortless expression of spontaneous wisdom benefit.

Universal language is a system of conveyance of the most profound meaning of truth. Universal language is particularly unique, in that its communications are unforgettable and are continuously deepening in meaning once aroused. Instead of the under-mutter in our minds of, "Oh, you're no good; you know you can't do anything right," the universal language is saying, "The benefit of all is where it's at!"

This language communicates what everyone wants to know, and within this open-intelligence community, we see this language developing and flourishing, so that it communicates in a way that people can understand. No matter how closed a person might seem to be, in every thought, emotion, sensation and experience they are seeking direct connection. We all get to share the terms and phrases that are naturally arising within the community, and this is a wonderful way of growing a language. What is more, we want as many people as possible to be affected in the way that we have been through clear, concise, direct words that come straight from the source, belonging to all beings. We want to support everyone in learning this universal language of the heart of love-bliss benefit.

OPEN INTELLIGENCE AS OUR BASIS OF COMMUNICATION

By the power of open intelligence as our basis of communication, we are able to learn in a new way. Whatever we read, we can instantaneously translate it into the new perfect knowledge of open intelligence. All the knowledge is already here and available to us. The only thing required is the humility to open up to the reality of what we truly are.

Through the power of open intelligence, our speech becomes infused with benefit. It actually becomes impossible for us to speak in any other way than in a way that is of benefit to all. Beneficial speech that comes spontaneously and automatically is the highest form of speech. We come to realize that what we are thinking and what we are doing with our thinking in terms of data streams directly influences our speech. The opening of our intelligence sets everything else free, so that our speech goes along with what is real, rather than what is not real. As open intelligence grows to be more beneficially apparent to us, we notice the growing influence it has on our speech. There are things that we say now that we didn't say before, and things that we said at one time that we no longer say.

The primordial sound of open intelligence pervades all sounds and is the basis of your own speech. Through the power of bliss-benefit potency, you see the reality of what your mind and body actually are. You see that your reality is the primordial sound that is present in all sound.

We do not automatically expect everyone to jump into our way of looking at things. We gently feel our way into where someone is and then we are able to communicate in a very direct way through the profound heart of reality *as it is*. We are able to communicate so easily and specifically in a way where they might begin to receive what they are being introduced to.

When you are intimately relating with yourself, then you are able to intimately relate with others, and when communicating with others, you see how these spontaneous expressions really hit the mark with a listener. Just by being who you are and by living in this totally refined condition of responsiveness, that alone has so much of an effect on other people. For instance, you can see the differences in the way you now live together with your family and friends when compared to before.

The before-and-after is very obvious, and maybe some people close to you will also notice that and want to know more about the change. The way that opening can best happen is for you to be fully connected with them, to listen to them carefully, to know how they are feeling and to see clearly what they might have going on in them. You are then able to directly speak to their exact situation.

TRUE FREEDOM OF SPEECH

The beneficial speech of open intelligence is based on a true freedom that always already exists and is potent and life-altering to the core. It is so basic; it is the simplicity of everyone everywhere. We are all born exactly as we are. Anything we might do, think or adopt is fueled by the open intelligence that is our very basis all the while.

Some believe that "freedom of speech" means the right to say anything one wants. That is one way of looking at freedom of speech; however, it is not true freedom of speech. Most often this type of "free" speech can degrade the individuals and the groups that are involved in it. Speech that comes only from limited self-focus is a denigration of authentic beneficial speech.

If people speak in a completely careless way, one can see very directly what the result will be, and this is especially evident online. It may begin with one or more individuals dominating the setting in a forum in a particularly negative and harmful way. Then very often things can deteriorate until beneficial dialogue is no longer possible in that setting. The only way to respond to the freedom of the internet is to realize that it is an aspect of the freedom of our own mind. We can see the varying levels of mind reflected in the different kinds of communication appearing online. People say just whatever they want to say, and there isn't any limit to it whatsoever. However, a person participating through wisdom speech brings an entirely new vantage to the dialogue.

The sort of aggressive speech one sees these days comes from a constructed identity based on an individualized self, but recognizing what we truly are gives us the potency to address one another in the most beneficial way possible. Do we really want to limit ourselves to this so-called "freedom" offered by holding to a limited self and thinking others to be the same, or are we willing to offer ourselves in complete humility to open intelligence?

Speech that is subsumed completely by open intelligence is completely different from the hate-speech that we see so often. Beneficial speech relies on the immediately available beneficial potencies of open intelligence to inform speech in each moment. At first this may require a commitment to short moments, pausing when agitated or doubtful about what to say, and then allowing open intelligence to inform what we are going to say. Living as the empowering and relaxing potency of open intelligence, we really know what true freedom of speech is, we know what freedom of thought is and we know what freedom of activity is, because all of it is an expression of spontaneous benefit.

In the universal language, only one thing takes place, and that is complete confirmation of our blazing benefit. Texts of the universal language bring something alive in us that has always been there but which probably had not been noticed. The teachings and texts composed in the universal language affirm and transmit what we are in a very simple and straightforward way. These texts are filled with words that we all have wanted to hear. They are simple and powerful words that cannot be forgotten. But, it isn't just the words themselves; it is the *profound meaning of the words* that gives the texts their impact.

In Dzogchen there are countless teachings and pith instructions—these heaps of jewels that give us such an evocative realization. Key points of the Dzogchen Teaching can be presented in some way in books and texts. However, the pith instructions of a Dzogchen master cannot be recorded in a book. Maybe a smattering of them can, but they are unique to the relationship between the student and their lineage guru and are not meant for a general audience.

Many who read texts like the Dzogchen texts described here are seeing something that they have not seen before and for which they may have no frame of reference. Maybe in the beginning when the texts are read, the meaning may not be at all clear, and one may not only not understand the words, but even find them nonsensical. However, it can happen that if the same text is picked up a few weeks or months later, somehow it will make perfect sense. All of a sudden one is able to clearly understand something that was not understandable at all a few weeks before.

It may be that at some point some phrase will pop up into our mind, and we will instinctively recognize exactly what it means. We see that what we have read in the text is now part of our own experience. These texts are generative of forever-complete relaxation opening inexhaustibly, and the world of complete relaxation has a vocabulary of its own. An experience like this is the beginning of the understanding that our current intelligence is being subsumed into something greater than itself.

The texts of the universal language involve an entirely new genre of writing, an authorless writing that has no reference to reification. There is not an indication in the texts of an individual person having written the literature. The precious words of these texts are spoken from a formless voice of flawless, exalted, unborn pure space and do not have a personified author. Open intelligence itself is the writer of the writing. That which is going to be of benefit to all and most responsive right here and now is what is being written.

In these sorts of texts, the writing may be incessantly repetitive, and as a reader goes through them, the repetition could seem to be burdensome, but the repetition is *purposeful*. Things are repeated over and over again so that they can take hold in a very deep way. Through the constant exposure brought about through the repetition, there will be a shift in understanding.

THE POWER OF THE INTERNET AND MODERN TELECOMMUNICATIONS

The power of this grassroots movement to educate the world in the nature of mind has become possible through the internet, telecommunications and electronic devices, as these innovations have allowed us to go beyond our national and cultural barriers. The power of all of us coming together with an incredible ability to communicate is really something grand. With the internet and modern telecommunications, we are able to communicate directly with each other in a way that was not possible before. We are able to see ourselves as globally connected in a very straightforward way, as opposed to merely thinking about some kind of abstract oneness.

We live in a time of incredible literacy, and not only the literacy associated with speech and writing, but the literacy associated with technology. One must know how to choose the new technologies that will work best for the present circumstances and which will also provide what is needed over the long term. Through these incredible technologies we are able to see our power as a global community to ask questions like, "Who are we really, and how do we want to live our lives?"

We can completely commit to directly experiencing the benefit of open intelligence in the moment and come to trust it, have faith in it and completely rely on it. It becomes so evident in us how beautiful, how powerful and how potent we are. Today we have the freedom to express it, whether it is on our smart phone, the internet or wherever it may be. We feel an increasing ability to free up our speech, and the very best way to free up our speech is within the context of its beneficial potency.

METAPHORS

Metaphors can really strike a person in a way that other words or phrases do not. In the Dzogchen Teaching there is a very specific set of metaphors, and when this specific set is used, there is a very forceful and meaningful power in them. Through the use of these specific metaphors, the essential meaning of the metaphor is laid open and bare.

We could use a metaphor such as, "Data and open intelligence are inseparable, like the sky and the color blue," but we might find it difficult to work our way into the instinctive recognition of that metaphor using ordinary logic. However, by simply allowing for a continuous opening of open intelligence, we will surely arrive at a point where we realize the essence of the meaning non-symbolically.

When ordinary words are coupled with these powerful metaphors, suddenly the decisive experience of open intelligence can hit home. When a very refined set of metaphors and similes is used, these skilled metaphors have a powerful impact and we can feel them strike our hearts. These aren't metaphors that are used lightly. "Like the flight path of the bird in the sky," "like a line drawn in water," "like sunlight outshining the planets and stars," "like a rainbow in the sky," these and so many others are very powerful metaphors that are chosen with great care.

In the Dzogchen Teaching only certain metaphors and similes are used. These are metaphors and similes based on things not created by human beings. For example, "the sun that outshines the planets and stars" is not an image of something that was created by human beings. In the metaphor "inseparable like the sky and the color blue," human beings did not create the sky or the color blue. Hence, these powerful metaphors are purposefully drawn from natural phenomena. In these metaphors we catch the essence, the spontaneous presence and the responsiveness of our beneficial wisdom-nature.

UNERRING INSTRUCTION

It is very important to have unerring instruction, and what is unerring instruction? Unerring instruction is instruction that has led to the swift realization of wisdom-open-intelligence for the most people throughout time. In each generation or in several generations wisdom-open-intelligence appears in some form, and it provides a teaching that is absolutely perfect for the people living in that era, spoken in a language that people of that era can understand, and providing a complete system of support for those particular people.

Unerring instruction evokes the decisive experience of the true nature of our own being to many people all at once. There are certain words that are like a sword with a diamond blade. These words cut through everything; they show the nature of reality *as it is.* They show it in a very definitive way where it is impossible to hide out from it. This is much different than instruction that is merely based on someone's personal experience or instruction that just talks *about* something. It is very, very important to know the distinction between this and unerring instruction.

Another aspect of unerring instruction is that it delivers the result, and it provides support for everyone who is facing not only overt data but also subtle data as well. So, there is support available for that. There is no one who has to be off on their own in a land where no one speaks open intelligence!

QUESTION AND ANSWER

Q. I have been involved in this teaching for some months, but one of my doubts is about the benefit of writing the value letters that we write after receiving a teaching. What if I or any participant can't quite see the value in what they have received in the teaching?

Ziji Rinpoche: Over the years we have found that writing value letters that reflect the benefit and value gained in trainings is a powerful way to gain fluency in the language of open intelligence in both writing and speaking.

A value letter is written by the participant in the training setting to express the value gained by participating in the training. It is incredibly empowering to write the value letters and then to share that writing with others. To be a person of outstanding openness is to understand the skillful means that are required in expressing value. As a group we want to honor those skillful means and allow them to be demonstrated in a safe setting.

One of the reasons that value is emphasized in this training is that very few of us have been trained to identify or express real value. This lack of training in real value is why we have been willing to

[handwritten margin note: I've never heard of "value letters" before. Interesting *]*

live in the way that we have been living. We have not trained ourselves to recognize the value within our own person or within other people, nor to value all the effort and sacrifice that went into providing the things we use, the clothes we wear or the food we eat. One of the most beneficial parts of the training is the ability to identify value and to speak articulately about it. To write articulately about value and then to express it aloud is a very exalted form of wisdom-speech.

The Dzogchen Teaching is not a place to list one's woes and all the things that are keeping one from following the instructions. It's a place to find out how to follow the instructions. When we begin to value ourselves and to value others, we are able to open up into an entirely new world. Rather than just having one person up on stage speaking and appearing to have all the knowledge, knowledge is empowered and activated and enlivened in everyone who is participating. Through the reading aloud of the value letters, that empowerment is reflected back to the other participants. Each unique and special value letter shows the growing and increasing fluency in the universal language.

These letters are an example of a call and response technique which greatly influences what will come next in the trainings, and in that way we are responding to the needs of everyone here and now. When I am participating in a training, I read each and every one of the value letters, and through that I can know where people are coming from and what is going on with them. It is very important to me to receive the letters, and no matter how long or short they are, I still do the same thing; I read every word!

I never see myself as some kind of remote observer of the value letters. They are for me like a re-living of everyone's life, and that is very meaningful, because through the value letters we develop a heart-connection with one another. The subsequent trainings can then be written as a direct response to what had been expressed in the value letters.

I have found that there is a great candor and honesty in the value letters that I have received. People have felt empowered to be frank and open with me, no matter what has been happening for them. I am touched by that honesty and openness to such an incredible degree that I could never explain it. Whatever it is that is written to me, I can receive it as, "Well, yes, I very much remember what that was like for me, too." Whatever it is that is being explained in the value letter, I have no problem at all relating to it.

You can write to your heart's delight whatever you would like to write in these letters, and every single letter is responded to. Even though you might not get a direct response from me referring to your value letter, each item or issue in the letter will be addressed and taken care of. Hearing directly from the participants in the training is one of the best ways to find what is working well for them, so for that reason alone the value letters are extremely important.

Everyone who practices Dzogchen is aspiring to come to a correct understanding, and this is cultivated in many ways. Writing value letters and sharing is one of those ways, and also asking questions is another way. Through asking questions, not only do we as an individual deepen our understanding of what Dzogchen is, and by asking a question in a public setting, a teaching is given that serves everyone. It serves the teacher and it serves the participant.

PURE EVOCATION

CHAPTER TWENTY-FOUR

Pure evocation is a simple disposition, whereby we allow the evocative power of open intelligence to be the reality of what we are. Evocation is pure knowledge of our own reality, and some people are very skilled at showing us that reality.

Pure evocation is a communication that arouses knowledge we already have but which might not yet be readily accessible to us. Evocation arouses the reality of who we are in a very rooted way, so that we no longer have any questions about it. Once we become comfortable with that as the reality of who we are, then the ability is available to us to receive communication that is completely fluent and readily accessible. "Evoke" is such an incredibly powerful word for me—evoking within culture the reality of what we are as precious human beings.

Evocation is not something that comes from someone else into us. It is not something that is over there that is going to hop in over here. Evocation does not come *from* or *to* us; it comes *through* us. Evocation, or another word that has often been used is "transmission," is always the primordial presence of totally great benefit, and nothing else other than that. This is crucial. Evocation is a simple disposition, whereby we allow the evocative power of open intelligence to be the reality of what we are.

There are all kinds of instruction, but evocation is the foremost instruction, and there is no other instruction that can so open in us comprehensive knowledge. When we are open and without preconceived notions, pure evocation is available to us. "Openness with no preconceived notions" is maybe not a place we have visited before, so when we go there we may not know what it is about or what is happening. But in fact, what is occurring is simply that we are opening up to the space of pure evocation.

For each one of us, this openness happens one moment at a time. The more open we are to the self that we really are, the more likely it is that perfect knowledge without learning will be evoked in us in full form. Depending on the way your participation unfolds, pure evocation may be a big part of your life, or not. If it is a big part of your life, then just like with any aspect of life that is being fully utilized, the power of its potential grows. Many, many realizations can occur, each one affirming the inexhaustible capacity of the pure evocation of open intelligence.

Through evocation, our entire slate of reification is somehow wiped clean, and we cannot really even say how it happened. This allows us to live as great benefit, to have a simple, pure knowing in each moment of what to do and how to act and to enter into the richness of the real meaning of life. This is where we really start to understand and comprehend the profundity of evocation.

As the communication of direct, pure evocation becomes more widespread, it cannot help but become obvious, evident and profoundly demonstrated by those who are open to it. This isn't something that can be packaged in a certain way of being. Pure evocation force speaks louder than words. It speaks with a range of sound not reachable through ordinary sound. Its appearances shine forth in a way that is not evident in the ordinary ways of speaking.

"Pure evocation" needs to become a household phrase, and it should not be seen any longer as limited to the merely esoteric and to the world of mystery. It needs to be understood and acknowledged for what it is, and it needs to be seen as a pivot point at this time in history, because the human species is in critical need of pure evocation.

Evocation is never-ending and inexhaustible. All we need to do is to be completely open to allowing it to occur. Yes, to be open, and also to want nothing. We are present with a total availability for receiving whatever there is to be received, and we come wanting nothing, because in wanting or insisting on *something*, there are things that might get in the way of what is being offered. To want nothing, to expect nothing and to know nothing is the most skillful way to approach pure evocation.

To want nothing at all is the most devotional disposition one can have, and the benefit of all is inherent in wanting nothing at all. Wanting nothing is the secret to the evocation of reality itself. To come to a training wanting nothing is the secret key to the inexhaustible treasury that will continue giving like an unending spread of precious gems. Open-ended knowledge and benefit creation—unending and superb, indivisible, spontaneously present, open and free of independent nature, with an unending flow of benefit to all—is given to mind, speech, body, qualities and activities through this inexhaustible treasury.

To open up to the reality that everything is great benefit is an enormous change from the common understanding of the world. When we are completely open without preconceived notions, we know how to receive, and comprehensive knowledge can be brought to bear in a very practical way, utilizing means and methods that are not used in an ordinary way.

THE EVOCATION OF REALITY

Through evocation we realize complete relaxation directly and decisively within our own experience. We do not need to do anything to be completely relaxed. Evocation is the essence of complete relaxation, and it is absolutely possible to live as that complete relaxation. Because the spontaneous beneficial energy that complete relaxation offers to us is unknowable, it cannot be traced backward to past knowledge that has been accumulated, and it cannot be projected forward as to what will happen in the future.

One can say things such as "primordial purity," "open intelligence is pure meaning," "it has nothing within it of a different kind," or "everything is pure," and on a certain level people can know that these are true in an intellectual way, but to instinctively recognize these things comes through the evocation of that reality. The words we use to describe open intelligence's beneficial potency are simply a way of communicating, but what is needed is the pure evocation in our own direct experience.

Evocation is comprehensive truth-telling about who we are, and that comprehensive truth always confirms for us *exactly* who we are. Words of direct evocation take hold permanently. The reality of who we are is evoked and can never be forgotten. It is completely enlivening and permanently empowering.

You could read a text of direct evocation and never think anything further about it, and yet what is written in the text will be evoked in you. It will open up within you. "Evoked in you" means that the meaning of the text is already naturally present in you; the evocation just makes it obvious. Pure evocation is the most powerful communication tool there is; however, it is only effective if the recipient is completely open and has no preconceived notions.

THE BENEFICIAL POTENCY OF PURE EVOCATION

Open intelligence's beneficial potency is not an object, an "it." This isn't "some other" apart from who we are; this is the only reality of who we are. As soon as anyone instinctively recognizes the beneficial potency of open intelligence, the spontaneous wisdom-benefit of mind, speech, body, qualities and activities is evoked. There is no need to work on each of these things individually. "Oh, got to work on my mind, got to work on my speech, got to work on my body, got to work on my qualities and activities." None of that. Resting naturally as the power of great benefit allows us to live as the pure evocation force itself.

When we acknowledge who we are, it is a very important moment. It affects our thinking and how we respond to our emotional life, because our emotional life is expanded to include the emotions of everyone. We start to see that everyone has the opportunity for recognizing open intelligence in the same way that we do. Whether we say anything or not, the fact that we know who we are evokes the same in others. The more we are grounded in this, the more all-pervasively this is our reality and the stronger the evocation.

Living as the complete relaxation of our native potency of benefit, we know what to do and how to act in all circumstances, but we don't know what it is going to look like! With growing experience of living as open intelligence comes growing trust, and with that trust comes the ability to know what to do and what to say. It is very important to allow ourselves to become fully acquainted with the reality of who we are. This is what complete relaxation means: friending our real identity. No longer do we mistake brass for gold. No longer do we consider that we are travelling west when we are actually going east.

Each short moment of open intelligence is a building block of wisdom. We can see in ourselves that with each short moment there is such a force of immediate benefit, and it is a benefit that extends beyond that moment. By open intelligence being evidenced in the people for whom the recognition is the easiest, other people will be attracted to it. Those who at first find it less easy to be open to wisdom are attracted to it through the ones who are more open.

PROFOUND MEANING

To receive expert instruction in the profound meaning of open intelligence is the greatest good fortune, and one of the wonderful things about receiving instruction is that it enables us to recognize the capacities and possibilities of open intelligence. Instruction in open intelligence has profound meaning, but to use that word "profound" isn't just a matter of attaching an adjective onto a noun. "Profound meaning" in this case is *the most profound of all meaning*; there is no meaning that goes beyond it.

To receive beneficial instruction in this way is so marvelous, so incredible and so beyond imagining! And what do we have to do? Nothing, because open intelligence already is. We relax body and mind completely for short moments repeated many times and see everything at the basis: pure benefit, pure relaxation, pure soothing. Open intelligence is the basis of all thinking, all emotions, all sensations, all experience whatsoever. Data are the radiant shine, the dynamic energy of this intelligence. One cannot be known without the other. They are inseparable like wetness and water, like heat and fire, like the sun's rays and the sun.

This profound instruction is like a range of golden mountains stretching back into the distant past and going on and on forever. It is an instruction that points to our innate capacity, endowment, authority and conviction. When we have been trained that we do not have profound capacity and that we do not have good fortune, that is how we see ourselves. We think we are in this body and mind, and that misfortune, meaninglessness and misery are in there too, and that we have to do something to overcome these things. However, we are not miserable by nature; we are power-born by nature! Power-born—born to be of benefit—with so much power that at times it might even feel scary to face it.

The good news once again is that there is nothing to be done. Leaving everything *as it is*, every datum resolves itself in its own actuality. In any moment of our life, when we feel any doubt whatsoever, we can show ourselves the pure benefit at the basis. In leaving everything *as it is*, we find that doubt, powerlessness, hopelessness, despair, excessive negativity—and all the joy and laughter—are all power-packed with beneficial potency that is both soothing and of great power.

Each of us is very potent by nature, and we have the innate ability to leave everything *as it is*. The profound meaning of this phrase is that everything is *as it is* as raw empty knowing and as primordial purity, and not as its reified definition. Soon we start to see that our mind, speech, body, qualities and activities are completely empowered by the potency of this raw empty knowingness of primordial purity.

THE LINEAGE OF DZOGCHEN

Just because we never learned about pure evocation doesn't mean that it isn't real. It just means that in the culture in which we have lived, evocation in this way was not something that was acknowledged or honored. However, not all cultures are created that way. There are a few cultures on earth that do acknowledge and honor pure evocation, and in those fortunate cultures there is the belief that the greatest thing that can ever happen for a person is to be introduced to open intelligence and to have an opportunity to experience pure evocation.

There are profound knowledge holders in human society, and these people are to be honored and respected. The precious, flawless, ancient lineage of profound knowledge holders is alive and well in human civilization. For many thousands of years specific people who are acknowledged as holders of the pure evocation lineage have been acknowledged to carry it on. They are not only acknowledged to carry it on, but to carry it on as they see fit through skillful means and wisdom.

It is a good fortune and a marvel to be exposed to a lineage of pure evocation. This pure lineage has been sustained by people who cared enough to keep it alive and vibrant. Some of those people chose to write down what it was that they had found. Why did they do this? Because the change in their life had been so immense and the opening so incredible that they wanted to make certain that other people who were living in their time and those in later times would be able to benefit from what they had realized. It is truly a great good fortune to have skillful people such as these who can serve as mentors and guides for others in this life.

There is an unbroken lineage of Dzogchen. That means the lineage has never been lost; the transmission of the lineage has carried on uninterruptedly over thousands of years up to the present day. Dzogchen began as an oral tradition, and those who could memorize well were given thousands of lines to memorize. In this way the Dzogchen Teachings and scriptures passed on from teacher to student and then on to the next generation, on and on. Over time Dzogchen Teachings began to be recorded in writing, on palm leaves in India and then carved into wooden blocks in Tibet, and the Teachings came to be pervasive in Tibetan culture.

For all of these generations, the Dzogchen lineage has had this systematic method for recording the Teachings and preserving them for those who were to follow. These masters of the lineage made sure that the Teachings that had been so important in their own lives would not be lost. In addition to the Teachings, a comprehensive record of the lives of the Dzogchen enlightened masters was kept, and these biographies are filled with great detail about the lives and wisdom of these marvelous beings.

I am so grateful for this gift. I'm grateful to everyone past, present and future for Dzogchen knowledge. If it had not been for the Dzogchen masters who carried the Teaching so lovingly and who cherished it and passed on to generation after generation up to the present day, we would not have this Dzogchen knowledge today. We are so fortunate.

The very great Dzogchen masters of the past are our energy right here. Their emanation is present; it doesn't go anywhere; it has no birth, life or death. The full force of Dzogchen lineage is our own sublime energy, throughout all times and directions, amidst all data that appear. Dzogchen practitioners are the living energy of the entire Dzogchen lineage, that of the entire universality of the many worlds. We practitioners are the living lineage power. The lineage is enlightened energy. The Dzogchen lineage isn't something that is separate from us. It pervades and exemplifies us; it is who we are.

There are all kinds of teachings, and the teaching that is considered to be the ultimate of all vehicles is direct pure evocation, and we now have at our disposal incredible technologies to empower evocation. What has been so rare, secret and hidden and the privilege of only a few is now potentially open to everyone.

QUESTION AND ANSWER

Q. I have heard of these terms "transmission" and "evocation" in other traditions, and now I am hearing about it here from you, but it has always sounded like some hocus-pocus to me that doesn't have any real relevance to everyday life as I know it.

Ziji Rinpoche: I have an illustration of transmission or evocation in my own life that may be helpful for you. I had learned Sanskrit because I had an interest in that language, and later on as I grew more and more in open intelligence, I also developed an interest in Tibetan Buddhism, because there is a natural trajectory from Sanskrit into Tibetan Buddhism.

At some point I went to a bookstore and bought some Tibetan Buddhist books written in Tibetan. I had never studied or learned Tibetan before, and I don't believe I'd ever even seen the language written down, but yet I took the books home. However, when I opened these books and began to engage with them, it did not seem like I would be able to get anything from them, so I thought, "Well, okay, I can't really use these books, so I'm just going to have to take them back to the bookstore."

Soon thereafter I had a meeting with a great lama, Wangdor Rimpoche, who had carried his guru on his back over the Himalayas in order to escape from Tibet when it was invaded. I didn't even talk to him about these Tibetan books I had. We were sitting together at the dining room table, and from this particular vantage we could look out over the ocean. There was a clear blue sky and there were birds cruising in the sky, just like in the teaching metaphors. He and I were talking about some very instructive Sanskrit and Tibetan words, and this great lama spontaneously said the word svabhavikakaya, which means "all-pervasive" in Sanskrit.

We had this great afternoon together, and after he had gone, I went to get the Tibetan books to return them to the bookstore. But then something truly incredible happened: I opened the books, and suddenly what was in the books was perfectly clear and obvious to me. Nothing happened, but yet, something very profound had happened. In the moment when Wangdor Rimpoche uttered the word "svabhavikakaya," beneficial potency of an extraordinary kind was ignited in me, beneficial potency that couldn't have been brought about, no matter how long I would have studied.

This is not something I had to try to learn; it is something that appeared as a gift within the space of my own mind, which is the space of your mind as well. All the knowledge is already here and available to us. It just requires the humility to lay naked and bare, and to open up to the reality that we hold the knowledge of everything in a usable way.

It was very important for me to have that experience, because there would be no way to teach without it, or to be a lama oneself. Even more important, I opened up to a complete understanding of what Dzogchen is and what it is not.

That's just one experience of many experiences I've had of what one could call profound non-symbolic communication, an evocation of knowledge that does not occur in an ordinary way. I had been exposed to very many evocations since the beginning of my life, but this one was particularly unique and particularly supportive of what I was doing. What can one say about that? So, this is one very instructive example from a real-life experience.

An Educational and Evolutionary Imperative

CHAPTER TWENTY-FIVE

This adaptation is coming about exponentially and through ways and means people have never thought of. Those ways are both educational and evolutionary. It is the first time the human species has taken part in its own evolution. We have said, "We are going this way and not that other way."

This incredible Planet Earth is a beautiful place to live, but we have created many messes here that we cannot ignore any longer. We are in a big muddle, because for most human beings the knowledge that is required to solve the problems before us has not been accessible. In order for this knowledge to become accessible, a great shift has to occur within human beings and within human society.

Regardless of whether it has been recognized till now or not, we live in a special period of time in which this shift *is* occurring, as we begin to recognize that we hold the intelligence of the universe in a usable way. Anyone who holds the intelligence of the universe in a usable way is an exalted creature with a responsibility. What responsibility? To claim their exaltation! That needs to be done before anything else can be done. To make the great discoveries that need to be made to rectify the harm that has been done to the planet and ourselves, we must claim our exalted nature, and this is what we are in the process of doing now.

We are becoming dissatisfied with many of our systems and organizations and our ways of doing things, and we are at a very crucial turning point in society where we can now choose a different path. We have been relying on systems that are hundreds or even thousands of years old that simply do not fit the time, place and circumstance of today. It is now imperative for each of us to take this simple action of seeing who we really are—to see how powerful and potent we are and how great our capacity is to be of benefit to all. It isn't a matter of governments, corporations or large organizations coming together and deciding this for us. Rather, it is a matter of each one of us becoming aware of the immediate benefit and potency that are available to us in each moment.

A great emergence of a powerful and comprehensive intelligence is occurring, and the reified lifestyle we are living today will in the future never be lived again, never again. As each new day comes, we will find that the change is coming much more quickly than we have expected and in ways we have not expected at all. We are crossing over and making a transition to a lifestyle for human beings that has never existed before.

Instead of using the old ways of relating to life—seeing people and circumstances as "good" and "bad" and then going between those two extremes—we bring reified life to a complete stop. Seeing things or situations as good or bad isn't going to be the choice for people who are refusing to live in this reified way. The nature of mind is inexhaustible and has no container, and data streams do not carry some kind of definition that makes a person wrong or bad.

In recognizing that, suddenly we as individuals or as a society are equal with the potency of benefit that is available right now. This recognition allows us to harmonize everything that is going on for us. Everything is consolidated in the potency and benefit of what is here right now, and from that vantage we can act skillfully to solve the problems we face. That is why the change is happening: we are refusing to live the old way any longer. Open intelligence is not about denial or blame. It is about getting down to business and taking care of things once and for all with the solution-orientation that relying on open intelligence provides.

The good news is that we have powerful skillful means to untangle the difficulties we have gotten into. In relying on our brilliant open intelligence that is inclusive of everything, we see that no matter what data come up, they are not separate from open intelligence and are indeed the luminosity of open intelligence. No matter what data streams appear, the sphere of luminosity is all that is known and is all that is seen, and all answers are to be found within that luminosity. Solutions that had not previously been known become available through true dedication to open intelligence and its luminous, beneficial potencies.

Thus, the main focus for us really has to be to unify in education in the nature of our mind. We are all essentially alike, and there is no getting away from that fact. No matter how we have perceived ourselves or others, we all have the same opportunity to see that our data streams are inseparable from open intelligence. If all our varied data streams, whatever they may have been according to culture, gender, country of origin or educational background, are clearly seen to be nothing other than open intelligence, the data streams are normalized right then and there.

We are in a time now when reality is revealing itself within human society, and people are becoming more actively involved in the agency of open intelligence. Open intelligence is the source of all agency anyway, and now it is becoming more and more evident to many people that agency does not come from a human being, but from open intelligence. Hence, very naturally many people are becoming more and more open intelligence-oriented through this collective insight.

We are spontaneously and globally united in open intelligence; however, if we are all wrapped up in self-focus and self-concern, that unity will not be recognized. A united human culture is based on each of us knowing exactly what the nature of our mind is. It comes from knowing that the nature of our mind is completely infused and pervaded by beneficial potency and that this beneficial potency is our natural state. The open-intelligence mind is foremost and of utmost significance; this mind informs the speech, the body and the qualities and activities. Mind is the great treasure of gold that twinkles and sparkles in every single thing, whether this is recognized by us or not.

Nowadays we as a human society are becoming much more open, and we see that there are all kinds of people living all kinds of different ways. People are opening up more to things that previously would have been seen as foreign or strange. We are seeing something emerging that is both new and very exciting, namely, that in fact we all live within a global human culture. Many of the insular ethnic and cultural structures are disappearing very rapidly, and we can see that national boundaries are also fading. This is no surprise, as so many things are now fading away and making way for a new way of thinking and being.

A NECESSARY ADAPTATION

We are creatures who through many generations have adapted for survival. Because we live at such a critical time where this adaptation, or evolution one could say, must come about surely and quickly, the adaptation is coming about exponentially and through ways and means people have never thought of. Those ways are both educational and evolutionary. It is the first time the human species has taken part in its own evolution. We have said, "We are going this way and not that other way."

Through the role-modeling of those who have already been trained up in comprehensive open intelligence, others can come to trust that comprehensive open intelligence is really something that works and that it will work for them. We will find that within a certain period of time this comprehensive knowledge will be accessible in a way that it is always on and totally available. In fact, it has always been available, but just not discovered. Once it is discovered, there isn't any need to search for it any longer.

Today we are very strongly linked to each other in a way that we never have been before. Many of the people in the world have had no copper wire infrastructure for telephone lines, so they could not get a telephone or online connection through that infrastructure. However, many now have mobile phones, and those phones have become their interface with the rest of the world. They can now explore the areas of interest that are most important to them.

What is more, people are now no longer limited to learning only that which has always been taught; they are being exposed to things they would have never had access to previously. From this access comes the possibility of an entirely new perspective. Now that we have a communication network where billions of people are globally connected, people who had been previously marginalized and ignored are now able to make their voices heard, and people with common interests and shared circumstances can speak with each other. People are being exposed to a life of empowerment that was not available to them before. No one wants to live a life of disempowerment, and we want to be where we are empowered and where we can utilize our gifts, strengths and talents in order to empower ourselves and others even further.

The reason that this can happen now is because of this amazing communication tool, the internet. The vast spread of the internet, where human beings have a worldwide forum in which they can state what they feel and think, has never before happened in human culture. This allowance of all sorts of opinions, all sorts of afflictive states and all kinds of other states to appear in this way is part of open intelligence opening itself within the human mind.

In using the resources we have online, we have many contacts and relationships with people that we will probably never meet face-to-face. We will never see them in a physical form, and we will never see a place where they begin or end. Hence, we no longer are relating to them based merely on concepts created by attributes such as race, physical appearance, gender or personality. In this way the internet really supports and affirms open intelligence, because we will have relationships with people online where none of the usual limiting categories are being applied. With this experience it becomes much easier to accept the possibility that open intelligence actually includes everything. Even though we were trained that we are isolated individuals with isolated minds, we prove this wrong over and over again every single day just by using the internet.

Among the many other benefits it has brought, the internet could become the greatest countermeasure against war ever created. When we think of war, we usually think of violence between nations, but the greatest war, the greatest violence, is the war inside ourselves, and that is the war we need to end. With the ending of that war, all other conflicts can come to an end. All the wars out there in the world are projections of the war inside ourselves, and the greatest response to that war inside and outside is education in the nature of mind that is simple, direct and empowering. Communication in which human beings stand up and take responsibility for who they are as individuals is what will defeat war, and when that communication becomes worldwide through the power of the internet, there is no telling what is possible.

To indulge peace and to avoid and replace things that aren't peace is not real peace; it is a pseudo-peace. Peace must first be made within oneself. All the data streams warring with each other must be outshone in the complete relaxation of love-bliss-benefit while totally engaged in profound positive action in the world. This is not positive action that is contrived and put together like a jigsaw puzzle. It is not a contrived activity at all; it is naturally and spontaneously responsive and easily engaged in what is of benefit to all.

AN EDUCATION THAT LEADS TO TRUE WELL-BEING

We as human beings have had very little education in this way, and it is now the right time to take action in this regard. The action to be taken is so direct, so radical, so potent, so powerful and so very, very simple. That action is self-placement in the reality of what we actually are, for short moments many times. To make this choice is so unlike what we have been taught to do before, which has been to do something, think something and be someone. To stop and rest for short moments many times in our beneficial potency is to get to know the beneficial potency at the basis, the actual comprehensive intelligence that governs everything.

For quite a long time, especially in certain specific cultures, people have been aware that the mind could be educated to reveal its power and its benefit. Because of the way most people around the world were living in the past—often illiterate and usually with very little training in terms of what we would call "education" today—any kind of system that was put together for education would usually be very limited and quite culturally specific. It would just naturally be that way because of the prevailing circumstances.

So for instance, if a specific form of education was to be formulated in one culture and it was saturated with all the values of that one culture, then that education would only be applicable within that culture. It would have to do with that culture and practice, and it would not necessarily have to do with the practices of another unrelated culture. As a result of social and political divisions, difficulties in travel and communication, a subtle or overt prejudice towards cultures other than one's own, and the divisions between many cultures and subcultures, an education that was suitable for all cultures and peoples was not available.

As a global human culture we have the same responsibility that all human cultures have had since the beginning of time: to provide an education in the nature of mind that leads to true well-being, life satisfaction and flourishing. However, what has happened over many centuries is that education in the nature of mind has occurred without clear insight into what true education really is. This was not done out of ill intent; it was done with the aim of providing an education that was suitable for that time, place and circumstance, but generally the education that was most needed was not provided.

BELIEF SYSTEMS ARE CHANGING

The belief systems and assumptions of the past about what a human being is may have been appropriate to that particular era, but they are not appropriate to this era. If these belief systems are no longer appropriate to this present era, then surely we need to have tools available to us that *are* appropriate for this time. We are going through a great change as a human society; a lot of the things that were required in the past are no longer required, and now the open-intelligence tools that are so desperately needed are becoming more available.

The belief systems of the present day have often been based on psychiatry and psychology, in which the mind has been described in a certain way. Mind was categorized and certain designations were given to it, and if a person did not have certain characteristics that were considered healthy, that meant that the mind was not working correctly. Hence, a successful human being would be one who had certain favored characteristics, and within the context of those characteristics one would live in a way that would hopefully bring about life satisfaction and flourishing.

However, the full satisfaction would never actually be found, and yet the same practices would go on with the expectation of a better result.

With this very short overview of the conventional use of the mind, we come up against a glaring fact: the education that has been trained up in us has not been sufficient to solve the problems that are coming up in ourselves or in the world. The mind has been trained up according to reified ways of dealing with data, but it has not been trained up at all in spontaneous non-learning. What is most definitely required is that people now be diligently, courageously and thoroughly introduced to the comprehensive open intelligence that is recognized through non-learning and non-effort.

FROM THE GRASSROOTS

For the first time in human history, at the very grassroots of human civilization, a revolution is taking place, a revolution uniting all in the beneficial potency that really is one human body, one human mind, one human speech, qualities and activities. This is a time like no other in history, and it is a time where people at the grassroots really take hold of what is going on.

We are in the early days of seeing how important it is to take this step into a new perspective, and there is no doubt that it is being taken, so it is not a projection any longer of something that might happen in the future. It is clear and obvious that the step has been taken, and more and more people who are looking for a new way of life are joining in each day.

This is a movement that has come from the grassroots; it has grown from the confusion and turmoil of a planet and species on the verge of extinction. Yet, it inexhaustibly emerges as the decisive empowerment of both the planet and the species to not only save itself but also to exalt itself, raising itself to its greatest power and exaltation. We thrive at the grassroots through the skillful means of education, empowerment and mobilization.

Education in the nature of mind is provided for everyone at their own level of ability and interest. This is actually what "a grassroots movement" means, which is that each and every individual is dealt with at their own level of ability and interest. The design is such that anyone can come in anywhere and leave anywhere; it is entirely up to them. With the Dzogchen Teaching for instance, if people wanted to just watch videos, listen to talks or read the texts, they can do that and never actually come to a meeting or meet another person who is involved. The longer people stay with this practice, in whatever way that practice may unfold for them, the more settled they will become.

This grassroots movement is mobilized through all possible means, including development and acceleration of new technologies that allow for radical change to take place. The way to strengthen human society from the grassroots comes through reaching out in a very specific way to individuals and communities everywhere and doing so with the use of a language that would not be subjected to censorship. So, spontaneously the beneficial intention arose that there would be a language that would not be censored and would not have an enormous pushback from existing institutions that have a great deal of strength within society. This is exactly what has occurred.

THE SHIP IS TURNING

For thousands of years, we have been relying on ideas such as original sin that have shaped virtually every institution. So, for example, when we go to our job, to the grocery store, to our place of worship, to the school or university, or when we do whatever we do, the institutions we are dealing with have been shaped in some way by very deep-seated ideologies. When we are told over and over again that we are a certain way, then we just kind of shrug our shoulders and think, "Oh well, that is what everyone says, so I must be that way then." We came to see ourselves as damaged goods because we accepted original sin into ourselves through this inherited bias.

We are loaded with all kinds of data that are really sad, even frightening. However, in the same way that we have trained ourselves to think that we are bad, we can train ourselves to know that we are exalted creatures. It is now time to free ourselves from the tyranny of dogmas that have led us into the mess we are in now.

When we come to the point as a species where we start to question the assumptions that led us to our present circumstance, we are really starting to get somewhere! Together we are looking at things in a new and innovative way, and we are testing things out in our own experience. What works and is of benefit to all we will keep, and what isn't of benefit we will leave behind. That we together are shaping our future in this way is a glorious thing to behold.

Education in the nature of mind will occur with each individual who is open to being educated in that way; however, the imperative is not only an educational one but is also evolutionary. At the same time that the educational imperative is coming about, the evolutionary imperative is also coming about. Evolution dispenses with what is no longer needed, and it does so in order for the species to survive. In this case evolution dispenses with structures and conditions that have resulted from the lack of education in the nature of mind.

Many minds are changing and being educated, and eventually many more will come to delight in open intelligence. Through the two skillful means, evolutionary and educational, over time everyone will be able to come around, so to speak. It is just like when our human ancestors went from moving about on all-fours to standing on two feet. The change was inevitable; even if some of them might have thought, "That weirdo is up on two legs, but I'm never going to do that," eventually the whole species came to stand on two legs. Not everyone stood up at the same time; the change happened little by little. It was a force from an evolutionary imperative from within; no one really knows how or why it happened. We could speculate about how and why it happened, but here we all are now up on two legs!

In a similar way, we are now going through an enormous transition where the ship is turning, and everyone on the ship is turning with it towards realizing our exalted nature. This transition just happens to be occurring now, where people are starting to see that we hold the intelligence of the universe in a usable way. We need to open up our idea of who we are out of the fixed status of a body-mind complex into the open intelligence of radical reality. This is an even greater shift than any of the other great shifts: standing upright, starting to speak, creating an alphabet, deciding that time and cause-and-effect exist or whatever it may have been. To repeat, it is an educational as well as an evolutionary shift, and it means that for the first time in human history humans are taking part in creating their own evolution.

When human beings came from all-fours to standing on two legs, there was no way to know what that would bring about for human society, and so too with opening up to the beneficial potency of open intelligence. We cannot possibly forecast the future. What we can appraise is the incredible benefit in our own life; what is more, we can also see the change brought about in others, plus we can see the organizing power within a very large group of people all over the globe that comes about without even trying.

This shift will happen very much in the same way these other forms of evolutionary adaptation have taken place. Human beings are pack animals and they copy each other. So, if one of them stands up on two legs, then another one will try to stand up on two legs. If we get a significant group together all on two legs, it is much more likely that the whole bunch will eventually stand up in that way. It is no different with the widespread recognition of open intelligence. It is about training up our native intelligence to its actual capacity, and when others see the benefits, they will want to do the same.

We are facing extinction as a human species, and so what have we done historically when we have faced extinction? We adapted for survival. Open intelligence is adaptation for survival, and for tremendous joy and connection with everyone and everything! The great exaltation of human beings is what can prevent the extinction of the human species. As long as we marginalize and diminish ourselves, we are on the road to extinction. We have not honored ourselves or the planet we live on; however, once we start to exalt ourselves, then we honor *everything*. We honor this beautiful place where we live and its waters and wonders and worlds and trees and all the other pretties and not so pretties. Open intelligence encompasses it all.

All of the things that would be useful for human society in order to take care of our planet and all its beings are best addressed from the perspective of open intelligence's beneficial potency. Anything we can think of that would be beneficial for human society—such as providing food, clothing and shelter for everyone, health care and education—can become an actual possibility. In order for social change to be genuine and authentic, it must come from the perspective of open intelligence's beneficial potency; otherwise, it will be fleeting.

This novel expression of what a human being really is is the cutting edge and the evolutionary leap that is like no other. This evolutionary leap can never go backward. It is an evolutionary leap that brings to human beings the fruition of the longing which has always been the most cherished: to be of benefit to all.

Q. I sometimes look at my life and it just seems so small and worthless. I don't feel that I am worthy to accomplish anything significant, and I don't really see that I have much to contribute. All this talk about joy and connection with others is nothing I can relate to. What can be said about deep despair like this?

Ziji Rinpoche: We rely on the perfect knowledge of open intelligence's great benefit to continuously reveal, unfurl and show to us the profound meaning in everything, in each and every step of life. We don't have to figure it out in advance. We just rely on open intelligence in each step of life, and this is a really wonderful means of complete relaxation. We don't need to be lying beside a swimming pool in order to be completely relaxed! We can rely on open intelligence for complete relaxation in all the circumstances of life.

People who live as the great benefit of open intelligence know without doubt that that is their identity. When people who are truly living as open intelligence have gone through extreme hardships, those circumstances, whatever they were, did nothing but increase faith in the power of open intelligence's great benefit. To me that is completely profound.

There is a story about a Tibetan monk who was in a Chinese prison in solitary confinement and tortured for twenty years. When he was released, the Dalai Lama asked him, "What was the most difficult experience you faced in twenty years in prison?" The monk said, "My greatest difficulty was maintaining compassion for the Chinese." Many people in this circumstance would be totally focused on self and what was happening to them. There would be so much self-centered apprehension which creates all kinds of reactions. This monk, however, in his complete relaxation, was interested only in maintaining compassion for the Chinese. Maintaining compassion for those who had imprisoned him had been his basic practice during the entire time he was in prison.

There is another great story, a story of a very great Rinpoche who taught thousands of other lamas. He sat on a golden throne in Tibet and all the other lamas would come to him, including the Dalai Lama. But when he was driven out of Tibet during the Cultural Revolution, he ended up alone with no one he knew and feeling very ill and depressed. He was living as a sadhu (*renunciate monk*) along the Ganges River in Rishikesh, and then he went to Calcutta where he ended up washing dishes in a hotel, and he still hadn't seen anyone he had ever known in Tibet.

He had gone from his golden throne to washing dishes and feeling sick and depressed. He was asked once, "So, if you were depressed and sick, how does that match up with the Teachings? How can you be a Dzogchen master and be depressed and sick?" He said, "Being depressed and sick? All it has done is to increase my faith in timeless awareness and in the Teachings." The golden throne—or washing dishes in Calcutta—no matter what it is, it is *as it is*. By allowing the key points and pith instructions of the heart essence to take over, everything is absorbed into pure perfect presence. Everything is *as it is*.

When we hear stories like this, we can share from the experience of people like this imprisoned Tibetan monk or this Rinpoche in Calcutta and gain strength and realization in regard to the different things going on in our own lives. Through this we each grow stronger, not only as individuals, but as the entire body of the movement of great benefit. The movement of great benefit itself grows stronger through each short moment, and each short moment is a revolutionary and skillful means of empowering all of human society.

When we hear stories about people throughout history who have lived in this way and we look at our own lives, we see that we have profound abilities we did not seem to have prior to introduction to open intelligence. Most importantly we see that we can live as benefit and that we know that we have a *choice* about that. We can live as benefit or live as misery, whatever we want. If we want to keep reifying data, we can do that, but at least now we know what the options are. We can continue to live accumulating descriptions and pretending that that is the nature of our existence, or we can let everything be *as it is* and just take off!

As everything whatsoever is indivisible, there is no "*your* greatness," "*her/his* greatness" or "*my* greatness." The only greatness is indivisible. So, for instance, we could hear about someone like Wangdor Rimpoche. He refused to leave his revered guru in Tibet when the Chinese invaded, and ended up carrying him on his back from Tibet all the way to India. He said, "I carried my teacher from Tibet to India, and I did that because I wanted these teachings to be available. If I had left my guru in Tibet, then he would have certainly died, and the teachings that he had would have gone with him." And so what did he do? He put his beloved guru on his back and carried him all the way from Tibet to India.

This is greatness; it is a vast living greatness. It is an inexhaustible greatness that belongs equally to everyone. Wangdor Rimpoche is not sharing that story to say "Oh, wow, I'm really something, and you could never do anything like that." It is a magnificent teaching, a teaching that is just so entirely beautiful, that relates to all of us.

Great good fortune! Great good fortune! Great good fortune!